The Travel Trivia
Handbook of Oddball
European Sights

The Travel Trivia Handbook of Oddball European Sights

Nino Lo Bello

A Citadel Press Book
Published by Carol Publishing Group

A Citadel Press Book
Published by Carol Publishing Group
Citadel Press is a registered trademark of Carol Communications, Inc.
Editorial Offices: 600 Madison Avenue, New York, N.Y. 10022
Sales and Distribution Offices: 120 Enterprise Avenue, Secaucus,
N.J. 07094
In Canada: Canadian Manda Group, P.O. Box 920, Station U,
Toronto, Ontario M8Z 5P9
Queries regarding rights and permissions should be addressed to
Carol Publishing Group, 600 Madison Avenue, New York, N.Y. 10022

Carol Publishing Group books are available at special discounts for
bulk purchases, for sales promotions, fund raising, or educational
purposes. Special editions can be created to specifications.
For details, contact Special Sales Department, Carol Publishing Group,
120 Enterprise Avenue, Secaucus, N.J. 07094.

Manufactured in the United States of America

10 9 8 7 6 5 4 3 2 1

Library of Congress Cataloging-in-Publication Data

Lo Bello, Nino
        The travel trivia handbook of offball European sights /
Nino Lo Bello.
                p.   cm.
        "A Citadel Press book."
        ISBN 0-8065-1333-0
        1. Europe—Guidebooks.   I. Title.
D909.L63   1992   92-30537
    914.04'559—dc20   CIP

For Lois, Patricia, Lucille, Susan, Bertha, Emilie, Rosalia, Milly, Anita, Karin, Anny, Barbara, Valerie, Melanie, Liz, Donna, Nancy, Vickie, Helga, Mary, Helen, Felizitas, Olive, Edith, Diane, Janis, Ruth, Frances, Rosie, Tatiana, Ursula, Mette, Elke, Juni, Elsie, Monica, Elfie—and Irene!

CONTENTS

vii

FRANCE

ITALY

AUSTRIA

INTRODUCTION

This book, by rights, should have been dedicated to the little girl in Kansas who took a trip to the Land of Oz and opened up new vistas to everybody who travels with imagination. A fantasy travel book with the wizardry L. Frank Baum cooked up for Dorothy is one kind of travel writing. Lotsa fun, lotsa good reading. This book, however, isn't fantasy.

For more than a quarter of a century, while covering Europe hither, thither and yon for one newspaper or another, I managed to find time to pursue a secret hobby of mine on the Continent. So now let me bare all—I collect oddball sites and sights. There, I've said it. My own wall map is full of green pins, orange pins, blue pins, red pins and even clothespins, each of which zeroes in on an oddball location I have already combed out—well over a thousand at this writing. They're the kind of obscure travel attractions that Robert ("Believe It Or Not") Ripley doted on—touristic curiosa, the unusual and the fantastic. Having gathered these while logging over 448,660.5 tourist miles on the Continent, I offer some of my choicest beauts in this unorthodox travel handbook.

Mind you, this is not a guidebook per se, but it can and will serve as a guidebook—with a gentle warning that (*a*) you should proceed at your own risk, and (*b*) there's no money-back guarantee. Roam the Continent with me, either by sitting in your comfy armchair and turning one page at a time or by carrying this modest collection in your hip pocket, somewhere in your knapsack or around your neck on a chain. If you're the kind of traveler who's forever busy going somewhere else, wanting to zip to the next well-worn, big tourist attraction in some other guidebook, then this field manual of offbeat targets—minus tips on the cheapest hotels and the best restaurants and the usual how-to's—will *not* be your cuppa. But bear in mind that every place cited in this book is *something special* which you won't find anywhere else.

If you're the curious type who, like Alice, keeps getting curiouser and curiouser, then this book *will* be your cuppa and maybe even your own road bible, a Baedeker of Europe's undiscovered wonders. It will travel well—or, as we used to say back in Brooklyn, the place that gave birth to my own special tapeworm for the unique, "it will travel good."

As with all compendiums of this type, an author needs help, and an inestimable number of fine human beings stepped forward. First, let me mention the late Jimmy Bedford of Missouri and Alaska, an intrepid global traveler and the author of *Around the World on a Nickel*. A number of other live-wire people helped: Bertha Smyth, Emilie Rooney, Mary Kaye Stray, Lois Shetler, Patricia Wise, Adele Ziminski, Alan and Valerie Levy, Dr. Gerd Baumgartner, Karin Gutleber, Dr. James Wilkie, Dr. Kurt Broer, Walter Wurzinger, Michael Knabl, Hans Gross, Ursula Frietzsche, Knud Jörgen, Gunter Winkler, Eckhart Brieder, Helga Stark, Georg Steiner, Karin Kunz, Max Scherrer, Melanie Sommer, Traudl Lisey, Wolfgang J. Kraus, Margit Klimscha, Josef Palffy, Catherine Althaus, Enrico Maggi, Dr. Giuliana Bartelletti, Lucilla (Cipriano) Szabo, my Aunt Milly Moscarelli and my peripatetic brother, Jit Lo Bello.

But above all, I am deeply grateful to my wife, Irene Rooney Lo Bello (oft referred to as Lefty), who deserves the biggest commendation of all, for with radar eyes she assiduously edited every one of the chapters several times over and gave birth to the final manuscript on her overworked computer, whilst several other pressing deadlines hung over both of us. No better editor in this world exists.

For any shortcomings, errors and bugs that may have crept in from the woodwork, however, the writer takes full responsibility.

Nino Lo Bello
Vienna
April 1992

The Travel Trivia Handbook of Oddball European Sights

WALES, ENGLAND
AND SCOTLAND

The Great Little Trains of Wales

Aberystwyth (Wales)

They toot and they puff and they are tiny and they wind and screech, like the nineteenth-century choo-choo trains that they are, through craggy and glorious—but always dizzying—mountains and cliffsides that provide tourists with some of the most magnificent coastal rides imaginable. Your steam engine may have the name of Kate or Muriel or Aylwin or the Prince of Wales, and it will lovingly chug you, with ample doses of the nearly forgotten fragrance of burning soft coal, through sections of Wales that automobiles can't reach and hikers wouldn't dare attempt.

Known as the **CAMBRIAN LINE** all together, the "Great Little Trains of Wales" are eight small railways that have routes that run from as short as two miles to as long as twelve. One of them climbs as high as 3,560 feet (where on a clear day you can see all the way to Ireland). There are a total of 30 steam engines in service that connect Aberystwyth in the south to Pwllheli in the north, 35 miles away.

For more than 50 years the Cambrian Line carried coal, copper ore, slate, lead, flour, timber, cattle and sheep from one place to another in middle and north Wales, mostly through the Welsh mountains, but after modern methods of transport were adopted the faithful little railways looked as if they would end up as history-book fodder. In 1956 a group of railroad buffs teamed up to "save" the trains. They wanted to bring in a passenger service that would be for local people, and also for visitors to Wales interested in savoring some offbeat delights.

Today, servicing some 50,000 passengers annually, the Cambrian Line runs year-round, with more frequent trains

3

when schools are open. The fares are no higher than fares on Britain's other trains, and the Cambrian Line does provide bargain round-trip tickets for holidaymakers and special tourist tickets with unlimited travel. Maps and time-tables for all the other lines are also available from each railway. Although some of the lines connect with each other, most of them do not, but are within a short bus ride of each other.

Whether you want to do all eight railways over a four- or five-day period or just a few, a good place to start your RR rhapsody is Aberystwyth, a splendid seaside resort with a "tourists-welcome!" university where Prince Charles (the Prince of Wales) spent a semester in 1969 to learn the language of the country.

Aberystwyth, reachable quite easily within a main trunk line from Shrewsbury, is the terminus of the **Vale of Rheidol Railway**, which runs for 12 miles to Devil's Bridge where there is a deep ravine with waterfalls and an enticing flight of 100 steps known as Jacob's Ladder (there are small admission fees for each attraction). Clinging to a scary hillside and screeching around curves so sharp you can get the huffing-puffing teakettle up front into frequent camera view, this same little wooden train—which used to haul lead and lumber when it first began in 1902—takes about three hours for its round-trip. It gives you CinemaScope views of the open Plynlimon moorland from more than 2,000 feet up.

Here's a mini-rundown of the other trains:

The **Snowdon Mountain Railway** (round-trip 9 miles—2 hours) reaches the 3,560-foot summit at a maximum speed of five miles per hour, but the spectacular ride can be quite chilly and windy, so bring a sweater. The **Bala Lake Railway** (round-trip 6 miles—30 minutes) hugs the largest natural lake in Wales into Bala, with its gorgeous tree-lined main street.

The **Ffestiniog Railway** (round-trip 20 miles—2 hours) climbs continuously above the Vale of Ffestiniog to a picnic spot at Ddualt with the sea on one side and mountain peaks on the other. The world's oldest steam passenger train, it began service in 1836 with horses pulling the cars up the steep slope and then the same steeds coasting back on one of the wheeled platforms. The **Llanberis Lake Railway** (round-trip 4 miles—45 minutes) operates on a track that is a mere two-feet wide and moves along from the ships at the Menai Strait to a serene picnic domain at Lake Cei Llydan.

The **Talyllyn Railway** (round-trip 13 miles—2 hours) infiltrates through eye-catching woods with coaches that have been used for over a century and takes you to the Dolgach station, which has three waterfalls in a nearby wooded gorge. The **Fairbourne Railway** (round-trip 4 miles —1 hour) is the smallest of the Wales's Little Trains and uses a gauge of only 15 inches. Skirting along a beach on Cardigan Bay with mountainous views through the window, it also was originally pulled by horses. The **Welshpool & Llanfair Railway** (round-trip 12 miles—1 hour and 45 minutes) is a sort of end-of-the-line type of railroad because at its main station it connects with a major highway.

A trip of any length on the Great Little Trains of Wales is a nifty experience cum tongue-twisting names with double consonants. And be sure to bring along a llight llunch.

*   *   *

Book City

Hay-on-Wye (Wales)

Ask not what the tourist attractions are, for there are either none or more than two million—according to how you read it. This tiny town just over the England-Wales border, 160 miles west of London, houses more second-hand books than probably any town or city in the world. And now you know why there is a steady flow of book freaks (call them tourists!) who come here on weekend trips with tour buses from other parts of Britain to blow their bibliomaniacal minds.

Nearly every other shop in this little town of 1,350 residents is a bookstore—plus, there are more than a million secondhand books in what used to be the local movie theater, the fire house, an old folks home, a Norman castle and three warehouses. As if that were not enough, every week new truckloads of old books are brought in to keep up with the demand. Yes, **HAY-ON-WYE** sells its books every day of the week. And in one shop, 24 hours around the clock, every night and day in the week, you can buy books. There are no clerks in attendance, and after you choose whatever book or books you want, you deposit the money into a box.

By peddling hundreds of thousands of books each month, Hay-on-Wye is now a name in the tourist trade, a booklover's paradise where the main commodity is for sale at the lowest prices anywhere on earth. In point of fact, the whole history of "Book City" reads like a book.

As recently as the early seventies Hay-on-Wye was just a remote farming town, a speck on some maps that showed it was located about 50 miles from Cardiff. It had narrow streets, stone cottages, one hardware store selling farm implements and not much else, except for some places that dealt in groceries. Then along came a fiftyish man by the name of Richard Booth who got the bright idea of really putting Hay-on-Wye on the map by declaring it a "kingdom." He also put a carload of books up for sale at the price of a pair of socks.

Bang! He got what he wanted: publicity in the British newspapers.

Then, when he began to ship truckload after truckload of used books into Hay, everybody knew that Richard Booth was "bonkers," that he was some kind of "nut." Well, yes, he was a nut—a nut about books. And wouldn't you know he began to sell the old tomes so quickly that he needed to buy up whatever indoor space he could acquire everywhere in town in order to handle the spillover of his fast business.

The more volumes this Barnum of books shipped into Hay—thousands of them from as far away as the United States and Canada and even, if you can believe it, from Australia and New Zealand—the more people flocked to the Welsh hamlet to buy. Hay-on-Wye was literally smothered in books and book buyers.

"We have books on every conceivable subject and even on subjects that are inconceivable," declares Booth from his upstairs office in the one-time cinema whose front sign reads, THE WORLD'S LARGEST SECOND HAND BOOKSHOP. "Old books never die—no matter how unattractive they are to ninety-nine percent of the people, there is always somebody somewhere who wants this book or that one.

"Of course, we make mistakes in pricing some of our books—the rare ones, I mean. For instance, I had a book, published in 1642, *Religio Medici* by Thomas Browne, that was marked for sale at £3, but one of my staff recognized its value because he knew that fewer than a dozen copies of it were in existence. So we jumped the price to £500, and sure enough it sold faster at that price to a collector. Yes, I've lost thousands of pounds by underpricing certain books, but that does not worry me at all. I'm in the business of selling secondhand books at all prices. We even run the 'Cheapest Bookstore in the World' here, where children and their parents can come in and browse among ten thousand adventure-story paperbacks for sale at less than the price of one cigarette."

People, adds Booth (who holds a degree in history from Oxford), will read anything, and many come to Hay to find books they can't find anywhere else—not even in London. In fact, he runs several tour buses out of London on weekends loaded with people who want to roam among the stacks to hunt down something in their area of special interest. That can run the range from books on criminal anthropology before the turn of the century to books on Victorian methods of dentistry.

Unlike most used-book sellers elsewhere, King Richard the Book-Hearted (as someone once dubbed him) makes a fetish of keeping every item on display completely dust free and neatly stacked on ten miles of well-lit shelves. There are no chairs, however. In all the stores, books are never upside-down and never on display with the spine facing the wrong way, nor will you ever find books tied together.

So let's hear it for Hay-on-Wye. This town is indeed one for the books!

* * *

The Laurel and Hardy Museum

Ulverston (England)

And now, ladeez 'n' gentlemun—the Laurel and Hardy Museum! LAUGHTER . . .

Although Stan Laurel and Oliver Hardy ended their comedy partnership in the mid-fifties and have been dead for years, they are still making people in all corners of the globe chuckle—just as they did in their heyday—thanks to television reruns and movie houses that still schedule Stan-and-Ollie golden oldies for surefire box-office bucks. And in Stan's hometown, Ulverston, here in England's Lake District (five miles south of Lake Windermere), we have a **LAUREL AND HARDY MUSEUM** crammed to the rafters with more than a thousand pieces of memorabilia of the beloved comedians. Laurel and Hardy are very likely the only Hollywood acting team in history who have an entire museum devoted to them—and them alone. Is everybody happy?

Founded in 1976 by one of Ulverston's former mayors, 68-year-old Bill Cubin (who, by the way, never met either Stan or Oliver), the memorial to the slapstick duo is the kind of tourist tempter that visitors to Britain get hooked on. Come here to Number 4c Upper Brook Street and find a half-timbered, seventeenth-century, slightly tilted building with a quaint courtyard that leads to the steps of the museum, where you will be bombarded by posters, programs, letters, models, movie stills and portraits of Fat and Skinny. The furniture on display belonged to one Arthur Stanley Jefferson, the name that appeared on Laurel's Ulverston birth certificate when he was born on June 16, 1890.

"I have Stan's voice on tape," explains the enthusiastic curator, "and he explains why he changed his name. He said that because Stan Jefferson had thirteen letters in it, he thought that would be unlucky and would also take up a lot of space in any billing, so one day when a friend happened to say that he should look to his laurels, Stan jumped at the word *laurel* and made it his stage name."

A not inconsiderable part of the charm of the Laurel and Hardy Museum is Cubin himself. Giving bombastic, personalized attention to every visitor, he is the self-installed ambassador for the famous lunatic pair. An incurable movie buff and a storehouse of lore about the two film clowns, Cubin handles about 10,000 visitors a year with his infectious zeal. The museum is open daily, seven days a week, from 10:00 A.M. to 4:30 P.M., and the admission is 1 pound, with a reduced rate of 50 pence for children and senior citizens.

During Cubin's two separate terms of office as mayor, he realized to his chagrin that Ulverston had never acknowledged the origins of its celebrated skinny son. So Cubin set the record straight by having a plaque erected on the wall at 3 Argyle Street, Stan's birthplace, and that sparked off the idea to start up a museum in honor of the immortal pair. Since then it has become an obsession with Cubin (also a member of the Town Council for over 30 years) and his wife Lucy, who together devote endless hours to the memory of the world's best-known comedy team. The couple used to have a fish-and-chip business when the museum was in its infancy (open one day a week and by appointment), but now they are "retired" and run the museum full time, with the projected idea that their two very eager grandsons will some day take it over.

In 1984 Ulverston and its environs hosted the convention of the "Sons of the Desert" (the name comes from one of the films), and it drew Laurel and Hardy freaks from fan clubs all over the world, many of whom were not even born when the twosome completed their last film in 1952. Each of the clubs represented was named after one of the Laurel and Hardy films, according to Cubin, who tells you ebulliently that the particular club called Pardon Us, which is housed in a Connecticut prison, was not, as far as he knows, represented at the congress. The 1990 centenary celebration of Laurel's birth created a great stir, when Ulverston went all out to pay homage to its native son.

The museum owns prints of 103 of the 105 films that

Stan and Ollie made over a 30-year-period, so two are still missing. During 1988 in Philadelphia, Cubin did manage to track down and acquire a three-minute segment of one of the errant films, *The Rogue Song*, and is now trying ever so desperately to unearth a complete copy, thinking it might be forgotten somewhere in one of the former Communist countries of eastern Europe. Cubin is offering a reward of 1,000 pounds sterling for the entire movie, a 115-minute Hal Roach production with Lawrence Tibbett, made in 1930 by MGM, which nobody in the United States or Canada seems to have a print of. Cubin has even checked with the heirs of Benito Mussolini, who collected Laurel and Hardy movies and screened them frequently. The other lost film is *Hats Off* (1930), for which Cubin is also offering a 1,000-pound bounty.

As you enter the museum, you hear over a loudspeaker whichever Laurel and Hardy film is being projected in a small cinema that seats 40 people. From there you are led to other rooms that use every available square inch of space, ceiling included, for the superabundance of Laurel and Hardy items.

"The secret of Laurel and Hardy is their evergreen appeal," the curator continues with unabated exuberance. "Their humor and routines are timeless and universal. And no matter how many times I see one of the films, I always find something new to laugh at. Ironically, not one of them ever got a favorable review from the critics. It's a pity, given the immortality of Laurel and Hardy and the persistance of their old films on the world market. I ask you, though—who has the last laugh now?"

* * *

London's Soapbox Parliament

London (England)

Listening to a debate in the House of Commons is a standard tourist come-hither—but nothing can match London's "Soapbox Parliament" in **Hyde Park** on a Sunday morning. The noisy orators, tongue-quick to insult anybody and everybody while deftly lashing yon heckler with knotted quips as the equally noisy crowds root pro or con, make Marble Arch corner (usually referred to as SPEAKERS' CORNER) the liveliest spot on earth, rain or shine, snow or fog. It's all for real, it's a lot of fun (no matter how many times you go back), and it's free.

If you are a tape worm, bring your cassette recorder and put down for posterity some of the dialogues that go on. If you are a photo bug, bring plenty of film because the picturesque characters and their antics will keep your camera busy. In fact, while you're taking a picture, the speaker will likely single you out and lambaste you as "a capitalist pig with that shiny Japanese camera you bought in Germany with U.S. dollars."

Don't let the ridicule bother you, for the creature atop his box is just trying to draw a bigger crowd so he can tell the world that Prime Minister John Major is a first-class nut and that President Bush is a first-class nut. "Not excluding the speaker himself," shouts a heckler in the crowd, "who's the biggest nut of all!" And so it goes—debate, English style.

Thousands of spectators have been going to Speakers' Corner every Sunday morning since 1872 when a law was enacted giving citizens the right to assemble peaceably, to say whatever they pleased, and to harangue on any subject, provided they didn't incite a riot to overthrow the government or use profanities.

Otherwise, everything goes in Hyde Park—all the way from the absurdity of calling the Chinese the dumbest people on earth (because they speak 106 different languages "and therefore need 106 different dictionaries") to predicting the end of the world because "dark-skinned people are allowed to become policemen and that's unfair to us burglars because we can't see them at night." More debate, English style.

Much of the oratory is indeed comical or tongue-in-cheek, but a lot of it is quite serious. You can pick which inflammatory jawsmith you want and join the standees gathered around. Many of the spectators turn up regularly each Sunday and come only to harass, an art that is highly polished at Speakers' Corner. But all of the elocutionists are just as sharp with the put-down comebacks, so that often you get an exchange of ad lib repartee that would do justice to a comedy scriptwriter.

Here's a sample dillie I taped on my cassette of a speaker wearing a pastor's collar dealing with a noisy bystander: "You have one last chance to repent, my son!" The bystander snaps back at him: "You were a better speaker, old boy, before the war—the Peloponnesian War!" The speaker: "My son, the Devil forgives you your sins!" The heckler: "You was up in Soho with me last night, pop, and you're the one who needs forgiveness!" The speaker: "Why don't you go back to the nut ward you escaped from?" The heckler: "I would, but they only have one place left, and it's reserved for you!" The speaker: "You are just a punk that's trying to set off some fireworks!" The heckler: "That proves you're no match for me!"

Speakers' Corner is less than a hundred yards away from the infamous **Tyburn Tree** from whose branches yesteryear's "dissenters" were hanged six at a time. That went on from the tenth century until 1783. Tradition has it that the condemned were given a chance to say a few last words, and out of this emerged the present-day speech-making that gives this patch of Hyde Park such an electro-magnetic pull on Sundays.

Using every kind of tactic to draw and then hold onto a group of listeners, the Sunday speakers often dress in a bizarre manner or rig up eye-catching signs. One speaker who shows up fairly regularly is tattooed from head to toe (he claims to be knowledgeable on all subjects—you name it for him and, boom, off he goes into orbit); another speaker hands out candy bars to anybody who can, quiz-like, answer fact questions; and others wave flags or screens or laugh hysterically or start to do long, drawn-out magic tricks. Sometimes it's hard to choose which one to listen to. They're all really good and sometimes really bad.

I recall, not long ago, one speaker and a heckler who kept at each other for nearly a half hour. They both gave a truly superb performance, because they both were so well informed. To my astonishment, later that afternoon I discovered them sitting together on a park bench peacefully eating ice cream cones.

*   *   *

The Queen's Dollhouse

London (England)

Once upon a time considered the secret and private realm of little girls, dollhouses with their wee charm and small-space fascination are coming back strong and beginning to bowl over all people, little and big. Tourists prowling around **Windsor Castle** should not overlook the world's most complete and magnificent dollhouse, which has been spellbinding visitors for nearly 70 years.

Under constant guard, 24 hours around the clock, and only a 30-minute bus ride from downtown London, the **QUEEN'S DOLLHOUSE** is a yes-yes the next time you are here with kiddies or not. Without exaggeration, this toy house is truly the most valuable plaything anywhere.

Designed in the classic traditions of Ancient Rome and Renaissance Italy as they developed in England in the seventeenth and eighteenth centuries and revived in the early years of this century, it has everything—complete in the minutest detail—from hot and cold running water, elevators and the tiniest imaginable door locks (all of which work), right down to a mini-gramophone that plays "God Save the King," albeit it a bit low in volume.

Constructed in the scale of one inch to the foot, this royal fantasy in a 12-foot-tall glass casing was the brainchild of the famed architect, Sir Edwin Lutyens, who not only designed numerous English country houses but also built the entire city of New Delhi in India. From that 80-square-mile project fun-loving Lutyens eagerly switched to a bite-sized undertaking when he was asked to create a gift for Queen Mary that would not only demonstrate the nation's goodwill but also serve as a fund-raiser for her Majesty's pet charity schemes.

Because of his tremendous influence, Lutyens was able to call on the talents of Britain's top artists, craftsmen and skilled workers of the time to help him concoct this dream palace. First shown to the public at the British Empire Exhibition at Wembley in 1924, since then the dollhouse has been on permanent display by itself in a room underneath the throne room in Windsor Castle.

On a base three-feet high that is divided into two parts—to contain the electrical machinery and the population of dolls that are stored in 208 interchangeable cedar drawers, each 11.5 inches long and 3.5 inches wide—stands the three-floor dollhouse mansion, which is about four feet in height. Directly on top of it rests the "outer shell." Like an outside skin, the exterior walls and roof (made of wood but painted to look like Portland stone, engineered so it can be lifted or lowered automatically) remain raised. Thus, when you walk around the entire house, you can see each of the 20-and-some rooms clearly.

From a well-stocked wine cellar with bottles of famous vintage years, beer casks and inch-high flasks (with real champagne inside), to mini royal crowns and precious jewels in a strong room with bars and locks, each item is as fine as British artisans could fashion it. In the basement you also see an astonishing array of perfectly made transformers and switches, a tank for bath wastes, a grocery storeroom, a central heating setup and an electrical system that lights up every room and runs all the contrivances, even the matchbox-sized elevator. The basement floor also serves as a garage with six miniature antique autos, including a Daimler and a Rolls Royce, plus gas pumps, a bicycle, a motorcycle with sidecar, a fire engine and two royal baby carriages.

Nearby is a fully equipped kitchen with a coal-burning stove, a floor that is tiled with 2,500 teeny wooden blocks (because in those days a stone floor would cut the hems of the servants' dresses!), cupboards with hinges and handles in sparkling steel, and a scullery with lead-lined sinks and tiny bars of soap next to amoeba-sized dishcloths.

On the ground floor the dining salon mesmerizes you. A 90-piece silver service of dime-sized plates and match-thin flatware decorates a dining table (5.5-inches wide when closed and 20 inches wide when open) that has tiny chairs of walnut covered in red leather parked around it. Postage-stamp-sized portraits of English kings and queens line the paneled walls.

Next to the dining room are the butler's pantry with perfect replicas of china and sterling silver, and the throne room, which is the largest and grandest room in the house. The walls are covered in a Queen Anne pattern, woven to the incredibly small scale of 120 silk threads to the inch. But even the linen room takes your breath away when you discover that the lilliputian linens stacked on the shelves were specially hand-woven in Ireland, each piece microscopically stitched in the corners with the royal monogram, all of which took one Franco-Irish woman 1,500 hours to do.

Containing peewee volumes written especially for the dollhouse by such famous authors as Rudyard Kipling, Thomas Hardy, Arnold Bennett and Arthur Conan Doyle, the 20-inch Italian walnut-paneled library also boasts its very own amazing and valuable collection of prints, watercolors and drawings. There are over 700 of these.

A tiny lamp on a night table in the queen's bedroom lights up a colorful painting representing Day and Night that covers the entire ceiling, the canopy bed glimmers in the same blue-gray silk damask that spans the walls, and a duplicate of a famous Persian carpet stretches over the floor. The king's bedroom is truly a royal room, sporting a painting on the ceiling that shows a garden trellis in the form of a musical staff—the notes are roses spelling out "God Save the King."

Queen Mary's granddaughter, the present Queen Elizabeth, keeps a royal eye on the dollhouse. Having once made new curtains for it herself, she visits the dollhouse from time to time with the younger members of her family, including Diana, the Princess of Wales. This happens when they are in residence at Windsor, and then the dollhouse is closed to the public. From mid-March to mid-October, the dollhouse is open Monday through Saturday from 10:30 A.M. to 3:00 P.M. (closed on Sundays).

When Queen Mary accepted the gift, she called it "the most perfect present anyone could receive!" It was truly a gift fit for a queen.

* * *

Wall Game—The Worst Spectator Sport

Eton (England)

Tourists who come to England usually want to see a game of cricket. Jolly good! But here's another British sport you ought to look into on your sojourn here, one that few foreigners know about. It's called the **WALL GAME**— and it has to head any list as truly the worst spectator sport in the world.

Yet it gets coverage by England's TV crews and writeups the next day in the British papers, even though most watchers don't know what in bloody blazes is going on. Neither will you. Nevertheless, it is an attraction that tourists should go to once for sure, though not likely for a second time. Once is enough, but once is a must.

What makes the yearly Wall Game at Eton the worst of the spectator contests is that fans rarely know where the ball is, nor can they determine the identities of the players once the action begins. Anybody who watches is baffled 99 percent of the time, but having a ball 100 percent of the time just locating the ball.

Having reached its 150th anniversary, the Wall Game is a fray that has no parallel anywhere. The annual contest at Eton, which is 30 minutes by motor west of London, begins at noontime on St. Andrew's Day, which takes place at the end of November. The two teams of ten Eton boys each are made up of the so-called Collegers (the students who live in dormitories) and the so-called Oppidans (who get their name from the Latin *oppidum*, because they live in town and not on campus). The rules of the game are rather simple and have come down to the present day, willy-nilly, from eighteenth-century mud-splashing contests.

At Eton the playing field is approximately 100 yards long and is bounded on one side by a high brick wall built in 1717 (the ground at its widest point extends no more than 15 yards). The object of the game is to drive a ball, which is about half the size of a soccer ball, along the length of the wall past a certain line called the Good Calx at one end or the Bad Calx at the other end, beyond which one team is legally allowed to try to score (there are no goalies).

No hands are permitted to touch the ball, which can only be nudged by feet or knees. Hands may be used, however, on an opponent. It is permissible for a player to clap a handful of mud or sand, depending on weather conditions, into the mouth of an adversary in order to distract him momentarily and encourage him to do one's bidding—which, translated from the Queen's English, means you want him to get away from the damn ball.

Yes, you guessed it: the Wall Game is the world's roughest sport, too. This is in spite of the fact that Rule XII disallows a player to cause a rival contender "excruciating discomfort." In American English, Rule XII forbids kicking, striking, tripping, stamping, knuckling, punching and elbowing. Oddly enough, the same regulation permits a player to grate the backbone of an enemy by running an elbow up and down his spine and also to grind the face of an opponent with a closed fist.

The highlight of a Wall Game is what is known as the "Bully." This comes when the three "Walls" on each side (a Wall is a gigantic-sized man chosen for his exceptional strength and not for his intellectual powers) take advantage of their advantage and prevent the bad guys from getting possession of the ball while said ball is forwarded in a controlled situation toward the unattended goal line. The frenzy over the disputed, and mostly invisible, leathery oval is marked by alternating possession throughout various forms of bodily argumentation to help impose the will of one team on the other.

One of the team members, usually the smallest boy available, is called the "Fly," and his job is to keep a running commentary on the whereabouts of the ball, which has a way of getting lost even to the players. Making up in trickery and viciousness what he lacks in weight, the Fly often steps on the opposition's hands and employs other forms of questionable coercion. The Fly, say the rules, may not be swatted.

As for the referee, he doesn't carry anything so impolite as a whistle, since his primary function is to see that no player is ever smothered to death. But perhaps the most astonishing thing about Eton's ungentlemanly Herculean tussle is the fact that no goal has been scored in over 60 years, at which time the Oppidans won 1–0. In fact, goals are so rare in the Wall Game that the first one was scored in 1842, the next one in 1885 and the one after that in 1928— a break of 43 years. This is the kind of sporting event that hardly ever gets to the point.

* * *

The Thirteen Heads of Oxford

Oxford (England)

A funny thing happened on the way to Cambridge: Oxford! So, please, Cambridge, don't think we don't love you, but the sanctitude of learning that is Oxford can indeed one-up you because of the THIRTEEN HEADS.

Made of stone, ponderous and weighing over a ton apiece, they gaze mischievously at passersby from their vantage outside the university's assembly theater. They have been, for all of three centuries, Oxford's best-loved curiosities—and a first-rate mystery as to who or what they are. Sherlock, where art thou?

What a shame that thousands of tourists who come to Oxford each week to visit the site of the world's greatest university with its thirty-four different colleges very often overlook this town's most unusual feature—thirteen enigmatic, giant noggins arrayed in a large semicircle that curves around the **Sheldonian Theatre**. They have variously been called the "Roman Emperors," the "Philosophers" and the "Twelve Apostles" (even though there is actually one more by count).

Generations of Oxford urchins have been warned by Dad or Mum that if they misbehaved, or were disobedient, they would not be taken to see the Roman Emperors having their beards trimmed. Among adults there has always been talk that at night the thirteen sneak down from their pillars to indulge in a nip or two of ale at the twelfth-century pub called the **Turf Tavern** after it has closed.

A number of Oxford's bright students have tried to track down the full story of the strange heads, but so far no convincing facts have emerged. There are, however, some credible, calculated theories: the main one is that the heads were not meant to be portraits at all but were simply intended to show different kinds of beards. Although each of the faces is indeed bearded differently, no one can explain why the sculptor, William Byrd, would have occupied himself with such a trivial subject on such a large scale.

Although Byrd carved fourteen heads, one of them had to be removed early in the eighteenth century to make room for a new, adjacent building. This missing fourteenth head has never cropped up, and most people believe it is lying on the bottom of the Thames River in the Oxford vicinity. To confuse the issue a bit more, the ones you see today—which are carved in Clipsham limestone—are not the ones Byrd sculpted, for those were twice replaced, once in 1860 when the poor quality stone had begun to deteriorate, and then again in 1972, when another set was carved by sculptor Michael Black after the 1860 heads had started to decay.

As for Byrd's thirteen originals, each one of them has been located, scattered in various Oxford gardens, except for one that used to be in the garden of the Corpus Christi College—that one disappeared over 35 years ago after a drunken student revelry.

So the heads you see standing guard around the Sheldonian (which was the first major building designed by the great Christopher Wren) were apparently modeled on the so-called boundary statues of ancient Greece, named after Hermes, who was the god of roads and doors.

When asked why Oxford University had bothered to go to the expense and the trouble of replacing what some people have termed "meaningless heads," Sir Alan Bullock, the school's vice-chancellor, pondered a moment and said, "Well, we like them, don't we?"

After paying a visit to the Thirteen, the best way to see Oxford is to take a two-hour walking tour that starts at the town's information center on High Street where former students serve as guides. You'll see everything Oxford has to offer a visitor as you get whisked through the academic and dormitory areas of the colleges (each of which holds onto its medieval autonomy), the impressive **Bodleian Library** with more than 3 million volumes, the oldest music room in Europe, the town's intricate system of underwater canals, the gardens and courtyards of the schools and Oxford's biggest bell, the **Great Tom**, at the entrance to Christ Church College. It tolls exactly 101 times at 9:00 P.M. every night, a carryover from the days when carousing male students had to run through the gates before the 101st toll, or else be locked out all night.

Established as a town sometime near the end of the eighth century, Oxford did not come into prominence until the founding of the university in 1140. With its great mixture of arches, spires, courtyards, rooftops, meadows, gardens, green quadrangles and medieval layouts (seen best from the vantage point of nearby **Bagley Hill**), Oxford is worth a side trip anytime, from either London or Stratford-upon-Avon, both of which are about an hour away.

What you'll find superb on your tour are the famed Oxford lawns, which are manicured like putting greens. A grizzled old university gardener explains how the fabulous lawns come about: "It's not really hard. You just grow the grass, mow it, fertilize it, feed it, baby it and preen it—for about 800 years!"

* * *

Edinburgh's Royal Mile

Edinburgh (Scotland)

A mile, officially, is 5,280 feet. Edinburgh's ROYAL MILE, however, is not measured in feet or inches but with another yardstick. Although the Royal Mile is actually longer than a real mile, it measures up to any street anywhere in the world because no matter where you decide to tackle it, you don't get off on the wrong foot.

There's much to see and do on the Royal Mile, which actually measures 1,984 yards of what is known as the Long Scots Mile, but before you plunge in, your best bet is to acquire a guidebook on the subject. Replete with Scottish words and phrases that provide a bit of local flavor, perhaps the finest one is a 48-page paperback called *A Guide to the Royal Mile—Edinburgh's Historic Highway*, written and published by Gordon Wright, Esq.

To conquer the sights, sites and shops of the Royal Mile you should really give yourself two days, though it's possible to do it in one chockful day. The Royal Mile, a cobbled street that slopes steeply, starts at the **Edinburgh Castle**, which is a fortress firmly plunked on top of a dead volcano and its massive slopes of hard rock. If you start at this point, then you walk downhill all the way to the end point at the **Holyrood Palace**, which was built in 1501 by King James IV and which housed Mary Queen of Scots during her feud with Queen Elizabeth I.

In between these two endpoints, the Royal Mile keeps you occupied with the past and the present every inch of the way. It has been compared to the skeleton of a big fish, and you see why once you start walking along it, down the lefthand side and then up again on the opposite side.

Edinburgh Castle, which has repelled every invasion throughout the ages, should get at least one hour of your time. Its esplanade, serving as the parade ground for the castle garrison and as the site of the annual Military Tattoo during Edinburgh's arts festival in August, provides a gorgeous view of the city and its horizon. This includes the broad span of the **Pentland Hills**, an extremely rich diet for the hungriest of cameras. With great halls, museums, chapels, shrines, dungeons and cemeteries (there's even a small graveyard for Scotland's regimental dogs), the castle has more history to it than any history book, and you are reminded of this by the one-o'clock cannon that has been fired each weekday since 1851.

Near the exit point of the castle, you should take advantage of the so-called camera obscura in the **Outlook Tower**, for it will give you a different panoramic picture of the city. This is done with a mirror on the tower top that jets a light through a tiny aperture onto a concave surface in a dark room, and a panoramic photo of the city appears, which an attendant will describe, point by point.

Listed here in no special order are *some* of the features and highlights of the Royal Mile that gloriously slow down your pace: **Golfer's Land**, which was built by a shoemaker with his winnings from a golf match when he partnered the Duke of York (later King James VII); the 1490 **John Knox House** (home of Presbyterianism) with its overhanging upper floors; the **Netherbow Port** (one of the six gates of old Edinburgh) where heads of criminals were eerily exhibited on spikes; the **Canongate Church and Churchyard** where Adam Smith, the economist, is buried near a number of other famous Scots; the **Holyrood Brewery** where beer has been brewed since the twelfth century when the monks discovered that the local water made first-rate ale.

Jenny Ha's Change House, a tavern built in the seventeenth century and famous for its claret; the **Museum of Childhood** (page 26), with a wonderful collection of old-time toys numbering more than 25,000; **St. Giles Cathedral**, with remarkable stained-glass windows, ancient battle flags and a tower shaped like the crown of Scotland; the **statue of King Charles II** dressed as a Roman Emperor (cast in lead in 1685); **Parliament Hall**, which was used until 1707 and once served as a stable for Oliver Cromwell; and **Cannonball House**, so named because a cannonball has been lodged in the west wall since the Jacobite siege of 1745.

Not to be missed under any circumstances is the seventeenth-century **Lady Stair's House**, a free museum honoring the literary agents of Scotland, like Sir Walter Scott, Robert Burns and Robert Louis Stevenson. Here is where you'll see original manuscripts and the printing press that was used to publish the works of Scott.

Along the way, dotted by tea shops, pubs and quick-bite restaurants, you'll be lured into kilt-making shops, bagpipe stores, sweater emporia and knitwear factories with the best prices in the British Isles. If you happen to have a name with a Scottish background, look up your tartan and purchase a scarf or a tie. You'll also come across sights and sites with enticing names like Queen Mary's Bath House, Horse Wynd, Shoemaker's Land, Bull's Close, St. John's Pend, the Tron Kirk, the Heart of Midlothian and the Upper Bow.

Indeed, to do justice to the Royal Mile is in itself a wonderful battle royal.

* * *

Greyfriars Bobby

Edinburgh (Scotland)

Here's the dog-umentary evidence on one of Edinburgh's supremely unique touristic lures. The words **GREYFRIARS BOBBY** are magic for thousands of people all over the British Isles who travel to Edinburgh to make a pilgrimage to the statue of the most famous canine in Scotland's bonnie history.

On any day of the week, if you come to the top of Candlemaker Row in old Edinburgh (along the so-called *Royal Mile* (page 21) and within barking distance of the monumental *Edinburgh Castle*) (page 21) you are bound to see whole classes of schoolchildren gathered around a teacher who is relating the fascinating story of Greyfriars Bobby in all its touching detail.

Several artists have painted the dog in oils or water color, and two books have been written on the subject (copies are available at a nearby souvenir/bookstore). Even Walt Disney once put out a film about the incredible dog, a scruffy little Skye terrier who made canine history and, with it, millions of fans throughout the Commonwealth.

Greyfriars Bobby was picked up as a stray one day in the mid-1850s by a shepherd named John Gray, known as "Auld Jock" to his friends. He and the dog become inseparable pals, but in 1858 John Gray died and was buried in a churchyard across the street from where the statue stands today. For the next 14 years, every day of the week, Bobby loyally spent nearly all his time at his master's tombstone. The bereaved little pooch died in 1872 at the age of 16 and today is buried in the Greyfriars cemetery, not far from his master's side.

Although the dog's devotion had made him a legend throughout Edinburgh, and eventually throughout all of the British Isles, the law's hard hand took Bobby into court on charges of vagrancy and trespassing. Had he been convicted, the faithful terrier would have been put to death in the city dog pound. But in court Bobby found himself among friends.

The Lord Provost, William Chambers, volunteered to pay Bobby's license fee every year, and Bobby was given a brass-plated collar that read: "Greyfriars Bobby, from the Lord Provost, 1867, Licensed." That collar gave Bobby the legal right to stay in the cemetery 24 hours around the clock to continue his constant vigil. Later, the city of Edinburgh officially adopted him, an unprecedented act for any government.

The monument to Greyfriars Bobby was built by a wealthy English woman, the Baroness Angela Georgina Burdett-Coutts who had heard about Bobby shortly before he died. As an animal lover, and fascinated by the dog's devotion, she offered to keep his memory fresh after his death by erecting a fountain at her expense—a gift the city gratefully accepted.

The fountain is of red granite, with drinking water provided for dogs and passersby. On top of the fountain is a life-sized bronze model of Bobby, and underneath is an inscription that reads: "A tribute to the affectionate fidelity of Greyfriars Bobby. In 1858 this faithful dog followed the remains of his master to Greyfriars Churchyard and lingered near the spot until his death in 1872. With permission, erected by Baroness Burdett-Coutts."

Tourists can see two of Bobby's possessions today in the **Huntly House Museum** on High Street. One is the collar given to him in 1867 by the Lord Provost, and the other is the metal dinner bowl that Bobby ate from in a restaurant run by a certain John Traill, who provided the dog with a meal every day at one o'clock when the daily cannon boomed. In the special showcase devoted to Bobby, the museum also displays several photographs of Bobby and John Traill.

Dogs hardly ever make the obituary columns. Not so, Bobby. A notice about him appeared in the *Scotsman*, Edinburgh's staid daily, on January 17, 1872: "Many will be sorry to hear that the poor but interesting dog, 'Greyfriars Bobby,' died on Sunday evening. Every kind attention was paid to him in his last days by his guardian, Mr. Traill, who has had him buried in a flower-plot near Greyfriars Church. His collar, a gift from Lord Provost Chambers, has been deposited in the office at the church gate."

A hundred years after Bobby's death, on a Sunday morning, a service was held in the cemetery by the minister of the Greyfriars Church in honor of Bobby, an event that was televised by the BBC. Bobby had made his niche in dogdom history as a tourist target.

So the legend of the immortal Greyfriars Bobby continues as every day visitors from as far away as New Zealand are drawn to the statute to pay him homage—truly a shaggy dog story.

*   *   *

The Museum of Childhood

Edinburgh (Scotland)

Inside everyone's brain is a compartment labeled "Childhood—Memories Of," and inside that is a special section of gray matter labeled "Toys," which is a good four-letter word for fun. In Edinburgh's West End, at Number 2 Rutland Place (directly across from the historic **John Knox House**, (page 22), you can visit the **MUSEUM OF CHILDHOOD**, which is not a museum for kids only, but for adults, tourists included, who can enjoy a fantasy flight into the frolicsome days of youth.

Started in the mid-1950s by a local bachelor-politician who claimed he "disliked children," this fascinating museum has over 50,000 toys, of which more than 15,000 are on display at one time on four floors of nostalgia, reminiscences and surprises. The Edinburgh collection of toys, games, puzzles, and other small-fry artifacts is without doubt the best of all possible toy museums, for it unlocks your mind to the past as you wander from object to object and showcase to showcase.

Annually attracting over 50,000 visitors—of whom more than 35,000 are grownups—the Museum of Childhood does an outstanding job of putting toys in their proper place (something few kids ever learn), largely in terms of yesterday, and according to five major categories: toys of movement, soft toys, small toys that reflect adult activity (like war), building toys and folk toys from various parts of the world. The games on display range from the kind that have passed into oblivion to the sophisticated board games of the modern world.

With a richness in nostalgic playthings that encourages lingering, the museum is great fun. Some of the things on display are not even toys at all—such as the "Secret Service" postcard (1932), which tells youngsters that "one of the easy ways to send a secret message is to write with a quill pen using milk as ink, and your pal heats the message so that it now comes out a readable brown." Thrilling stuff.

Perhaps the most awesome toy of all is the huge, impressive dollhouse with electric light and running water. Six feet long, four feet high and two feet deep, this exhibit is always so crowded that it's rather difficult to take a photograph of it all by itself. The miniature toy shops and the tiny kitchens—which mothers used to introduce their daughters to the domestic skills—are other favorites, as is the vast collection of dolls (an exhibit that draws, by the way, more scholars and serious students than other items do).

A mere listing of all the museum's attractions would be a challenge even Hercules might have balked at, but here's a random sample from A to Z:

Archery set, ball games, bells, billiards, blocks, books, bottles, bubble pipes, carousel horse, chemistry sets, children's newspapers, Christmas cards and Valentines, cigarette and chewing gum cards, cinema toys, clay handwarmers, comic books, costumes, cut-out paper figures, dominoes, erector sets, fairy-tale books, fire engines, German clockwork toys, hats, jigsaw puzzles, knives, magic lanterns, magnets, marionettes, mathematical games, medals and buttons, minitheatres, model airplanes, musical instruments, paintboxes, painting books, paper assembly toys, picture books, piggy banks, playing cards, railroad trains, rattles, rocking horses, sewing things, story books, stuffed animals, talking dolls, tea sets, tin soldiers, tiny tableware, warships, wax fruits, weapons, whistles, Wild West items, yo-yos and zoo creatures.

Charming and ingenious beyond description are the homemade toys, particularly the ones that were made in foreign countries by people who could not afford the price of store-bought ones. Running the full gamut of human imagination, these handcrafted playthings include a doll made from an old shoe (Egypt), fully dressed dead fleas set in a half hazelnut shell (Mexico), tiny garments made from seaweed and onion skins (Spain), painted human figures made from corn husks (Czechoslovakia), and wooden tops made to spin with whips (Italy). There is also an array of makeshift toys made by prisoners of war who intended to bring them home for their kids.

Here and there are scattered some of the oddest items ever made for children. Among other beauts these include: a child's hot-water-bottle cover in the shape of a rabbit, a multiplication table stitched by a six-year-old girl, various mechanical banks that include one of a soldier shooting coins into an iron safe, a one-eyed teddy bear and a billiard player whose ball is returned to him until the action ceases.

Not to be overlooked when you are finally leaving this time-thieving collection are boxes of kiddie cookies on sale at the main desk. They taste good, but they don't look particularly appetizing—they're in the form of mud pies!

* * *

Alexander Selkirk, Robinson Crusoe

Lower Largo (Scotland)

For years travelers have been touring Scotland, almost tiptoeing along well-defined paths so as not to disturb certain places where the twentieth century seems never to have happened. Such a place is the waterfront town of **Lower Largo** on the south coast of the Kingdom of Fife, which last year clocked in fewer than a hundred tourists. Alas!

This is the town in which a certain cobbler's son, born over 300 years ago, ran away to sea in 1695 when he was 19 years old . . . was stranded in 1704 on a tiny island off the coast of Chile . . . and only got back to civilization some five years later. Then he met the famous essayist, Richard Steele, who, after listening to the unblievable yarn, wrote a story about it that was later used by yet another London author as the basis for an adventure novel.

The castaway was **ALEXANDER SELKIRK**; the London novelist was Daniel DeFoe, and the book he wrote—you guessed it!—was *Robinson Crusoe*. But maybe you don't know that here on High Street in Lower Largo stands

Selkirk's cottage birthplace. In a niche above it is a bronze statue of him clad in skins, with one hand holding a gun and the other raised above his eyes, hopefully scanning the horizon for a distant ship.

Beneath is a plaque that has the following inscription: "In memory of Alexander Selkirk, mariner, the original Robinson Crusoe who lived on the Island of Juan Fernandez in complete solitude for 4 years and 4 months. He died in 1723, aged 47 years."

Reachable in a couple of hours by bus from Edinburgh—also only a 15-minute drive from the hallowed turf of the renowned **St. Andrews golf course** and **St. Andrews College**—Lower Largo deserves a green-light asterisk on your travel schedule.

With a little luck you may well meet up with the descendant of DeFoe's model for one of the most enduring literary figures known to every schoolkid and adult alike. He is Selkirk's great-great-great-grandnephew, one Allan Jadine, a retired sixtyish farmer, whose knowledge about his great-great-great-granduncle is fascinatingly encyclopedic.

Did you know for instance, that Selkirk (whose real name was Selcraig before he changed it) was not shipwrecked the way the fictional Robinson Crusoe had been, but actually began his true adventure after an argument with his captain? He demanded to be put ashore on one of the Juan Fernandez islands (Más a Tierra) with all his possessions because he was wary of the seaworthiness of the ship he was on, the *Cinque Ports*.

And did you know that once he set foot on the island, he had a quick change of heart, saw what isolation he had in store for him and realized what a mistake he had made? He desperately shouted to be taken back aboard ship, but his shrieks were ignored. In the novel his adventures as a castaway on the island for over four years and how he coped with his solitary dilemma are all accurate—except for the part about meeting Friday, who DeFoe invented, using literary license.

Selkirk was eventually rescued in February 1709, a miserable figure dressed in goatskins, unable to speak coherently. He had become an antisocial eccentric, and when he finally returned to his hometown, he burst through the door of the village church on a Sunday morning looking like a fearful character and shocking the congregation. After that, Selkirk spent most of his time in Lower Largo as a recluse in a cave he made behind his father's house, often rowing across Largo Bay to the uninhabited Kincraig Point to be totally alone. In 1717 he went back to sea, and six years later died aboard his ship from a fever, never to know that his true story would live on for centuries to come.

Selkirk's coconut drinking-cup and his wooden chest are on display in Edinburgh's **National Museum of Antiquities**, but his long-barreled flintlock went astray in 1895 when a member of the Jardine family auctioned it off to a Philadelphia woman who gave it to a restaurant where it hung for many years. In 1926 the weapon was returned to Britain by the daughter of the deceased restaurateur, but was once again "lost." Trying to track it down, Mr. Jardine has instituted a publicity campaign for it on the assumption that it is in some Scottish basement or attic.

When you come to Lower Largo, especially during the summer months, you'll have a chance to enjoy the sea and the sandy beach of Largo Bay, which has always been a haven for seamen, especially when storms threaten, for the waters are perfectly safe for a swim. The tiny beachside Crusoe Hotel runs a fine kitchen and serves up some intriguing dishes named after you-know-who. That's seven days a week, including Friday.

* * *

The Highland Games

Braemer (Scotland)

If you're the kind of tourist looking for action, you'll get multiple doses of it at the **HIGHLAND GAMES**, where the action is everywhere. That includes flying tree trunks, sky-soaring hammers, heavy stones floating in air, tugs-of-war,

uphill foot races, pillow fights, chin-to-shoulder wrestling
and slippery grass-racing on bikes. All of them are arduous
novelty sports going back, in most cases, as far as a thousand years. So don't knock 'em until you've tried 'em—but
better still, why not see the Highland Games in their natural habitat?

Every year during the height of the tourist season, in
dozens of cities and towns gracing the blue and purple hill
regions of Scotland, the traditional Highland Games are
staged to give kilted giants, "strong in limb and tough in
endurance" (to borrow a Scottish phrase), a chance to show
their stuff with their feats of strength, skill and beauty—all
with uniformed marching bands dishing up local music on
bagpipes and drums. Few spectacles can claim to be as
colorful as these games, which are staged in the Scottish Highlands during the months of June, July, August
and September in one rose-covered-cottage village after
another.

Finding out when a village has the games is as easy as
pie. If you're in Scotland, the nearest tourist office will give
precise dates and places. To find out well ahead of time,
before you even go to Scotland, you can write directly to
the Scottish Tourist Board at 23 Ravelston Terrace, Edinburgh EH4 3EU, and you'll get a folder telling you where
each of the games is being staged, and when, for several
years in advance. Most of the contests, generally speaking, are held on Saturdays—with the very last ones usually scheduled for the second Saturday in September at
Pitlochry.

The Highland Games at Braemar in Aberdeenshire,
which take place on the first Saturday in September, are
considered the most important because the Queen of England, her husband and members of the Royal Family attend the proceedings. This has mostly to do with tradition,
since in Queen Victoria's day the Royal Family was always
in residence at the nearby Castle of Balmoral when the
Braemer games were scheduled.

Another nice thing about the Highland Games is the low
admission fee. This is partly to reflect Scotland's reputation
for thriftiness, but whatever price you pay, you get a lot of

pageantry, a lot of entertainment and a lot to cheer about. The usual spectacular finale, which includes the grand marching parade, makes a day at the Highland Games a grand family outing no one ever forgets.

The origins of the games are mixed in with Scotland's austere past. Since the Scots had to do everything by hand and cover all distances by foot, muscle power became the means by which a poor man could cope with life in the Highlands. If a man could not cut timber, lift rocks or chase across the moors for his food, life would be impossible.

Credit for starting the games goes to King Malcolm Canmore, who, to find new fleet-of-foot messengers for his staff, had the idea of arranging a hill race to the top of Craig Choinich, a mountain overlooking Braemar. Winners could get a purse of gold, a sword and a job with the king's troops as a runner. Then the sporting contest was staged in subsequent years, and as time went on, various new athletic events of a typically Scottish flavor were added, not to mention dancing exhibitions and musical interludes.

Easily the most exciting of the individual games is the one called "tossing the cabar." The cabar is an 18-foot-long tree trunk weighing about 150 pounds. Actually, the object is not to toss the trunk for distance but as straight as possible according to the face of an imaginary clock—so that if a tosser throws the pole from a six-o'clock position, the bottom end must turn a full semicircle in midair and land as close as possible to the twelve-o'clock position. Cabar-throwing, by the way, originated from the practice of Scotch lumbermen who pitched trees across streams to avoid carrying them long distance.

Stone-putting is much like the shotput in the Olympics, except that the stone must weigh between 13 and 28 pounds and may vary in shape—some of them even being boulders from the nearest river. The hammer throw is not to be confused with the Olympic hammer; here the contestant is not allowed to turn but must stand with his spiked boots firmly in the ground, swinging the hammer around his head three to five times before letting go.

Other exciting events include the Cumberland-style wrestling match where the contestants stand chest-to-chest with their chins on each other's right shoulder and grasp one another around the waist with hands clasped. When the loser touches the ground with anything other than his feet or when he breaks his grip, the contest is won. The pillow fight pits two men sitting on a horizontal pole, each with one hand secured behind his back, while they try to knock each other to the ground with straw-filled sacks. For thrills and spills there is no equal to the cycling event held on slippery grass or on muddy tracks where contestants are permitted to hold onto their rivals' bikes.

All things being equal, not to be overlooked is the proud marching and counter-marching of the pipe bands, which make for a stirring sight—rivalled only by the complex, athletic folk dancing of the Scottish Highlands. Going back to the eighteenth century, the Highland Fling is derived from the antics of a courting stag. The Sword Dance, which has its origins in Scotland's martial tradition, hies to the eleventh century and involves a nimble set of complicated steps done between the blades of swords. A dance called Flora MacDonald's Fancy is for women alone, and it stresses elegance and the swing and rustle of the skirt.

Any tourist who seeks out the games on the next trip to Scotland has an easy choice on how to get to them. Simply follow the good advice from that song—you can take the high road or you can take the low road.

GERMANY

The Sparrow of Ulm

Ulm

This vest-pocket city on the banks of the Danube has a hardy little feathered creature as its main symbol. Known as the **ULM SPARROW**, the bird is perched prominently in the center of town on top of the world's largest Protestant cathedral—and therein lies a charming tale. When you come to Ulm, you'll not only get a full dose of the celebrated sparrow but also, more important for the tourist, an unforgettable dose of Ulm itself, probably the most underrated city in Germany.

Ulm doesn't spoil a good thing with promotional overkill, for unlike nearby Stuttgart, 44 miles north, this toy box of a town looks just about the way it did a century or so ago. The postwar restorations made sure the city was put together the way it was before being bombed out. There are neither mega-bulb signs to assault the eyes, nor mega-decibel night clubs to assault the ears. Indeed, Ulm is the kind of city where you stand downtown at the main intersection and mentally drink a toast in its honor.

But first, what's this about an ornithological tourist sight, the sparrow of Ulm? The way the folks here tell the story—which you are supposed to believe, no matter how much it taxes your credibility—is that the workmen who were building the cathedral centuries ago were faced with a problem that a sparrow finally solved for them. It seems the men who were lugging the timber could not get through the narrow town gate because the planks were too long.

While the workers were deciding whether to cut the logs into smaller lengths or to tear down the gate, a sparrow, taking a bird's-eye view of all this, figured she'd show the workers what to do. Gripping a piece of straw in her beak to build her nest, she turned her head so that the straw was now pointed in the other direction, thereby demonstrating to the men that all they had to do to get the wood inside the gate was to turn the planks around longways, instead of sideways. So the story goes.

For this historic helpful hint, the sparrow achieved immortality, becoming Ulm's first honorary citizen and the number one heroine of the city. You can see her with the strand of straw in her mouth atop the roof of the **Münster Church**, probably the only bird in Germany's history enjoying such a distinction. But it doesn't end there, because the Ulm Sparrow is found everywhere today—you can buy kitschy and nonkitschy statuettes of her in every souvenir store; marzipan and chocolate facsimiles of her and frozen chocolate-coated ice cream reproductions of her in candy shops; plus paintings and/or postcards, photographs, pennants, stickers, glassware, buttons, jewelry and whatnots of Ulm's beloved critter.

All the same, in time you'll discover that the sparrow isn't Ulm's only charm. The cathedral has the world's tallest spire, a Gothic structure that reaches 530 feet into the sky—and if you have the yen-cum-stamina to do the 768 steps to the top, you are treated to a panorama of Germany you won't forget, a view that extends as far as the Alps. While up there, you get a superb photographic close-up angle of the sparrow, by the way.

Ulm's Protestant church, second in overall size only to Cologne's cathedral, took many centuries to build (from 1377 to 1890), and it contains the exquisitely carved wooden choir stalls by the fifteenth-century master, Jorg Syrlin the Elder. When this work of art was smashed to kindling wood by World War II bombs, the pieces were painstakingly glued together again.

With its own leaning tower, Ulm's **Metzgerturm** houses the smallest theater in Europe. Tilting nearly seven feet and casting a slanted shadow on the river bank, the tower, a former prison, is not slated to go the way its more famous relative in Pisa is supposed to. Nearby is Ulm's renowned "crooked house," called the **Schiefes Haus**, an enchanting half-timbered dwelling whose thick beams are completely bent out of shape, but despite its dangerous look, people still live inside.

To get to both the crooked house and the leaning tower, you stroll on a city-wall footpath that, over 500 years old, is the only one of its kind anywhere in Euope. This utterly delightful elevated walkway takes you to the Blau River at a point where it narrows to a width of about ten feet. Also not to be overlooked is Ulm's fascinating **astronomical clock** that dates back to 1520 and Ulm's **bread museum**, which is dedicated to the staff of life.

And last but not least, on the outskirts of town is a street called Albert Einstein Strasse, named after the great scientist who was born in Ulm in a four-story house at Number 20 Bahnhof Strasse. Ulm proudly boasts about its genius son and its bird-brained sparrow—two extremes that show that all things are really relative!

*   *   *

Oath Monday

Ulm

"**OATH MONDAY**" just doesn't sound tourist-tempting. Well it is.

Score one point for yourself if you knew that Ulm was the birthplace of Albert Einstein, two points if you have ever heard of Ulm's Oath Monday. Give yourself a full ten points if you've ever jumped into the Danube River while 160,000 people watched during the so-called *Nabada* that is held every year in July.

It's on Oath Monday that Ulm lets its teutonic hair down for some of the nuttiest nonstop merrymaking that makes the rest of Germany's beer busts look like girlscout campfire soirees. Called in German *Schwörmontag*, Oath Monday begins around noontime when the Lord Mayor of Ulm stands on the balcony of the Schwörhaus, as required by tradition, and swears to every resident of his fair city, most of whom are gathered in the square below, to uphold the municipal constitution as it was written nearly seven centuries ago (although Ulm actually started up in the ninth century).

Once the Lord Mayor has recited his oath, now begins the spectacular *Nabada*, which is a dialect word meaning "to bathe while floating downstream." While Ulm's 100,000 residents, together with some 60,000 visitors from everywhere, line up on both banks of the Danube to watch dozens of gaily colored boats bob by in procession, men and women of all ages, not excluding some city officials, jump into the drink for their once-a-year Danube dip.

This particular tradition started in 1811 as the result of a poor tailor's fantasies. Far from being one of those disputable folklore yarns, the story of Albrecht Ludwig Berblinger is a true tale. Possessing a lot of guts and ingenuity, the tailor fashioned a pair of silk wings that he hoped would enable him to soar into the air. The statue of Berblinger in the center of town, by the way, gives him credit for being the first German who actually tried to fly. Anyway, Berblinger and his homemade wings plopped into the gray waters of the Danube as the whole town turned out to watch his aeronautic fiasco.

Despite his failure, Berblinger became a hero of sorts, and though he never tried to fly again (his wife sold the makeshift flaps to an umbrella maker), the young people of Ulm took the occasion of his ill-fated pioneer effort to plunge into the Danube every year after that—and thus was born the *Nabada*.

Another picturesque event is the frantic *Fischerstechen* (literally, fishermen stabbing at each other) that also takes place on Ulm's resident river. Dressed in white costumes and armed with long wooden poles, sturdy youths stand upright—or try to—in the back of boats and do glorious battle against each other as they are rowed by three plume-hatted men. The object is for one "water knight" to knock his opponent into the wet. This particular type of contest actually began in 1662 and took place every year since then as a separate event until the river gladiators were eventually included as part of the Oath Monday events.

The water of the Danube is not the only important fluid that runs on Oath Monday, however. When the river show comes to a close by late afternoon, it's time for King Beer to take over. The city forthwith adjourns en masse to the beer gardens, the squares, the cafés, courtyards, rathskellers, hotels and restaurants where Germany's liquid asset reigns supreme.

If you can get in, the "in" place for the action is the biggest of the city's some 50 food emporia, the rathskeller in the basement of the town hall. Also a very popular place is Ulm's oldest restaurant, a celebrated fisherman's inn called the Weinstube Forelle. In both these locales, as in every other Ulm restaurant, Swabian specialties are served. Don't pass up another Ulm treat that goes well with or without beer—thumb-thick soft pretzels, swabbed with butter chunks and available in any bakery.

On Oath Monday the revelry goes on and on and on. Indeed, in Ulm, that Tuesday has an inexorable way of vanishing so that the day that follows Oath Monday is always Wednesday. Predictably, this kind of folklore event is enough to make you want to pay court to it. So why not swear you'll come here, witness Oath Monday for yourself and be your own judge?

*   *   *

Hamburg Harry's Bazaar

Hamburg

Wanna buy a shark? Or a polar bear that growls at you in total silence? The place to go is where the world's wandering sailors dock, sooner or later, to sell bizarre items they have picked up in their travels. They need the pocket money during their stay in this Hanseatic port, where the naughtiest mile in Europe provides the tars with a nightlife that beats anything yet.

Next time you're in Hamburg and you have some spare time on your hands, pay a call on what is easily the world's most unusual antique shop—**Harry's Hamburger Haf-enbasar**. It's been in business for more than three decades already, and its 30 showrooms are crammed from floor to ceiling with the most outrageous items man or God has ever assembled in one place. Everything is for sale at Harry's—or, to put it in his own words: "We are a museum, yes—but, no, we are not a museum!"

Indeed, a lot of tourists do go just to look, but it is almost inevitable that they end up buying one of Harry's curios. During a recent visit, a newspaperman watched two giggly teenage girls from Canada buy a shrunken head of an Ecuadorian Indian the size of a tennis ball. This reporter ended up acquiring a hand-carved Dahomey warrior girl carrying a war club menacingly in her left hand. The doll had been carved in Africa a few months earlier. Harry had paid $25 for it and sold it to me for $30. That's one of the nice things about Harry's bizarre bazaar—his prices range from cheap to reasonable. He just doesn't like to skin people.

Harry's Hamburger Hafenbasar is located very close to the waterfront on Bernhard-Nocht Strasse 63 in Hamburg's St. Pauli District. His place is open every day of the week from 9:00 A.M. to 10:00 P.M., and when customers or sailors selling something are still drifting in late in the evening, he'll even stay open past midnight.

"We buy anything that could conceivably be classified as art or eligible for a collection," explains Harry Rosenberg, who started his strange business in the late 1950s when he opened up a store that specialized in coins, paper money and stamps.

When foreign sailors in need of extra cash began visiting him offering to sell such things as a Chinese rice-paddy hat or a South American boat carved out of a peach pit (with teeny windows that could swing open), Harry weakened and bought them for his own pleasure.

Word soon got around among the maritime fraternity, and before long every man working on the high seas knew about the port of Hamburg's Harry and his generous wallet. It also became a mail-drop where sailors could leave messages for their buddies at sea due to arrive later.

In most cases, however, Harry doesn't really buy anything from a seaman outright. He actually runs a kind of
pawnshop for sailors, who can deposit some items there for
as long as four months, following which Harry can legally
sell them if they're not reclaimed. Rarely is any item left
with him ever claimed, and that explains why more than
100,000 items are usually up for grabs. Quite often you'll
find some of the curiosities and rarities being played with
as toys by children when wife Lilli is minding the store.

On any given day, Harry's oddball collection might include stuffed animals from all countries, native Indian
masks from the Philippines, coral chunks from the South
Seas, spears from Africa, books and magazines from
Hitler's Third Reich, a collection of personal effects that
belonged to America's yesteryear cowboy star Tom Mix,
three-thonged whips from Russia, parts of oldtime automobiles or ships, toys from any country on earth, long
rifles from the Spanish-American War, bound volumes of a
Swiss newspaper printed in Romansch, military uniforms
from the First World War, the dried-out penis of a whale,
obsolete stock and bond certificates going back a hundred
years, unusual jewelry of all kinds and all values, a bottle of
Portuguese wine from 1925, ancient movie and/or propaganda posters, thousands of postcards from the Kaiser's
time, gas masks, daggers, bayonets, handguns, obsolete
tourist guides for places that don't even exist anymore (like
the nation of Moresnet in Central Europe), chipped and
nonchipped beer mugs in all sizes and shapes, old bus and
tram tickets, statues and statuettes, old telephones, type-
writers, and what-have-you, gulp and phew!

You name it, baby, and Harry has it!

Some of Harry's best clients are big companies and film
producers. Quite often companies wanting to put on special displays in their lobbies need the kind of props that can
only be found at the *basar*. As for the movies, nearly every
week a director desperately seeks to borrow (at a price, of
course) an exotic prop or a variety of such rarities—and so
it's off to Harry's to scour around among his offbeat gems.

But when all is said and done, the most interesting item
in the store is . . . you guessed it: Harry himself. Harry is a

selling point, all right—but Lilli lets women customers know that Harry is the only item in the place that is not up for grabs.

* * *

Passau the Beautiful

Passau

My quest of over a quarter of a century for the world's most beautiful small town climaxes now in an eye-opening end. Eureka, it has been found. Pass the word on; the password is . . . **PASSAU**.

To have discovered Passau sooner, more attention should have been paid by me to some clues that had already been spread around, such as: (1) Napoleon Bonaparte, who had besieged the town in 1807, confided to his biographer that he had not seen a more beautiful town in Germany; (2) The renowned world traveler Alexander von Humboldt classified Passau, shortly before his death in 1859, as among the seven most beautiful towns in the world; and (3) Composer Richard Wagner, eager to build a music temple to honor his own works, had already decided Passau would be the proper place to commemorate his operas before he abruptly changed his mind and opted for Bayreuth, where he was promised eager financing from the city fathers.

Leaving out a bag of superlatives, I do nevertheless want to paint Passau as beautiful. So let's just have the facts bring the message home to every veteran traveler and would-be tourist who's looking for the "bestest" of the best.

Mapmakers and geographers describe Passau as a "floating city." And a better designation could not be made for this town of 52,000 people. Known as the "Bavarian Venice" and moored in the southwestern-most corner of Germany just over the Austrian border, Passau embraces three rivers that meet in a unique natural spectacle. Coming to a junction at the Passau peninsula are the blue-green

Danube (which originates in the Black Forest), the muddy gray Inn (which rises in a mountain lake in the Swiss Alps) and the peat-brown Ilz (which flows out of the Bavarian Woods).

In a town that is hugged by these three very active rivers, there is, as you could guess, a history of floods, floods, floods. For a devastatingly graphic picture of the lineup of Passau's most destructive floods, go to the city hall building, flanked by an outdoor café on the banks of the Danube, and there at the righthand corner is a large thermometer-like drawing with visual markings of how high the water rose in specific years. Officially, the three worst floods ever are the ones that took place in 1501, 1595 and 1954. In all three instances, both the Danube and the Inn surged over their banks simultaneously, literally filling every house in town with water up to the second story.

As for the pin-point view where the three rivers mingle, swirl and embrace, the best spot for a visitor to zero in on the hydro-trio is the venerable **Veste Oberhaus**, 345 feet above the Danube. This imposing old stronghold can be reached by car, taxi, bus or on foot (uphill). Built in the year 1219 by the prince-bishops, the fortress is a mighty tourist attraction in itself. The citadel contains a museum, art gallery, observatory, battlement parapets, torture chambers, dungeons, a weather station, a youth hostel and princely halls. This stone symbol of power, serving as a retreat for yesteryear's politicos with many tales to tell, also provides a glorious panorama at its knees below.

Even if it weren't for Passau's remarkable location, the town would draw its lion's share of curiosity-seekers anyway. Just before noontime, for instance, every visitor to Passau heads automatically toward the reconstructed baroque-style **St. Stephen's Cathedral**, one of the most significant Christian monuments of the lower Alps and the Danube region, to hear the world's biggest church organ—with 17,388 pipes and 231 stops.

Come early in order to get a seat for the twelve-noon explanation and concert (daily except Sunday) of this incredible, massive musical instrument. The main organ and the two side organs date from the early eighteenth century,

while the organ under the church's roof and the choir
organ were built between 1924 and 1928. All, however,
were thoroughly renewed and enlarged between 1979 and
1980. If you're late, you'll always find standing room along
the sides.

After a detailed explanation of everything you ever
wanted to know about the mammoth organ, the chief organist gives a resounding concert that lasts about 25 minutes. Thine ears have not yet heard such rich echoing
tones, sounds that you begin to believe are coming from
heaven with God Himself at the keyboard. Luckily, you can
take this sound experience home with you, for there are
several recordings of different programs available in the
souvenir shops (nine feature works by Johann Sebastian
Bach, Max Reger, Jean Langlais and Leon Boellman).

Recommended ways to imbue yourself with Passau are
walks through the picturesque alleys and lanes reminiscent
of Venice. Besides doing the inner town on foot, make sure
you saunter along each of the two long riverside promenades, one flanking the Inn and the other paralleling the
Danube—especially *wunderbar* if done at dawn and/or at
sunset. Rewarding as these are, don't miss taking the ultra-
spectacular **Three River Tour** aboard a ferry boat that
bobs along the Danube, the Inn and the Ilz for 45 minutes.
Boats leave daily, every half hour, from March until the
end of October, and most visitors do the boat thing before
they chase down Passau's museums. These include the
Museum of History and the Arts (exhibits in 50 rooms),
the **Cathedral and Diocese Treasure Museum** (in the former residence of the Prince Bishop), and the **Passau Toy
Museum** (housing the Ivan Steiger collection of old European and American playthings).

No doubt the most fascinating museum in town, the
Passau Glass Museum is housed in the Wilder Mann Hotel, whose owner, Georg Holtl, keeps a private collection of
arty nineteenth-century glasses from Bavaria, Bohemia
and Austria. In some 150 showcases on four majestic floors
there are more than 10,000 beautifully crafted drinking
glasses dating from 1780, most of which are classified as
true masterpieces. In the same hotel, located on Rathaus

Platz, Herr Holtl runs a gourmet restaurant that equals the fame of his museum, and warm-weather dining on his terrace overlooking two of the rivers can't be duplicated.

As for the history of the City of Three Rivers, Passau dates back over 2,000 years to when settlements were made on the embankments where the Danube, the Inn and the Ilz converge. No matter how you look at it, Passau—the city built on the banks of three rivers—is a three-time winner. And you can bank on that.

*   *   *

Munich's Thrice-Yearly Fair, the Dult

Munich

Okay, everybody, all together now. Let's hear it for the super-duper **AUER DULT**.

Hold it! The super-duper *what?*

Why, the Auer Dult of Munich—haven't you heard?

Some travelers develop touristophobia, and over the years even cultivate an aversion to throngs, hordes, multitudes and crowded events. So why send people to the Dult of Munich?

Well, for one thing, it's been going on for more than 730 years. For another thing, each Dult draws more than 450,000 Germans because it is actually a mixture of the worst and the best of bazaars, close-out sales and flea markets. The Dult is a shopper's bliss and it swings three times a year—in April, July and October, each time for nine days, without any publicity.

In its own way more authentic than the famed annual Oktoberfest, the Dult is a colorful folk fair that will key you into what makes the Bavarians really tick. Since there is probably nothing to match it, the Dult is the event minus the glitz that preserves the true atmosphere of yesteryear Germany in a way that makes Munich the unique city of Germany.

Held alongside the old Maria-Hilf-Church (built in

1630, but heavily bombed in the last war and reopened again in 1953), the Dult covers the largest square in Munich, not far away from the sprawling **Deutsches Museum** (take Bus 52 from City Hall at Marienplatz and get off when everybody else does).

The Dult operates according to ancient, unwritten rules dating back to the thirteenth century. It opens on a Saturday, and nine days later, on a Sunday night, it closes. The regulations prescribe that of the 320 stands permitted there be 46 stalls dispensing patent medicines, 43 antique dealers (also selling secondhand books), and 28 crockery merchants. With the rest of the stalls, almost anything goes—leather goods, jewelry, toys, straw goods, clothing, cheeses, sausages and sweets, not to mention souvenirs and an incredible variety of white elephants and fascinating junk that would make most flea markets green with envy.

And let's not forget what flows steadily—beer, Munich's trademark. The Dult has its own beer tent, and a tent like this you have to see to believe because it's so spacious inside it looks like a building. Need anything be said after that? Well, yes, actually, since there are 17 other kinds of entertainment, again according to Dult traditions, some of which include a pony track, a ferris wheel and carnival rides. Organ grinders, too.

Apart from the shopping, another thing that gives the Dult flavor is that you can snack to your heart's content. There are, of course, wursts, popcorn, cotton candy and loads of yum-yums, but the three Dult specialties (recommended) are split-roasted fish, jam- or jelly-covered waffles and fruit chunks dipped in white chocolate—for which you nearly always have to queue up on a long but aromatic line.

Open from 9:00 A.M. to 9:00 P.M. each day, the Dult used to be a favorite with composer Richard Wagner, who often found the right props there for his stage productions at Bayreuth. Another eminent German composer, Richard Strauss (himself a Bavarian), was a familiar figure at each of the Dults, and it was not uncommon to see him swilling beer with pals while some pulsating orchestra banged out the latest teutonic hit parade numbers. Ironically, both Strauss's and Wagner's operatic arias get the oom-pah-pah treatment in souped up, but delightfully listenable, versions.

A few of the vendors are themselves straight out of show business—particularly a quip-lash huckster who sells umbrellas, stockings, leather belts and what-have-you. He has a line of patter and fast-on-the-trigger comebacks and putdowns that keep crowds five-deep roaring with laughter. His awning-covered stand, which is his nonstop stage, advertises him as *Der Billige Jakob* (The Inexpensive Jakob), and if you don't spot the awning from afar, just follow the echoing laughter that fills the air every 30 seconds. Whether you understand German or not, you'll go away smiling.

Where do the words *Auer Dult* come from? There are two opinions on this: one views the origin of the word *dult* as descending from the Latin, *indultum*, which means indulgence, and the other says that it derives from the old German word, *Tult*, which means church festival. The word *auer* is from the name of a small community called Au, which is the neighborhood where the Auer Dult takes place today at Maria-Hilf-Platz.

Junky? Maybe. Tawdry? Hmmmmm. Irresistible? Yes! Kitschy? Call it what you will, but the thrice-yearly Auer Dult is the best family shown in town, not excluding the Oktoberfest, because you cannot resist the impulse that you may find something exciting.

So, it's been said that there breathes not a single Munich resident who has not been to the Dult at least a dozen times in his a-dult life.

* * *

Germany's Gem Route

Idar-Oberstein

The main attraction to these twin cities on the River Nahe—a mere 40-minute drive from the Luxembourg border—is that, like a splendorous diamond, they have many facets and should be described with a word not yet in the dictionary.

IDAR-OBERSTEIN, as one of the greatest gem centers in Europe, can boast over 600 gem shops, employs over 10,000 people in the gem business, runs an exciting gem museum and is located strategically on Germany's so-called Gem Highway (clearly marked with gem signs to let you know you're on the right track). And what, pray, is the word that is not in the dictionary to describe Idar-Oberstein? Bravo, you guessed it—"gem-dandy."

Long before Columbus discovered America, the residents of this area had discovered high quality jasper, agate and amethyst and, doing what comes naturally with such things, in short order Idar-Oberstein flourished as a gem center, eventually becoming *the* gem center of Germany. For more than 500 years the locals here excavated rough gemstones.

The diggings, by hand, created vast labyrinths of interconnecting caves in the hillsides, which can be viewed easily, and also brought on an array of would-be highwaymen who, instead of digging like everybody else, took to robbing. Little by little, the busy guillotine of Idar-Oberstein cut short the career of these nefarious gentlemen. They were not, however, the biggest problem for the gem twin cities.

That problem was that the deposit of gemstone materials was exhausted by around 1850, and many of Idar-Oberstein's gem workers migrated to Brazil, Ceylon, Australia and South Africa. But then they began shipping gems back home—moonstones from Ceylon, opals from Australia and tigereyes from Africa—and these imports enabled the centuries-old tradition of grinding gems to continue, guaranteeing the future of Idar-Oberstein as far back as the turn of the century.

What intrigues tourists who come here, besides the fantastic purchase possibilities of gems of all kinds (bargains included!), is to watch the gemstone workers as they grind the stones. In the past workers used to lie horizontally on a special tilted bench as the big, water-bathed sandstone grinding wheels for carving and polishing whirred away.

Visitors can still get a demonstration of this method in the **Weiher-Schleife grinding mill**.

As for the **German Museum of Precious Stones**, located at 34 Mainzer Strasse 34 in Idar, it is open from 8:00 A.M. to 5:00 P.M. every day, including Saturdays and Sundays. Maintained by the area's gem dealers, the museum has a spectacular display of rough gemstones, crystals and hundreds of magnificent, colored gems that excite the passions. They're enough to move some people to hunt down a precious stone to buy—cut or uncut—in one of the many shops.

How Idar and Oberstein became gem cities is a story in itself—a love story, if you please. History reports that a Count Wyrich of Oberstein, who was in love with a beauteous damsel called Bertha of Lichtenberg, was uptight over the attentions his brother, Emich, showered on Bertha. As things turned out, Count Wyrich unceremoniously threw his rival sibling out the castle window, and then the errant nobleman had to leave town.

This all happened way back in the twelfth century. Years later, Count Wyrich—eager to show his repentance and wanting to return for absolution—came back to Oberstein and began building a stone church into the cliff under the castle from which Emich had been given the heave-ho. During the excavations, wouldn't you know that precious stones popped out here, there and everywhere—quality jaspers and amethysts. Thus began the gem industry here.

Count Wyrich's "guilt-church," set in a grotto in the cliff's face, is a notable landmark today. Irresistible indeed, the **Church on the Rock** is a very steep climb, but a rewarding one. The castle from which poor Emich began his final count-down is called the **Alt Schloss** (old castle), and on an adjacent cliff you'll find a more impressive one, the **Neue Schloss** (new castle). The walk between the two castles is a must-do at all costs!

But de rigueur under any circumstances is a guided tour to the **Steinkaulenberg**, an underground gem dig that goes back to medieval times, the only historic mine of its kind in

Europe. Its large gaps and big caves are explorable from mid-March to mid-November but should be done with an experienced tour leader. Available from him is a brochure called *Where the Precious Stones Are To Be Found.*

The guide makes quite clear that if you happen to find a stray gem, you are legally entitled to keep it. In Idar-Oberstein, remember, that a good rule of thumb (and forefinger) for any tourist is never to leave a stone unturned.

* * *

Kansas City in Germany

Plech

If you think you're seeing Wild Bill Hickok or John Wayne acomin' down Main Street here in "Kansas City," look again 'cause this is not Kansas City, USA but **KANSAS CITY, GERMANY**. Unlike K.C., Missouri, this Kansas City is strictly a cowboy town—a hop, skip, and a five-mile-horseback ride from Nuremberg.

Practically in the shadow of Wagner's festival town of Bayreuth, the Old West has been recreated in a lookee-here style by Ernst Schuster, a Bavarian farmer, whose hobby, since he was knee-high to a chuckwagon, has been the frontier days of America and the legendary cowpokes who shot their way to distinction and extinction.

Fulfilling a long-cherished dream, Schuster opened up his own idea of a *Wunderland*, Western style, complete with a lynching tree and hangman's noose, a choo-choo railroad and station, a sheriff's office and a jail, an ole corral, an operating gold-mine (where you can do your own panning), pony-express horseback rides for kids, a gambling casino, a shooting range, a ghost city (with a scary electronic show in total darkness every hour), a drugstore (that carries only Wild West gear, T-shirts and souvenirs), a daily *High Noon* shoot-out at 1:00 P.M., knife-throwing acts (with real pros who can also throw some pretty mean butcher's cleavers all around their human targets), a carousel called "Whisky," a Mexican café, a photography studio (where you can have your picture taken in old time American costumes), and a typical cowpunchers' saloon where any tenderfoot can down a jigger or grab some grub.

When you get here, you're likely to meet Sheriff Billy (Karl Heinz Brunner of Neuhaus am der Pegnitz), hitching up his gunbelt and greeting you from under his ten-gallon hat with a teutonic "Howdy, Herr Podner!" Sheriff Billy keeps the key to the two-cell jail and will oblige everyone big and little who wants a photo taken in the slammer. By the way, he's quite a trick-rider and proves it during the Wild West show.

Kansas City goes back to the summer of 1977 and has turned out to be a goldmine for its hobbyist-owner who draws an average of 10,000 people per weekend and figgers that's about a half-million folks each year. Upwards of $2 million is what he reckons he has invested in Kansas City with new features being added all the time.

What really is a golden winner is the saloon—a quality restaurant/café/bar—run by saloonkeepers Roland Sigl and his sidekick chief cook and gal-friend, Margie Zeltner. Margit (her name in German) is as handy with a six-gun as she is with the frying pan and serves up two kinds of roasts, Kansas City Braten and Texas Braten, with other choices like Little Joe's Nudelsuppe, Buffalo Bill Steak, Cowboy Lasso (that's spaghetti with meat sauce), and something called Rancher-Snake (which is not dangerous at all because it's a melt-in-the-mouth grilled sandwich, ham *mit* cheese). Margie ain't the kind to speak English with a drawl—but what maverick would want to tell a gorgeous pistol-packin' mama how to shoot off her mouth? (She's a real Dorothy Maguire look-alike, by the way.)

Known also in German as the *Frankisches Wunderland* and as a leisure-time adventure park (open from Easter till mid-October), Kansas City has a kind of backyard to it that is for kids of all ages who want to go off into fairy-tale land.

The entertainment setup includes "the land of the dwarfs," a start-it-yourself fire-breathing dragon, a summer-sledding run, a real lookout tower to climb, characters like Red Riding Hood and Hansel and Gretel, etc., straight from Grimm, and a variety of playground gimmicks and rides for kids to let off energy. (There's one for kids up to eight with a slide delving into an enclosed area containing 16,000 varied colored soft plastic balls.) Well under way is the completion of a larger Dinosaurland to incorporate the dozen dinosaurs already prowling the park, where Mr. Brontosauris and Mrs. Tyrannosauris and their families and friends (and enemies) will be your hosts.

Other recent additions include a Pony Express Hotel with at least 20 bunks, a community church, and a stage-coach that takes visitors around the countryside (Hey, mister, is that Randolph Scott up on top riding shotgun?). Where there are cowboys there must be Indians. So . . .

Watching over one corner of the six-acre Kansas City is a bona fide Mexican Indian in his Indian camp with real teepees and tom-toms. A 36-year-old Aztec by the name of Xokonoschtletl (called Xoko for short, and pronounced "Shoko") does a daily Sun Dance, barefoot (to commune with Mother Earth) and wearing a magnificent feathered head-dress—inside a cave that seats about 100 people on wooden benches. He is more than a professional dancer; he has dedicated himself to a specific cause, that of getting back a centuries-old (1524) ceremonial headdress that was stolen from his people almost 470 years ago and is to be found today in Vienna's Volkerkunde Museum. (He has written two books on the subject, published in German.)

The hombre who runs Kansas City today as its manager and foreman is Hans Lothes, who's been keeping an eye on the ole corral since the beginning. In 1982 the mayor of Kansas City, Missouri, awarded Lothes the key to the city. Considering this as a great honor, Lothes has one more lifetime wish—that varmints like Wyatt Earp and Anthony Quinn could one day, hankering for a fight, just breeze into the Deutschland Kansas City.

* * *

Dinkelsbühl's Hero Children Festival

Dinkelsbühl

And a child shall lead them. . . .

Though more than three centuries have gone by, the people of this ancient Bavarian town are still grateful to its children for having rescued them from enemy invaders.

Every third Monday in July hundreds of smallfry recreate, for the townsfolk and visitors, the rescue incident that took place in 1632 during the Thirty Years War by acting out the heroic event that saved their town from the conquering Swedish army that had come to pillage and burn. For over 90 years, Dinkelsbühl, an hour's drive southwest of Nuremberg, has been staging the historical pageant (called the **KINDERZECHE**) to pay homage to the children who saved their town.

Thousands of tourists focus eyes and cameras each year on what everyone visiting Dinkelsbühl considers an unforgettable experience.

According to documented historical accounts, the victorious Swedish soldiers had gathered before the village gates, preparatory to burning Dinkelsbühl to the ground and massacring the burghers. The Catholic residents of the town wanted to fight to the last man, but those of the new Protestant faith preferred not to think of the Swedes as enemies.

While perplexed city fathers argued in the council hall to work out some kind of solution, a beautiful girl named Lore, the city gate-keeper's young daughter, made her own decision. Little Lore—intent upon kneeling before the enemy's top brass to beg for the safety of Dinkelsbühl's people—gathered up all the children of Dinkelsbühl and marched to the edge of town under a flag of truce, singing prayers of peace, asking "gentle Jesus, Thy mighty help award!"

In the meantime, the troops were just about ready to

begin the assault when the sound of children's voices, coming from afar, made them pause. As the song became more distinct and louder, the Swedes stayed put. History tells us they were charmed. Leading the band of kids, Lore approached Colonel Sperreuth resolutely and knelt before him.

As the army commander listened to Lore's pleas that he take pity on the town, he spotted among the youngsters a tiny fair-haired boy who looked like his own deceased son. Sperreuth's wrath melted away. Pardoning the village for the sake of its brave children, the commandant proclaimed:

"Listen, ye all, listen. The children are the rescuers of Dinkelsbühl. Let the Herr Burgomaster always remember the debt of gratitude Dinkelsbühl owes them."

This scene, brought to the fore in 1897, has been reenacted every July since then, with ten successive days of celebrations that include parades, festival plays, folk dances, fireworks displays and unusual gastronomic offerings. The procession of children, led by a rose-crowned, dirndl-wearing girl playing the role of Lore (a most highly prized honor each year), also features a boys' orchestra that wins hearty applause every time. Famous throughout Germany, the sprout musicians wear white wigs, black boots and red-and-white uniforms as they march in perfect hoof-beat through Dinkelsbühl's narrow cobblestone streets, past the wine and leather markets.

Following the procession on foot comes the town's population—women wearing red or blue dirndl dresses and men in cotton coats. Also marching are the master guilds in their picturesque garb, complete with tools. The bakers, bent under their special load, lug along Dinkelsbühl's prize delicacy, a gigantic raisin cake *(Schnecken-Nudel)* rolled up in the shape of a snail. Naturally, every visitor in town is expected to munch on some of this tasty mammoth dessert—and no fair asking what the calorie count is!

Dinkelsbühl has hardly changed its appearance since the Thirty Years War. One of the few German cities undamaged by World War II bombs, snug Dinkelsbühl is a jewel of medieval Teutonic architecture that has remained un-

changed and unspoiled by modern times, yet is not a musty
museum.

Rich in touristic rewards as a genuine romantic hamlet—with a romanticism that was not artificially produced,
but that grew naturally over the centuries—the town provides a serene sojourn in history and waves a come-hither
invitation to bask in the enticement of picture-book Germany. That it gives all visitors the opportunity to feel what
it was like to live during Germany's golden days provides
this town's big plus today.

However, Dinkelsbühl is more than a fairy-tale place to
look at. The town is not only ringed by a medieval wall with
turrets and towers, but also by a thick growth of lush
forests whose soaring trees form giant arches over wide-
wide paths—dreamy perfect for cyclists and hikers. Want
to relax and unwind for two or three days?—go fishing?—
play tennis?—paint that picture you've always promised
yourself you'd do?—take the kids along and stay in your
camper on a lake for swimming and sailing?

Yes, Dinkelsbühl is indeed a Romeo and Juliet star on
Germany's famed *Romantische Strasse* (The Romantic
Road).

As one of Europe's most delectable hideaways, Dinkelsbühl is in the nostalgia sweepstakes as the childhood
dream of yesterday, today and tomorrow.

*   *   *

My Shangri-la, Mittenwald

Mittenwald

My Shangri-la has been my secret for three decades.
And now I'm confessing. It's *the* spot wifey and I opt for
first when we want to disappear from civilization, unwind
fully and completely undergo rejuvenation. Our storybook mountain land, perhaps every tourist's lifelong wish
of finding an undiscovered vacation hideaway where life
approaches "perfection," is in the mountains of Bavaria—

and it's called **MITTENWALD**. There, the secret is now out. . . .

Nestled in a 3,000-foot-high valley and surrounded by the massive rock wall of the 8,800-foot Wetterstein on the southwest side and on the east by the mighty face of the Karwendel Mountains (7,825 feet), Mittenwald is a four-seasons beauty for visitors. Yes, it is a "Lost Horizon" all year round, guaranteed to give you the bloom and vigor found in that mythical fountain-of-youth land.

North of Innsbruck, the German village of Mittenwald is located just beyond Austria's border on the Isar River, about 11 miles from Garmisch-Partenkirchen. Completely free of fog, even in winter, Mittenwald is strong on sun and looks. It is a hive of activity, as all the slopes for the ski crowd are kept perfectly sculpted and all walking paths for the hikers are carefully ploughed and smoothed out. For the cross-country buffs, Mittenwald is a utopian dream. To keep everybody comfy there are countless cafés, modest restaurants or "huts" sprinkled just about everywhere. Friendliness is the key word.

Twenty-four miles of pathways, some as high as 4,600 feet, are rigorously kept in walking order and 250 seats and benches along the way are brushed clean of snow daily. An additional 24 miles of courses are reserved for cross-country skiers only, and let's not forget the fun-filled sledding run. For those who do serious skiing in every rank of expertise, there are so many cable cars, chair lifts and T-bar lifts that things usually move along ever so nicely.

As a market town lying on an old Roman trade route between Venice and Augsburg, medieval Mittenwald flourished for two centuries, until 1679 when the halcyon days ended—the market was transferred to Bolzano and economic hardship hit. To the rescue came one Matthias Klotz (1653–1743), a native son of Mittenwald, who as a child was apprenticed to the master violin-makers, Nicolo Amati in Cremona and Johann Railich in Padua. Klotz blew the breath of life into his hometown in 1684 by introducing violin-making to the locals. With this new source of livelihood, Mittenwald tuned up to this tremendous economic pizzicato that plucked it from disaster, and for over 300 years violins, violas, cellos, zithers and guitars are have been made here.

You can see Matthias Klotz at work on a violin in the form of a bronze statue, a memorial to the genius violin master, standing in front of Mittenwald's landmark **St. Peter and Paul's Church**, right at the mouth of the narrow street leading to the **Violin-Making Museum** (*Geigenbau-museum*). To the strains of a Brahms violin concerto—one of the many violin pieces played around the clock—you wander through the museum where you not only see finished masterpieces in glass cases and others in various stages of preparation, but also some typical rooms and objects reflecting the history and the culture of the local people.

Of the some 20 marked winter walks (many more in other seasons) in and around Mittenwald, one outstanding day's outing will truly cast a spell on you—to **Elmau** and the **Partnachklamm** (Partnach Gorge). An early start at 9:00 A.M. gets you, in about three hours of easy walking from Mittenwald to Elmau, a tiny, humble village with a nearby famous and most unusual castle-hotel **(Schloss Elmau)**. After an hour's pause for an abundant home-cooked lunch at the inn in the village, you are indeed well fortified, calorie-wise, to hit the trail to yon gorge.

This walk, no kidding, battling for first prize in scenery nwith the sun and blue sky pitted against the evergreens, snow and mountains, keeps you company for the next two hours up to the entrance of the gorge. Once here, you walk single file along a four-foot ledge cut into the rock wall (yes, there are protectives fences and railings) and gaze down into the speeding waters bumping over rocks and boulders, or stare up at the one-foot thick gargantuan icicles, like giant ice stalactites, hanging all over at all levels, even from the cliff's edge, way up above your head. No matter what you photograph during this hour-long venture-adventure, it gets "ooh-aah" results because "somebody up there" has thrown together all of nature's cutesy tricks. Now you learn why this super-attraction has earned the nickname Gorgeous Gorge.

As you leave reluctantly, you needn't be a math whiz to calculate your outing and eating time have added up to six

or seven hours. Don't fret. It's easy to get back to Mittenwald proper without hoofing it. An easy 20 minute walk
(horse and carriage is quicker) to a local bus stop enables
you to catch a ride to the Garmisch train station, and in a
jiffy you are back in Mittenwald as the sun begins to set—
feeling healthy, happy and hungry.

Eating in Mittenwald is another treat supreme. At the
elegant Rieger, Alpenrose and Post hotels, the cuisine is
superb. The same goes for the small restaurants, inns,
cafés and take-out places—all of which are furiously com-
petitive, which is why the standards are inordinately high.
Important also to keep in mind are the bustling bakeries
and *Konditorei*, which burst with crispy, plump pretzels and
breads in every shape and size. Not to forget the pastries
and cakes, a specialty in Mittenwald is the so-called Black
Forest cherry cream cake, which many gourmets claim is
even better than what you actually find in the Black Forest.

Mittenwald is the kind of town that everybody likes.
Nearly all of its tourists come from other parts of Germany—and the foreign visitors can usually be counted on
the fingers of one hand. Which simply means, the outside
world just hasn't discovered this snow oasis with its plusses
and plus-plusses.

*   *   *

The Forest of Fairy Tales

Wambach

Kids from the age of 8 up and adults from the age of 88
down can now meet some of their oldest and nicest friends
by plunging into a vast piece of woodland in Wambach that
sprawls over 50,000 square yards. Here you'll meet "old
friends" like Robinson Crusoe, the wicked old witch who
wanted to bake Hansel and Gretel in the oven, Sitting Bull,
Cinderella, the Seven Dwarfs and a stegosaurus who lashes
its spiny tail while creepy-crawling hither and thither.

The **TAUNUS WUNDERLAND** was founded by a Wiesbaden publisher, Erich Maxheimer, who had visited

amusement parks in Luxembourgh, Sweden, Holland, and France and found them wanting. Although he knew he could never out-Disney Disney, he nevertheless put his imagination to work in the Wambach Woods at a cost of over $600,000, to make a truly "German" amusement park in a way that perhaps Walt Disney might not have. That he succeeded is attested to by the fact that on any given week-end more than 20,000 Germans show up—and better than half of them are adults.

A mere 15-minute drive from Wiesbaden brings you to Germany's only forest full of fairy-tale and literary person-alities from the good old days when all of us devoured kiddie books. Besides being the biggest fairy-tale park in Europe, what makes the Taunus Wunderland a fascinating afternoon tour is that many of your "old pals" are pro-grammed to talk aloud to you. (Just press the button, please!) Okay, so they talk to you in German, *ach Du lieber*, but so what?—when in Germany, do what the Germans do. They all go to Taunus because as a place for grown-ups and growing-ups, it takes you back, back and back into time and fantasy. After Taunus, who wants reality?

In addition to all those bedtime celebrities, Taunus abounds with some well-known places within its wooded bosom: there's the pond where the prince turned into a frog; there's Sleeping Beauty's Palace; there's the house in which Snow White lived with her septet of peewee pals; there's the house where Hansel and Gretel almost got baked; there's the good ship *Santa Maria* that Columbus crossed the ocean on; there's the Santa Fe Express that will choo-choo you six miles across the Wild West—not to men-tion Robinson Crusoe's island home with its shipwreck provisions that include whisky and corned beef, or the longest, most thrilling slide in the world, that twists like a circular staircase.

One of the most popular attractions is the live concert given by the famous "Traveling Musicians of Bremen." To refresh your memory, this quartet consists of an old roost-er, a woebegone cat, an itchy dog and a lame donkey who all wanted to make a career as musicians after their master threw them out of his house. Perched on top of each other, the rhythmic foursome gives out with some squeaky, hilarious numbers that would never remind you of the Berlin Philharmonic.

For some foreign visitors, a number of the Taunus celebs who occupy the enchanting woods will be unfamiliar because they never made it big outside Germany, though every German kid knows who they are, backward and forward. You'll meet up with the cricket on a harp, the frog blowing his trumpet, the Meadow Express pulled by snails, the giant Rübezahl who weighs 20 tons, and the red-topped mushroom with the white polka dots that wishes you good luck.

Open daily the whole year round from 9:00 A.M. to about 7:30 P.M., Taunus has several restaurants and many snacking facilities all over the place. Its best restaurant is located in the middle of a fantastic re-creation of the historic Rothenburg ob der Tauber, which is a pivotal town on Germany's famous Romantic Road. Most tourists who have been to the real Rothenburg marvel at the Taunus replica, and some even brag that the food is better.

Another magnetic draw is the Stone Age cave with its bevy of friendly Neanderthal men who [sic!] speak good grammatical German. Their monster pals are true-to-life reproductions of the mighty tyrannosaurus and the huge, dangerous stegosaurus. Neither of them can bite you, but watch out for the stego's whiplashing fairy tail. Don't fail to make the observation that one of the big beasts roars in a tenor voice while the other sounds off in baritone.

An afternoon at the Taunus Wunderland and you find it's good to be a kid all over again discovering brand new characters and renewing some Grimm memories.

*　*　*

Germany's Leaning Tower

Kitzingen

Are you ready for this? A virtual "secret" up to now, Germany can boast a leaning tower of its very own. That's right! It's called the LEANING TOWER OF KITZINGEN—and though it doesn't tilt as much as Italy's now-dangerous Leaning Tower of P/sa, it certainly provides German tourism with a new slant/.

Constructed more than four centuries ago, the crooked fortress turret here in this north Bavarian town, midway between Frankfurt and Nuremberg, looks like a pointed party hat that is about to topple off. In fact, one legend has it that since Kitzingen is the wine capital of Franconia, the wine went to the tower's head, hic!

If you go for that yarn, here's yet another one to mull over: Kitzingen lies smack in the center of an area called *Wasserschatten*—which means a region with little rain. Thus, while the tower was being built, legend says, there wasn't enough water to mix the cement, so the city fathers used some of their abundant wine stock, some of which had gone bad. To show distaste for the sour wine, the tower's top hat bent its head.

Another story relates that the man (name unknown) responsible for the portion of the tower that tilts did it on purpose so that when one looks at it from any point, the dunce-cap part always leans in another direction. It is more likely, however, that the lean, which is exactly 3.6 feet and has not varied one bit in 400 years, is the result of a construction error.

Whatever the lean truth, one thing is sure: Kitzingen's tower (called the *Falterturm*) once was 50 feet higher than its famed cousin in Pisa. A little over a century ago, the tower showed a height of 300 feet, but the moat in which it stood had to be filled in, so that what used to be the ground floor became a basement and a sort of dungeon. Though this action removed 65 feet from the tower's measurement, there are still eight stories remaining to the tower itself.

Visiting each of the eight stories is fun, albeit a little dizzying at times as you wend upward on creaky, narrow one-way wooden stairs. The tower serves as the seat of the **German Carnival Museum**, and as such gives you some fascinating looks at what Germany's age-old *Fasching* or *Karneval* period was and is like.

Stocked with pictures, costumes, masks and documents, the museum follows the pre-Lenten public bash back to the

Nuremberg of the sixteenth century when the butchers' guild started it all with an annual street parade and dance. Actually, Germany's wild carnival period can be traced back to mythology and the ancient rites of spring, judging from the figures and masks on display one flight up.

Replete with faces and face masks collected from the local regions, the second floor has one such mask from the Odenwald Forest that depicts the type of clown who danced in the streets wielding a broom. According to *Karneval* scholars, this indicates the connection between carnival and the ritual of spring cleaning. Some of the masks on display were also created to scare away that bad guy, the Devil.

A panoramic Brueghel painting on the third floor demonstrates all the carnival celebrations popular in the sixteenth century, and you can see the Flemish master's idea of villagers drinking, dancing, playing, clowning, cooking, baking and even arguing. Some of the people are portrayed with black sacks over their heads, a sign that they need to do penance and think about their evil ways.

On the next three stories you go through an array of badges and medals awarded to politicians, both German and foreign, for displaying a sense of humor during their term in office. Extremely fascinating are the samples of eggs and nuts that were filled with perfumed water to be thrown at fellow fun-seekers. Today it's confetti, candy and flowers that pelt you. And to add a grim note, there are a few showcases devoted to "policemen" dressed as harlequins who wielded blackjacks in case the frolic got out of hand.

Other displays include documents and literary works on carnivals, with writers like Goethe and Schiller holding prominence in this field. Not to be overlooked is the Nuremberg shoemaker, Hans Sachs (immortalized in Richard Wagner's *Die Meistersinger von Nürnberg*), who wrote more than 6,000 poems and plays, many of which dealt with fools, foolishness and folly.

From all this you get the impression that the carnival spirit captured in Kitzingen's Leaning Tower has really gone to its head.

* * *

Museum to a Big Liar

Bodenwerder

Now for some truth about a liar—the world's greatest liar!

You've got to believe it: Baron Münchhausen was not fiction or fantasy or fib but indeed a real, live person who used to spin his world-acclaimed tall tales right here in this quaint postcard-photo town in Lower Saxony. Truth, man, truth!

Are you still skeptical? Well, then don your best tourist togs and come to *Bodenwerder* on the Weser River, 45 miles south of Hannover, and visit the house where the popular prevaricator first saw the light of day. It is now the city hall where reigns a fascinating **Münchhausen Museum**, in the room where the Baron was born in 1720.

Called the Room of Memories, the delightful chamber is guarded over by the world's greatest expert on Baron Münchhausen, one Kurt Ostfeld, a charming, witty raconteur who serves as the official curator. Containing many personal belongings of the Baron, the room boasts a number of splendid murals that recapture the best known of Münchhausen's improbable adventures, not to mention an array of Münchhausen books in many languages.

During the summer months, mostly on weekends, Baron Münchhausen's teutonic whoppers are retold on the city hall grounds among statues depicting incidents from the tales. The silver-tongued gentleman spinning the stories is Curator Ostfeld himself, elegantly decked out as the Baron was wont to dress—in a dashing blue and red uniform and white wig. And if this comes at you as a bit touristy, why let's face it—where else will you ever get a chance to hear Baron Münchhausen's tall tales told by Baron Münchhausen's dead ringer? Truly, it's a banquet for both your cassette recorder and camera.

Since audiences never seem able to get enough of the

outrageous yarns, the "Baron" keeps drawing on his end-less supply as he impersonates the manner and style of the real Münchhausen to relate now-familiar stories about the horse cut in half, the stag from whose head a cherry tree grew, the Baron's two trips to the moon (one by cannonball and the other by way of a bean plant that grew and grew and grew . . .).

Who indeed was Baron Münchhausen? His full name was Hieronymus Karl Friedrich von Münchhausen, a Ger-man of old aristocratic stock. While a captain in the cavalry at the age of 20, he fought in several campaigns against the Turks. Later he hooked up with the Russian army, and in recognition of his gallantry in action was promoted to major. He once had the distinction of being tabbed for the team of escort-bodyguards for Empress Catherine the Great (truth, man, truth!) when she made a journey from St. Petersburg during the winter of 1774.

After Münchhausen ended his military career, he re-tired to Bodenwerder to spend his time hunting, managing his ancestral home and spinning impromptu stories based on his experiences as a cavalryman and a hunter. Over jugs of tongue-loosening wine, the talkative nobleman often let his vivid imagination go beyond his credibility gap. But since they provided hearty laughs and were dished out only in the intimacy of his circle of friends, he kept telling the far-fetched narratives time and again.

Münchhausen never intended that these embellished epics be published—but in 1781 someone anonymously put out a book in Berlin using 16 of them. Four years later in London an archaeologist by the name of Rudolf Erich Raspe, who had had many a merry evening with the Baron, compiled a volume on the Grand Old Liar's "travels." It became a bestseller.

Perhaps the most unbelievable thing about the real Münchhausen is that he never thought of himself as a purveyor of mendacities, but as an amiable storyteller. Baron Münchhausen would have certainly lost his cool had he known that one day his name would enter the dictionary (with one "h" instead of two) as a synonym for a liar.

Bodenwerder, feeling it owes a lot to its most illustrious

son, bills itself as "The Münchhausen City." Tourists are given a map that cites the points of interest connected with the fabulous fibber's life—such as the four Linden trees he himself planted. Today, under their leafy branches, you can sit on a bench and enjoy a grand view of the Weser as it winds through the surrounding countryside.

But here's a hot tip. If you stay long enough—truth, man, truth!—you are certain to get a glimpse of the old Baron traveling to Turkey, re-lying on his favorite cannon-ball. . . .

* * *

The Teddy Bear Museum

Giengen

The teddy bear is a VIP here in town and lord of the animal kingdom in the museum dedicated to the plush version of genus Ursidae. He's not a stuffed shirt, however, and tourists are flooding the place like a tidal wave. Situated on the eastern edge of the Swabian Alps on the river Brenz, some 20 miles northeast of the Danube-kissed town of Ulm (page 34) and two hours northwest of Munich, Giengen's **TEDDY BEAR MUSEUM** is home and palace to the cuddly bruin, the world's most cherished toy fur animal.

Yes, teddy bears were born here, thanks to the imagination of a young woman paralyzed by polio at the age of two—Margarete Steiff, who from her wheelchair founded a cottage industry in 1880 that eventually grew into a stuffed-toy dynasty. Margarete began by making little elephant pincushions for the children in Giengen who used to go to her place to hear her relate fairy tales and be fascinated with the stuffed animals she made from pieces of felt leftover from her dressmaking.

But why the name "teddy"? Well, no greater personality than the twenty-sixth president of the United States, Theodore (Teddy) Roosevelt, is behind it all. Because America's chief executive was fond of big game hunting, the story of how Teddy Roosevelt shooed a bear cub back to the safety of the woods one day prompted a political cartoonist to insert a small bear into his daily caricatures.

Then someone responsible for decorating the White House breakfast tables for the wedding of Roosevelt's daughter in 1906 saw some tiny life-like Steiff bears with movable legs, arms and heads in a New York toy store, which had bought up 3,000 of them at the Leipzig Trade Fair. Dolled up as hunters and fishermen, with miniature rifles and fishing rods in their paws, the bears were placed alongside mini-tents on all the tables. With the President having beamed approval when asked if they could be called "teddy bears," the White House correspondents picked that up—and forthwith the teddy-bear boom burst forth.

Thunderstruck at the sudden publicity, the Steiff family did not have enough time to get all the teddy bears out to fulfill the thousands of requests and orders, but by 1907 the company managed to produce a phenomenal million teddy bears for the hungry global market. The teddy continues to be the number-one stuffed toy of the Steiff factories here, with more than 250,000 sold directly to people who visit the museum each year. Even today, the bearish family still adheres to the concept of the handmade toy with the special magic and individuality of an Old World artisan's work. The little gold button in each animal's left ear constitutes their trademark for quality (*Knopf im Ohr*, or Button in the Ear).

Because teddy bears are not just for tots, the museum's visitors number among them junior and senior "kids" of all ages who have never lost their fascination for a huggable bear. A kind of paradise or Noah's Ark, the museum displays are laid out like a string of toy-shop windows, all filled with the stuffed animals that the company has been creating for over a hundred years.

The bears range in size from big-brawny to teeny-tiny, each one endearing. Mirroring the history and the evolutionary changes in the appearance of the fuzzy stuffed creatures, bears from the time of the kaisers look like quaint pets, while those from World Wars I and II are more stern-faced.

The 1945 genre, however, brought back and kept forever a "new look"—actually the old smiling self-assurance of happy toys that have the ability to respond to hugs and kisses. Myriad expressions on their faces grab you and you are zapped, inextricably in love with the whole menagerie: tame lions, playful rabbits, kittens and puppies, mischievous monkeys, not to forget rhinos, giraffes, donkeys, birds and, of course, legions of bears, especially the cinnamon, black or brown varieties called teddies.

Open only on weekdays from 2:00 to 4:00 P.M. (closed the first half of August—admission free), the museum also offers an excellent 25-minute movie that chronicles the saga of the family business with old photographs and stuffed toys—Steiff's very first teddy bear is the narrator. Also on view are objects that belonged to Miss Steiff, including documentary photos from the beginning of toy-making by the family, plus the original drawing of the teddy bear as dreamed up by her nephew, Richard.

Since no greater hero exists for Giengen than Teddy Roosevelt, in this town's auditorium you'll find a bronze bust of him, unveiled by a U.S. State Department official when Giengen staged a "Teddy Bear Festival" because it is the Teddy Bear Capital of the world.

Adjacent to the museum are the factory and the showroom shop (the shop is open from 9:00 A.M. until noon and from 1:30 to 4:30 P.M.). In addition to individual visitors, busloads of tourists come to the showroom every week, but there is never any pressure to purchase anything. In spite of that, company officials tell you that rare indeed is the visitor who doesn't melt and pick up at least one furry fellow. The teddy is the one that sells the best, however, because most owners of a bear feel an unexplainable closeness to this lifelong companion, which some psychiatrists today are still trying to figure out.

Yes, the winsome, easy-to-love expression on teddy's face, the upright ears and the outstretched arms tell you at the museum that you can bare your soul to teddy. Bear in mind, however, that the bear facts do bear out the bare facts at the Teddy Bear Museum.

* * *

The Beethoven Birth House

Bonn

Tourists who come to visit the house where Beethoven was born invariably arrive all keyed up, for the name of *Der Grosse Komponist* is truly music to everybody's ears. Like a haunting melody, the ghost of Ludwig van Beethoven roams over this city where all roads lead to his place of birth—at Number 20 Bonngasse—which attracts over 100,000 visitors a year. The **BEETHOVEN HOUSE**, now a museum, is open seven days a week the whole year round.

A call at these stucco quarters in Germany's capital city—a green-shuttered, yellow building where red geraniums and vines share the exterior decor—is a don't-miss pilgrimage, because it is a place where Beethoven the composer and Beethoven the man really come alive in every way. One peers into the showcases displaying the genius's ear trumpets (made for him by the inventor of the metronome), his razor, a lock of his hair, a pair of glasses, original manuscripts with his numerous penciled corrections (Beethoven never wrote a piece of music outright—he rewrote it dozens of times), his visiting card, a magnifying glass, his piano from Vienna, his viola from Bonn, and a death mask made when he died in Vienna at the age of 57.

The room in which baby Ludwig was born—an attic room with a sloping ceiling in the rear part of the house—still contains the original floorboards, as does the hallway. The **St. Remigius Catholic Church** nearby, where Beethoven was baptized in 1770, has donated to the museum-home a console from the old organ that Beethoven used when, at the age of 11, he was already a professional organist. During Mass he would accompany the choir, and an anecdote tells how, at a Holy Week function, Beethoven as a 12-year-old boy threw a singer off stride when he began to insert his own imaginative ideas as to how the score should have read.

It's Beethoven's piano, however, that strikes a sour note, for its gives the city fathers a few headaches. They can't keep it in tune. The wires sag too much, so that it's difficult to play it at the concerts during Bonn's triennial Beethoven Festival.

On display in a chamber on the second floor is Beethoven's last piano. Given to him around 1823, it was made by a master piano maker in the Viennese court, and unlike modern pianos, it is a multistringed instrument—that is, each note has four strings and it has a very different sound from the later pianos of the nineteenth century. The master of the symphony had a sounding board fitted over the opening and the striking mechanism to amplify the tone quality and counteract (he hoped) his deafness. But it is doubtful if Beethoven ever heard any notes from this piano since by 1818 all conversation with him was done by written messages—which writings, by the way, eventually became a unique biographical source.

To give admirers an idea of what Beethoven's works sounded like in his day, the Beethoven House displays and sells several LP discs of his music recorded from the Vienna-made piano. Unavailable anywhere else except in the house and in two stores on the same street, the records include several sonatas played by Jörg Demus, seven Bagatelles played by Erich Appel, the *Moonlight* Sonata played by Ernst Gröschel and a String Quartet in G Major (Opus 18/2) played by the Sizer Quartet.

Similarly, the last record is done with Beethoven's own stringed instruments—two violins, a viola and a cello that are on exhibit in a showcase near the piano and that still bear the marks of seals put on them personally by Beethoven. Many of the composer's string compositions were performed on these very instruments for the first time by famous soloists of the period. Unfortunately, some of the instruments, three of which were made in Northern Italy, are cracked.

One particular sonata that the young Beethoven wrote for one of these instruments was dedicated to Countess Giulietta Guicciardi with whom he fell deeply in love while she was a beginning student of his. He believed her to be "the most beautiful woman in the whole world" and dedicated to her his Opus 27/2, which he called *sonata quasi una fantasia*.

In one of the rooms there is a bronze bust of the young Italian contessa. Her father rejected Beethoven because he believed the youth was unworthy of his daughter's hand, maintaining that "that chap Beethoven will never amount to anything."

FRANCE

Bridge to Nowhere

Avignon

Even the French have an expression to the effect that you should not cross your bridges before you get to them. But the French have a bridge that beats anything yet, for when you get to it, you can't cross it. It doesn't go anywhere. In spite of that, the bridge is the delight of every tourist who aims his camera at it to get proof-positive of the only half-bridge in existence that's named after a kid!

Called the **PONT SAINT-BENEZET**, the Romanesque bridge was built between 1177 and 1185 and originally crossed the wide Rhone River on 22 powerful arches. Then, early in the seventeenth century a series of violent floods weakened the structure that connected the city of Avignon on one side with Villeneuve-les-Avignon on the other. One of the big arches collapsed, but not until 1669 did the half of the bridge flop into the water with a great big splash.

That's the way it's been for over 320 years now—a bridge that doesn't reach the other side but ends right in the middle of the river. Some people in Avignon take the view that the Pont Saint-Benezet should really be put into the Louvre, alongside the Venus de Milo (page 91) with its missing arms. Others, however, believe the bridge should be restored. But that, say most of the Avignon folks, would be like trying to complete Schubert's *Unfinished Symphony* or straightening up Pisa's Leaning Tower.

When during its better days the bridge was really a span that went somewhere—as all dutiful bridges are supposed to—it straddled a little island in the Rhone called Ile de la Barthelasse. This toe of earth served as a Sunday picnic ground where people would feast on fried river fish and merrily drink up Rhone reds and whites before they took to dancing underneath the shady arches. This gave rise to a song that every French kid learns in school and still knows by heart when he grows up, "Sur le pont d'Avignon, l'on-y-danse, l'on-y-danse. . . ."

About fifteen years ago a movement got underway to have the bridge fixed up so that Avignon would get a badly needed additional transportation connection across the Rhone. Led by a business tycoon, who was also prominent in cultural circles as a part-time painter, the campaign to get signatures on a petition got considerable publicity in the French papers, but in the end nothing came of it. The truncated ruin is still a city monument that is more of a touristic oddity.

Today it's possible to go for a stroll atop the Pont Saint-Benezet. There's a small admission charge, and you walk along a pathway that leads to a chapel on one of the arches. Since the path is barely wide enough for a horse and wagon, you are made aware almost immediately that if the bridge were ever to be repaired, the whole structure would have to be substantially widened to handle modern traffic and pedestrians.

Besides having achieved fame near and far through the children's song, Avignon's oddball bridge bears a legend every Frenchman also knows. It seems a 12-year-old boy named Benezet stopped the bishop of Avignon one day to relate that during a dream an angel told him a bridge should be built across the Rhone. The boy also said that Christ had sent him to talk with the bishop. Incensed, the bishop commanded one of his orderlies to take the boy away and whip him for being insubordinate and irreverent.

But the boy was stubborn. When he kept insisting that the Lord had sent him, the orderly facetiously asked the kid to prove it by lifting a nearby boulder, and if he didn't, he'd get twice as many whiplashes. Although the big stone was more than 13 feet in length and 7 feet in width and would have required a dozen strong men to raise it from the ground, the little boy lifted it up and carried it all the way to the spot where the angel had told him the bridge should be built. Not only did all the onlookers fall to their knees, including the bishop and Avignon's city officials, but the lad was declared a saint and the bridge was forthwith erected with his name on it.

Most tourists come to Avignon (a one-hour train ride north of Marseilles) to see the mammoth **Palais des Papes** (Palace of the Popes), a soaring fortress that served as a home and refuge for seven pontiffs and as the seat of the "second Vatican" during the fourteenth century. After visiting the lofty structure, don't miss the spectacular ride in a train of open-air wagons drawn by a tractor that climbs to the top of a solid rock and provides a breathtaking view of the papal palace, its ramparts, all of Avignon, the Rhone River and the bridge to nowhere.

Looking from this point makes you see that in the city fathers' game of bridge-or-no-bridge, Avignon's trump card and best deal is not to bridge the gap.

* * *

The Museum of Women

Neuilly

Freud once said that a question that had never been answered in his 30 years of research into the feminine soul, was "What does a woman want?"

The answer to that might be forthcoming at France's **MUSÉE DE LA FEMME** (Museum of Women), the first one of its kind ever, and you'll get other answers about Eve and her sisters in the extensive collection of "femininia" valued at nearly a half-million dollars that took over 40 years to assemble.

Put together in the former town house of a Chilean millionaire by a retired antique dealer, who serves as its curator, the Museum of Women is housed in three rooms that will keep you busy and fascinated, on the one hand, and fascinated and busy on the other hand. The museum, located at 12 Rue de Centre, Neuilly, barely outside Paris and just a four-stop Metro ride from the Champs Elysées, is open six afternoons a week (closed Sundays) between 2:30 and 6:00, with a guided one-hour tour beginning at 3:00.

Having nursed the idea of a museum to the glorification of womanhood for over ten years, curator Jacques Damiot finally got the go-ahead sign from Neuilly's Mayor Achilles Peretti, who used his political clout to find a locale for the project. One of the outstanding things on exhibit is the bed used by France's most famous courtesan during the reign of Napoleon III, an item that originally cost 100,000 gold francs.

An imposing piece of furniture, the bed is shaped like a large shell with a painting of its owner on the back. The courtesan (known by her professional name, La Paiva) had herself painted sitting in front of a small lake, fully dressed and flanked by some gold cupids. When museum visitors say they are flabbergasted that the bed cost so much money, they are reminded by the curator, who serves as his own tour guide, that the Marchioness de La Paiva reportedly charged a fee of 10,000 gold francs a night. Of her it was also said that she knew all the secrets of the state.

Visitors to the Museum of Women are lovingly taken around by Damiot, and in a short while it becomes apparent which objects rank among his personal favorites. The bronze cast of the legendary ballet dancer Katherine Dunham's feet, which she autographed for Damiot, dominates the first room and takes up a goodly part of his rather spirited presentation, charming storyteller that he is.

Another object of curiosity is Marie Antoinette's corset, which France's last queen wore in prison before being guillotined. Salvaged by her daughter, who took it to Spain where it remained in the Bourbon family, the corset was purchased by Damiot from Jaime de Bourbon for the equivalent of $3,500. Made of blue linen and embroidered with delicate white curlicues, with the royal crest emblazoned on it four times (twice in front and twice in back), the corset is proof of Marie Antoinette's very tiny waistline.

Other interesting items include a letter from Nobel prize winner, Marie Curie; a silk jacket that belonged to China's last empress; the menu of a testimonial dinner given in honor of actress Sarah Bernhardt; a sculptured fountain dedicated to motherhood; and a biscuit box with the portrait of Paris's revered music-hall star, Mistinguett. As for the last item, Damiot hastens to explain that the brand that Mistinguett was advertising was a product manufactured by her brother-in-law.

The museum has a good collection of valuable paintings, one of which is a portrait of Olympe Pelissier who started her career as a model for Horace Vernet, then became the mistress of Honoré de Balzac, and later married Gioacchino Rossini. Damiot's commentary about her: "Some woman! She had it all—painting, literature and music!"

Other objects and curiosities on display, about which the curator recounts details that keep you entertained, include eyeglasses belonging to Utrillo's mother (herself a painter); the saddle of Eleanor of Aquitaine; a manuscript of George Sand (whose maiden name was Amandine-Aurore-Lucie Dupin); a hand sketch of Marie Harel (a heroine in France because she invented Camembert cheese); a pair of black stockings belonging to the beloved movie actress Arletty; the drapery used to cover Salvador Dali's wife while she posed as his model; slippers that were once owned by the classic ballerina, Ludmilla Tcherina; the flamboyant feathered hat of actress Elvire Popesco; Sarah Bernhardt's cane, and the inimitable Zulma, the snake-charmer automaton, who, when you deposit a coin, does a sensational dance with a serpent. (This mechanized doll has given over a million performances so far and still works.) The Museum of Women works well, too.

* * *

The Robert Louis Stevenson Trail

Le Monastier-sur-Gazeille

It's called the SUR LES PAS DE R. L. STEVENSON (Robert Louis Stevenson Trail), and it begins here in this fascinating-in-a-sleepy-sort-of-way town some 15 miles from Le Puy in France's southland regions. Over a hundred years ago the famous Scottish author of *Treasure Island* and *Kidnapped* set off from this spot with a ladened donkey named Modestine, and, during a 12-day period, hiked 120 miles through the Cevennes Mountains. The book he wrote about the walking trip, *Travels with a Donkey in the Cevennes*, has recently come out in a new edition.

The Robert Louis Stevenson Trail today, indicated along the way with markers of a silhouette of R. L. S. and a donkey, is not an easy walk even for dedicated hikers, but in recent years several hardy, trail-blazing groups have done the trip. Since Stevenson's journey in September 1878, however, certain parts of the route have had to be changed because there are now enclosed fields, barbed wire and automobile roads not present in his day. These changes add about 20 miles to the trail.

Nevertheless, anybody who wants to retrace Stevenson's steps, even with the few modifications, should be in good condition before attempting the trek. Don't try it during the winter months, and if possible, go with another person or with a group of people, and by all means inform town officials of your intent. Monsieur Jean Pradier, president of the local Syndicate d'Initiative—which is very proud of the famous nineteenth-century visitor who put Le Monastier on the map—may even be able to give you a lot of help and trot out the town's only donkey (also called Modestine) if available.

Stevenson, then 28 years old, spent a month in Le Monastier planning his journey. Against the advice of everybody in town, including the Mayor, R. L. S. set off from what is now the front of the village post-office building. A small granite monument has been erected under an acacia tree with an inscription to commemorate his departure. Nearby, the hotel in which he stayed is also marked with a notice. And in the downstairs lobby of Le Monastier's city hall, a huge wall display shows the 12 towns R. L. S. went through, graphically indicated with a thick rope snaking its way past each stop.

"When Stevenson set out from Le Monastier," explained

Mayor Marcel Bocquin, who had agreed to pose with Modestine for my camera at the point were R. L. S. commenced his historic march, "everybody here thought him a lunatic because such a thing was unheard of at the time. But he did what he said he wanted to—and we have officially named the path he took after him."

Sparsely populated, the Cevennes, an area of highlands squeezed between the Alps and the Pyrenees, is gashed by plunging pine-clad valleys, gorges and streams and is dotted with relics of the past, not excluding some ruined castles and ancient bridges. Throughout the Cevennes, tiny hamlets (the kind with narrow zig-zag streets) cling to the sides of the mountains, and small hotels and inns abound in each town. Part of the Cevennes massif, which Stevenson trudged through, now forms a portion of a national park whose main town, **St. Jean du Gard**, is where R. L. S. ended his journey and sold the faithful Modestine, saddle and all, for 35 francs. Known as the Pearl of the Cevennes, St. Jean du Gard draws regular tourist buses all the way from Paris.

The most majestic part of the Cevennes, between the towns of Bleymard and Florac, where the Col de Finiels stands, is best described in Stevenson's own words:

"These are the Cevennes with an emphasis; the Cevennes of the Cevennes that, in clear weather, commands a view over all lower Languedoc to the Mediterranean Sea. It is visionary highland country: steep woods of scented pine giving way to bare moorland, heath, rolling grass or scree; rushing streams and deep green and gold terraces of chestnut trees."

Le Monastier has put together a special museum on Robert Louis Stevenson, who died of a stroke at the age of 44 in 1894. Also set up are two tours—one for backpackers wishing to camp en route and another for hikers preferring to stay in hotels or inns along the Robert Louis Stevenson Trail.

Whether you opt for a tour or not, just a visit to Le Monastier will make clear to you why the unofficial theme here is the "Donkey Serenade."

*   *   *

Lascaux II

Montignac

LASCAUX II is a superb forgery. . . . But legal, because it was ordered by the French government.

Opened in the summer of 1983, the youngest underground art gallery on earth—encased in a man-made concrete bunker—houses copies of some of the world's oldest wall drawings, an array of prehistoric bulls, deer, horses, bison, oxen, bears, a lion and a unicorn creature, all reproduced down to the most infinitesimal detail. In fact, it's such a perfect fake that it draws 40,000 tourists a month, who come here to see the prehistoric counterfeits because the real thing in the nearby **Lascaux Cave** had to be closed to the public in 1963.

Discovered on September 12, 1940, by four boys looking for a dog that had fallen into a hole, the cave held the most substantial, most elegant and most notable grotto paintings anywhere, drawn by Stone Age hunters more than 15,000 years ago. But the cave had to be shut down 20 years later when the frescoes began to show a green mold, a mysterious bacterial growth that had been triggered by human visitations. Thus, it appeared that the greatest collection of prehistoric art, a unique heritage, would become "the treasure no one sees."

All that is changed. The full-sized, pin-point-exact duplicate of the Lascaux Cave takes all visitors on hourly tours (including several a day in English when enough requests accumulate). Lascaux II, which is only about 200 yards down the road from the original, allows tourists to experience the overwhelming magnificence of the authentic cave paintings. France spent a goodly million dollars to build the art bunker. And Lascaux II is the kind of attraction and art rarity that delivers.

Lying in the Dordogne region of France's southwest,

Montignac is about 280 miles from Paris, and the famed cave is just a mile away from the town's edge. Closed from mid-December to mid-February, Lascaux II runs its hourly tours from 10:00 A.M. to noon and from 2:00 P.M. to 5:00 P.M. As for the original Lascaux Cave, about a dozen people a month do get special permits to visit it.

Whether you see the actual thing or the superbly perfect facsimile, you come away from your visit with the feeling that the cave dwellers who did those frescoes during the Aurignacian period were no half-apes. Indeed, they were sensitive artists, and though working with crude tools and simple pigments, they provided proof that great art is timeless, that art rises out of basic human emotions and experience.

Very little, if anything, is known about the artists who did the Lascaux paintings. Nor does anybody explain why the paintings were found in such excellent condition, other than to guess that they were sealed airtight from the damp, the dust and the air poisons for centuries on end, and that the ochre, charcoal, ferrous oxide and manganese used as the pigments became slowly encased by the calcium on the walls.

In the chamber known as the Hall of the Bulls, there are huge black and brown beasts, one of them about 18 feet in length. Two very striking pictures show a hunted bison with seven arrows in him, and the most brutal bull of all, a muscular, threatening monster that seems to stomp out at you, full of rage and hatred. Its eye has been very cleverly painted inside a small hole, and it penetrates you if you stare at it long enough. The artist scored a "bull's eye" with this one.

In another section you find numerous horses of all sizes, some of them galloping and others grazing. One of the most curious is the "upside-down horse," which apparently depicts a common event in the life of primitive man— hunters driving a horse to the edge of a cliff and forcing it to jump. The artist captured in paint the dead horse lying at the bottom.

Many art critics who have visited Lascaux believe that the most remarkable drawing is that of the row of deer heads going up a jagged stone wall. Life-sized, these antlered heads belong to animals swimming across a river—those at the right in midstream with their noses raised high in order to breathe and those at the left with their noses down because they are emerging from the water.

Lascaux II, like the original, is about 90 feet long, 30 feet wide and some 15 feet high. Along the rocky walls and also on the ceilings, you see murals of beasts that look as fresh as if they had been done less than a week ago. Altogether, there are more than a thousand paintings and engravings on the Lascaux walls, all of them showing animals in motion.

How Lascaux II was constructed is a miracle in itself, one that your tour guide glowingly explains in all its fascinating detail. The actual work began in 1972 when the bunker was built. Photographs of every five square centimeters were made of the original Lascaux Cave, and then these were put into a computer from which a printout of minute grid lines emerged. Soft concrete in tiny dibs and dabs was poured into five-centimeter molds so that every pimple, each hole, all the bumps and waves and the tiniest curves were reproduced in the minutest detail.

Once the cave and its inner contours were erected, then the exact copying of the Cro-Magnon art began when professional artists were brought in to do the painting. Putting into use the same color mixtures and the same substances that the cave dwellers had, and working from magnified color photographs, they gave life to Lascaux II. All this was done under the supervision of finicky, disciplinarian experts who oversaw the work for 13 years.

Bearing witness to the birth of art thousands of years before Christ was born, the genuine Lascaux frescoes are sometimes called "the Sistine Chapel of prehistory." And Lascaux II is a twentieth-century work of art that gives you the whole picture.

* * *

The Foreign Legion Museum

Aubagne

Human cast offs. Wastrels and misfits. Rowdies, cut-throats, refuse from the earth's worst gutters, hell-bent scoundrels. Such is the image of the French Foreign Legion, thanks to movies like *Beau Geste* and dozens of novels and articles about the world's toughest band of mercenaries. Is it all true?

Yes and no. But mostly no! If you trek-tourist yourself to this sleepy village in the southeast part of France, about ten miles east of Marseilles, do pay a call on **Le Musée De La Legion Etrangere** (Museum of the Foreign Legion) and find out the "truth" about the most elite military organization on the face of the earth. The famed Legion Etrangere, which has the distinction of having fought more dirty wars than any extant military unit (including the U.S. Marine Corps and the notorious Gurkhas), has set up the memorial museum in honor of the more than 35,000 men who lost their lives fighting with the legion.

Visiting hours for the Foreign Legion Museum are a bit tricky. From June 1 through September 30, it is open from 10:00 A.M. to noon and from 3:00 P.M. to 7:00 P.M., Tuesday through Sunday. From October 1 through May 31, the museum opens from 10:00 A.M. to noon and from 2:00 P.M. to 6:00 P.M., Wednesdays, Saturdays and Sundays. There is no entrance fee.

More than 3,000 objects involving the victories and defeats of the Foreign Legion are on display, many of them rare military relics, like the wooden arm of Captain Jean Danjou. He lost his left arm when hit by a Russian shell at Sevastopol during the Crimean War. Some years later, while fighting with his force of 50 men against 2,000 Mexican troops at Camerone, he was mortally wounded. Though his body was never found, the wooden arm was recovered and it now holds a special place, together with Danjou's portrait, in the museum's Hall of Honor.

During the century and a half of its existence, the Legion has seen action in big wars, little wars and any number of police actions in such countries as Algeria, Morocco, Tunisia, Spain, Mexico, the Crimea, Italy, France, Germany, Austria, Africa, Libya, Syria, Madagascar, Turkey, Greece, Serbia and Indochina. More than a million men from almost every country of the world have served in the Legion's ranks—and, as the museum makes clear, there have been more Germans than any other nationality.

Of the 35,000 U.S. citizens and Canadians who were Legionnaires, at least 70 of them were killed in action. One in particular, a certain William Moll of Chicago, has his ashes inside a monument in the museum. His last wish was that his remains always be with the Foreign Legion, and the high command granted this request. If you ask the museum curator who William Moll really was or what his particular story was, you get a shrug and a strange look. If the museum has not put it down in black and white in a showcase, hard legion policy dictates that it will accept no inquiries whatever. A tight lip has always been a trademark of the legion.

Another American who died on the battlefield (he fell in 1916 during the summer offensive in the Somme) was the poet, Alan Seeger, a Harvard graduate who wrote the poem "I Have A Rendezvous With Death." Intellectuals like Seeger were not alone in the Legion. In truth, the Foreign Legion has attracted many unlikely recruits, such as priests, millionaires and royalty; even Prince Ranier of Monaco did a tour of duty during World War II. The sword of Prince Aage of Denmark (a descendant of the Duke of Chartres, who also served in the legion) is given prominent attention in the museum.

One of the most enticing exhibits concerns Colonel Paul Rollet, who was called "the father of the legion." He headed the most decorated unit of France's fighting forces during the First World War. To stay in command of his regiment, and remain with his men, Rollet turned down

promotions, one after another. The museum claims him to
be the all-time favorite commanding officer of the Foreign
Legion. Rollet, whose real name and nationality are not
known, has been immortalized in several novels and films
that have glamorized some of his exploits on the battlefield.

Nor have the "legion's women" been overlooked. The
Foreign Legion may be the only army in history that officially encourages its men to seek the comfort of sex. On
most marches to a military campaign, the Legion took
along its *Bordels Militaire de Campagne*, most of whom were
vibrant Drouard women who followed on mules, donkeys
and camels (some did become frontline casualties).

The point is also made that the legion turns down three
of every four applicants. Though enlistees have the right to
assume a new name and nationality upon joining, corps
officials assert that the legion is not an army of hopeless
incorrigibles or criminals hiding from justice. Watch the
men at one of their frequent parades here, a treat for any
visitor. Ever so proudly do the legionnaires march in their
white kepis and green ties to their distinctive slow cadence,
singing their famous bawdy songs at the top of their lungs.

In battle, of course, they sing a different tune.

* * *

Monet's Gardens

Giverny

Masterpiece is the word often used for Claude Monet's
impressionist paintings. It's also the word that best describes his gardens here at **GIVERNY** where he lived and
worked for over 40 years, some 30 miles northwest of
Paris. Then, still another word, *genius*, applies to the many
Monet canvases that hang in the world's major museums,
and that same word can be ascribed to him as one of the
great gardeners.

You can visit Monet's "masterpiece, genius" garden,

which opened to the public in June 1980, from 10:00 A.M. to 6:00 P.M., six days a week (no Mondays). And be prepared to stay all day because it's not an easy place to leave. In fact, the bearded artist's four acres of water-garden environment must rank today as among France's five best tourist attractions, not excluding Paris' big-league offerings.

What did the "father of Impressionism" do with plants and flowers that could possibly upstage his immortal art works?

Well, for one thing, he diverted the meandering river Epte (a tributary of the Seine) onto his land to feed his lily pond. Because he had a love affair with water lilies, Monet managed to import, over four decades of daily care in his garden, every known variety of water lily. He even captured their beauty in a set of 19 large paintings. Monet also planned his garden in such a way that flowers would be in bloom all the year round, so that at any time of the year he could set up his easel and paint what appealed to him. In addition, Monet provided an atmosphere in which wildflowers and hybrids could bloom side by side.

No, Monet's gardens do not in any way resemble the traditional, formal gardens you see in France's great palaces and châteaus. His strategy was to capture the ephemeral effects of light, water and flowers in a melange of ever-changing colors that today give the impression he personally selected the colors from his palette.

Prime Minister George Clemenceau, in his book on Monet, wrote that the painter's gardens must be counted among his works of art. "He made his garden to satisfy his sense of colors, and his profusions of blooms were planted in single-color masses—blue irises, big gold sunflowers, blazing red poppies. . . . His garden is an array of flaming cascades, violent and tender hues spreading boldly beneath the climbing roses."

Monet, who was born in 1840, did not really start selling his paintings until he was about 50 (he died at the age of 86). When he was 43 years old, broke and almost destitute, he moved to Giverny and with a loan of $1,000 installed his wife and eight children in a rundown farmhouse. He weeded the land himself and dug and planted flowers and worked like a beast to get his new home into shape. Untiringly, he trundled his wheelbarrow day in and day out until he accomplished what he set out to do.

Once he had become world famous for his impressionist paintings and his home and gardens were the way he wanted them, intimate friends like Clemenceau and artists like Rodin, Matisse, Renoir, Pissarro and Sisley were regular visitors. Giverny even became an international artists' colony. But after Monet's son Michel died in 1966, the property fell into shambles, the lily pond was black with pollution from a nearby paper factory, and the gardens were engulfed by thorn bushes. His Japanese footbridge (which is one of the most famous scenes of modern painting) had become covered by the wild foliage.

Since the land had been willed to the Institut de France of the Academie des Beaux-Arts, the government appointed the former curator of Versailles (Gerald van der Kemp) to restore the gardens. This he did at a cost of $2.5 million. Apart from bringing back to luxuriant life the water-lily pond and, of course, the Japanese bridge, Van der Kemp also restored Monet's modest two-story cottage, which you can also tour today.

Completely furnished in exact detail as it was during Monet's time, the fiesta-pink stucco house contains his collection of Japanese prints, his priceless array of china and his copper pots, all arranged in a row on kitchen hooks. The artist's hat and pipe take a place of honor in his studio, a huge room with a skylight ceiling 50 feet high where he worked on the mammoth water-lily paintings that now hang in the **Orangerie Museum** in Paris. Today this studio serves as a souvenir and gift shop where Monet reproductions, books, postcards and other Monet-iana are for sale, including copies of Monet's custom-made Limoges dishes.

When you come here one day, try to catch the whole and the parts of its sum with a color camera, or with paint and canvas if you've got a good hand with the brush. Monet captured his flowers successfully directly from nature— and it's a sure bet his flowers will capture you.

* * *

France's River of Secrecy

Fontaine de Vaucluse

If it's true that 50 million Frenchmen can't be wrong, then it's also true—at least when you visit touristdom's number-one super mystery here—that 50 million French-men *can* be baffled. And that includes Jacques Cousteau who came here with a team of intrepid divers and went away without any answers.

But who needs answers when you are a tourist on a fun trip? Come here at any time of the year and get the low-down on Europe's only mysterious underground river. No ordinary river indeed, it disappears in the summer, and from a baby trickle comes back later on in the spring as a surging, gushing, churning, bouncing, spraying, Niagara-like tumbling torrent that bounds over a stretch of massive boulders and mesmerizes everybody who comes to be wowed. But everybody!

Where the river comes from, or where it goes to when it disappears from view is anybody's guess. The sheer walls of rock that form a semicircle around the basin do not pro-vide any clues as to the source of the hippety-hoppety H_2O. And in August, when the water in the basin is less than a foot deep, you still can't figure out the *why* and the *how* about the **FONTAINE DE VAUCLUSE**, which is also the name of the town about 25 miles of east of Avignon (page 70) (where the Popes used to live in exile).

Should you ever come here when the water is at its lowest point, you can clamber down into the deep cave right to the place where a tiny trickle is oozing out, and you don't even get your shoes wet. The water level of the river, which is known as the Sorgue River, never ever goes to zero. Many Frenchmen and other Europeans come to Fon-taine de Vaucluse in the summer just to see the Sorgue when it's dry. Then they make it a point to come back someday when the Sorgue is at full blast, bombarding the

Springtime is one of the two times to visit the Sorgue, for then you see it as a long ribbon of agitated foam with a water depth of better than 24 meters, which corresponds to an average rate of 150,000 liters per second. Measurements are constantly being made and records kept by France's National Office of Geological and Mining Research. So far, the gushiest time in the Sorgue's history came on the November 9, 1907 when more than 200,000 liters per second were measured. On an annual basis the Sorgue jets out over 880 million cubic meters of water.

Although the Fontaine de Vaucluse has been fascinating people from time immemorial, the first scientific explorations began in 1878 when a professional diver went down to a distance of 35 meters and then had to be rescued. The next formal attempt came in 1938 when another pro went down to what he considered the bottom. Still no luck. Then in 1946, a research team from the naval base of Toulon came to Vaucluse, headed by Lt. Jacques Cousteau, and four dives were made, the deepest ever—still with no results. Cousteau came back again in 1967 with highly sophisticated equipment to penetrate the mystery. Putting into play a robot diver hooked to a TV transmitter that he had used on ocean research, Cousteau went down 106 meters and was able to ascertain the true bottom. But again, no clue about the source.

Cousteau now believes that diving will never supply the solution to the mystery. He is of the opinion that only speleological research will discover the mystery of the Fontaine de Vaucluse. Indeed, several such studies and explorations were undertaken in recent years, but none of the presumed aquatic underground networks was found.

So the scientists continue. The villagers, meanwhile, are 100 percent unanimous, down to the last man and woman, in their hope that nobody will every really solve the mystery, because as long as it remains the only river of its kind anywhere in the world, the tourist business thrives. Everybody in town is concerned with his liquid assets. . . .

* * *

The Mysterious Stone Men of Corsica

Filitosa (Corsica)

Close Encounters of the Corsican Kind could easily be the name for a film about the mystery statues of this hunchback island. The **STONE IMAGES OF FILITOSA**, as mysterious as the ones on Easter Island, are a phantasmagoria that will make you run out of exclamation points, inasmuch as they suggest the culture of an outer galaxy.

Vro-o-o-ommmm! Yes, when you come to Corsica, you get the feeling you have been dropped into the Mediterranean from the interplanetary system. The first thing that hits you is the odor—or rather, the perfume. Corsica is the nicest smelling piece of real estate ever, and Napoleon once wrote of his birthplace while in exile that he could recognize Corsica "with my eyes closed just from its perfume."

All things considered—location, climate, terrain, friendly people and a bit o' mystery—it is not easy to explain why this island of 200,000 souls, 110 miles in length and 50 miles at its widest part, is not overrun by tourists. Ethnically Italian, but politically French, Corsica is best described as a "mountain plunked in the sea," and most visitors who do come nickname it the "Scented Isle."

Just where does this marvelous aroma that hangs like sunlight in the air come from? It emanates from the *maquis*, the dense undergrowth made up of myriad plants, shrubs, wildflowers, aromatic herbs, ferns, juniper, arbutus, myrtle, lavender and bay. This floral bouquet also provided the name of the French Underground during World War II. Corsica's pockets of aroma waft hither and thither and come at you in a mysterious way.

Nothing here, however, is more mysterious than Corsica's puzzle. Ponder, if you please, the question, "Who are the mysterious stone men who watch you when you come to Filitosa, a half-hour drive south of Ajaccio?" Little or nothing is known about these perplexing, ancient, stern-faced creatures, except that a prehistoric civilization going back to about 3000 B.C. (even before the rise of the Romans) gave "life" to them and provided, according to some archaeologists, an insight into Etruscan art.

As to their identity, the only clue scientists have is to be found on the top of each statue's head: above the line marking the base of the helmet are usually two holes that some scholars believe held Viking-type horns. Still other experts maintain that these silent men from the past were carved by Stone Age farmers as monuments to a dead man or as a symbol of men who had been killed.

But some of the stone-men figures (dating back to 1200 B.C., unlike the others) carry swords and daggers that were brought onto the island by a hostile foreign invader. Since weapons of that kind were unknown to the Corsicans, no one has been able to figure out who these invaders might have been. They did, however, leave a fortress with massive Cyclopean walls near the cliff-hanging town of **Cucuruzzu** (a very short distance from Filitosa).

It's worth a trip to this enigmatic stone castle. You walk up the narrow steps into the fort with its small windows and rooms, now all open to the sky, and from the top you get a panorama of the valleys and a hundred hilltops capped with similar forts, which have not been visited or reached in centuries. As you look at these through binoculars, you wonder how the unearthly guests ever got to these high points, much less put huge buildings up there.

Still hungry for more mystery? Then drive to the medieval town of **Cauria**, in the middle of a maquis heath, and visit the lineup of stone warriors, many of whom are ignominiously fallen. Strewn about are heads, faces, hands, swords, daggers and armor. Looking at all this, you are bound to let your imagination wander about the fascinating jigsaw puzzle that offers no solution.

But let not the strange stone men sidetrack you from another Corsican man who dominates the island. Once back at Ajaccio, de rigueur is a visit to the humble house on

Rue St. Charles where Napoleon Bonaparte (original family name, Buonaparte) was born on August 15, 1769, a few months after Corsica—which for at least 300 years had been in the hands of Italians from Genoa and Pisa—had become a French province.

There are two floors of exhibits that include the red couch on which Napoleon was born, a collection of relics, his birth certificate and other memorabilia, much of which has to do with his mother, brothers and sisters. His death mask, however, is at city hall where you can buy a booklet with facts and trivia about Napoleon.

Having taken in the Napoleon exhibit and done the stone-men bit, you will leave Corsica pleasantly perfumed, but not stoned.

* * *

Sewer Tour of Paris

Paris

If it hadn't been for the famous chase scenes both in Victor Hugo's *Les Miserables* and Carol Reed's *The Third Man*, not a single tourist would ever have dreamed of wanting to invade a sewer to see for himself the tunnels of swishing, murky waters that the runaway prisoner Jean Valjean or the fugitive Orson Welles desperately plowed through. Well, if you're still fascinated with this hidden world the next time you get to Paris, the underground maze is yours to visit on a guided tour—with a well-scrubbed sewer worker as your host.

No, you won't have to bring a flashlight, boots or special clothing because the segment of Paris's sewer system that you are taken through has been cleaned up and is well lighted, although the unfavorable odor is still perceptible. Paris's sewers run for better than 1,300 miles, and you are given a good picture of them in a special documentary film and historical exhibit that precede the tour, which attracts many thousands of visitors every year, not excluding a quota of schoolkids on field trips with teacher.

To get on a sewer tour is fairly easy, no advance bookings necessary. Get off at the Metro stop Alma-Marceau at the Place de La Resistance and find the stairway alongside the Rhone River that's marked SYSTEM DU TOUT A L'EGOUT. Wend your way down either at 2:00 P.M. or 5:00 P.M. (when the daily tours are scheduled) and take a seat in the tiny movie theater until the show begins. Twenty minutes later, your guide picks you up, and off you go. The permanent exhibit in the showcases is something you look at after you return from the tour itself, which lasts about a half hour. There is also a souvenir stand down below—with the biggest sales being color slides.

Once you accustom yourself to your surroundings, walking at times behind your guide four abreast on ramps flanking the water and sludge flow, you find the complex of tunnels that also carries telephone cables, post office pneumatic tubes for express letters and fresh-water pipes amazing. In addition, the sewer network has a 160-acre purifying plant that is the largest in Europe.

Unlike the sewers in other cities, the Paris system is unusual in one respect: the tunnels were designed almost entirely on the gravity principle so that the flow does not require any pumping. You'll be shown a catch basin that is wider than the sewer to slow down the water and allow sludge to sink to the bottom so that it can be hauled away in trucks later on. Let it be said that the Paris sewers service more than nine million people very efficiently.

Although you are usually some 65 feet below ground, at no time will you have to stoop. As for falling into the surge of water, the guide waits for that inevitable question and informs you that it has not happened yet to any tourist— and even if it did, it is not particularly dangerous since the water is never deep. You'd need a new set of clothes, however, and a good shower (the latter is available in the locker rooms for the staff near the entrance).

One of the points that interests all visitors is the spot where, back in 1976, a team of bank robbers descended into the sewer with electric drills and welding torches and opened up the steel vault of a bank from beneath, getting away with the equivalent of $10 million in cash—which your guide facetiously refers to as "dirty money." Sewer authorities are aware that terrorists could do the same thing to blow up foreign embassies from underneath, so special security measures, including the use of concealed guards, are in operation.

Paris owes its magnificent unified sewer setup to Napoleon, who established a water board in 1807, but it was really one Baron Haussmann who designed the whole network in the middle of the nineteenth century, together with a web of grand avenues. For easy identification, the sewers bear the names of the streets under which they run. They are patrolled by an army of over 900 male workers. (Women have never applied for a job.)

Seventy-five of these men are part of a special team, an emergency squad whose job it is to retrieve valuable objects that end up in sewers. It's hard to believe, but in a typical year the retrievers fish out more than 3,000 keyrings, some 200 tourist's cameras, and at least a dozen sets of false teeth. Several years ago, some kind of record was set when the sewer recovery team ferreted out two glass eyes, a wooden leg, a motor scooter and a pearl necklace that accidentally slipped off the neck of the wife of a cabinet minister and fell into a sewer. The woman desperately called in her loss at 10:24 P.M., according to the logbook, and at 12:02 A.M. the necklace had been reported in hand. Beneath the log entry was the footnote: "Necklace returned quickly, but Madame forgot to say thank you!"

* * *

The Venus de Milo Puzzle

Paris

She stands in the **Louvre** as perhaps the most famous statute in the world, yet the thousands upon thousands of visitors who view the armless, seminude masterpiece are hardly aware that the **VENUS DE MILO** (considered as the ultimate in feminine beauty by European standards) is a patch-up that underwent extensive repairs. Next time you visit here, stop and give the goddess a closer look.

Unknown to nearly everybody is the fact that the statue is made of two marble halves that have been skilfully joined together at the waist. Now take a look at the nose. When discovered in Greece in April 1820, the nose of the famous beauty was broken and needed to be restored when she reached Paris. Also damaged were Venus's lower lip and her left foot, which were both reconstructed, a missing lock of her hair was replaced, and innumerable minor scratches were cleverly obliterated.

As for her missing arms, even the best French experts could do nothing about these. No one can prove what she might have been doing with her arms, though many theorists believe she was holding an apple with her left hand and clutching her garment with the right. Others hold to the view that originally she was brandishing a spear or a shield like a Greek amazon. Yet another guess is that she was embracing someone.

Among these experts believing the Venus to be only part of a more elaborate statue was a French sculptor who actually created his idea of the man at her side—a helmeted warrior holding a sword in his right hand and a shield in his left. For several years that figure stood next to the Venus de Milo until it was taken away for good.

But there are other puzzles and questions about the Venus. Nobody knows who she is. Speculations have even been made as to why she has such a serious look on her face. And as for those missing arms, where are they?

When the Venus was first dug up, an arm holding an apple was found, and though initially this was believed to have belonged to her, closer inspection made it certain that this could not possibly be so. The ultimate question today is: how can arms be placed on the Venus de Milo without destroying the beauty of the statue's lines?

Then there's the intrigue about how the Venus got to

France. When the statue was originally discovered by a peasant and his son on the island of Milo (Melos) while digging in some ruins to find stones to build a house, a young French naval officer, himself an archaeology buff, had been excavating nearby. Having taken a strong interest in the discovery, he reported the find to his government, and herein lies the "mystery" about the statue's sea voyage to Paris. Why do French government officials still today give out the following two conflicting stories?

On the other hand, according to written reports, France sent out a ship, the *Estafette*, to pick up the statue, but the French sailors had to fight a pitched battle against Greek and Turkish boats that had sought to kidnap the work of art. The report goes on to say that at the captain's orders, swords and pistols were drawn and forthwith blood flowed. In the end, the French successfully delivered the statue to Paris.

On the other hand, another official declaration relates that the beauty of the statue so impressed the crew of the *Estafette* that they took the Venus on a four-month tour of the Mediterranean Sea. At each port as the ship docked, the Venus was brought to the deck and displayed for all to see. After the statue was presented to King Louis XVIII, he eventually turned it over to the Louvre.

To add one final puzzle to the Venus de Milo, mention should be made about the inscription on the statue's base. When exhibited to the public for the first time in 1882, the inscription had been removed because France said that part of the base did not belong there. No explanation was even given as to *why* it did not belong, and yet, strange as it may seem, the base was never seen again after it arrived in Paris. The inscription had read: "Alexandros son of Menides, from Antioch in Maander, made this."

Perhaps some day the French government will come clean and provide some clarifications that a lot of people are waiting for. Whether explanations about the Venus de Milo are ever forthcoming or not, one thing is certain:

tourists who visit her admire the shape of her torso and are awed by the aura of her world fame.

Even without arms, the Venus de Milo grabs you.

* * *

Lafayette's Grave and the American Flag That Never Came Down

Paris

Away from the bright lights of the Champs-Elysées is a tiny cemetery at Rue de Picpus 25 where the body of Lafayette is buried in soil that was brought from the United States, and the American flag has flown over his tomb every day for about 160 years. During the Nazi occupation of France in the Second World War, it was the only American flag to wave anywhere in occupied Europe.

Behind that snug cemetery with the flag that never came down, there is an incredible story of a woman, Lafayette's wife Adrienne, who lovingly built the cemetery in 1800. It can veritably be described as one of the world's most unusual burial grounds. Inside the small enclosure in memory of the 1,306 beheaded victims of the French Revolution are their graves and that of the immortal, idealistic French poet, André Chenier, about whom Umberto Giordano wrote a masterpiece opera that is still done today in Europe.

General Lafayette died in 1834, and at that time the state of Virginia shipped to France the earth in which he was to be buried—so that he might lie eternally under American soil. Equally remarkable is that, for more than 190 years, two or more white-robed nuns have always been stationed to recite prayers 24 hours around the clock in the cemetery convent, designed by Madame Lafayette in honor of the victims of the Reign of Terror in 1794.

On the Fourth of July every year, direct descendants of Lafayette—who have had honorary American citizenship conferred on them by the U.S. Congress—proceed for official ceremonies to Lafayette's grave, for which the U.S. ambassador and his staff are in attendance. The current spokesman for the great French general who fought in the Revolutionary War for American independence is Count René de Chambrun, the great-great-great-great-grandson of Lafayette.

Count Chambrun has been working with a cache of Lafayette's papers. These were found hidden in the attic of his fifteenth-century castle home at La Grange after nearly a hundred years. What comes through strongly in the Lafayette papers is what a remarkable woman his wife was. She died in 1807 and is buried alongside her husband. Hers is a story that has not yet been told. . . .

As the daughter of the Duke d'Ayen'Noaille, Adrienne was a woman of nobility, and at the high point of the Reign of Terror, she saw her mother, grandmother and one of her sisters taken to the guillotine. Though she was scheduled to be the next victim, she was saved in the nick of time by the American minister in Paris and, coincidentally, by the fall of Robespierre.

On the day she was freed from the French prison, after languishing three years in a cell, she took her two little daughters to join her husband who was locked up in an Austrian dungeon. Lafayette had been a major general in George Washington's army and had served gallantly on many a battlefield (on one of which, Yorktown, he had played a key role). He had been imprisoned by the Austrian Emperor when captured by Austria's troops that were part of a counter-revolutionary allied army.

With great difficulty, Adrienne managed an audience with the Austrian emperor, and, although he flatly refused to liberate Lafayette, he gave Adrienne permission to join her husband in his prison cell in Olmütz. Cooped up for two long years, the Lafayettes shared a miserable life of hardship in the bare dungeon that had neither a toilet nor water. The Lafayettes were released after Napoleon's victories over the Austrians.

Once back in Paris, Adrienne sought to find the hidden

pit where the bodies of her family and the other guillotine victims had been buried. After she located the huge common grave, she conceived the idea of creating a memorial cemetery around the burial hole. Having built a new chapel on the site, she arranged for the walls to be built that now enclose the PICPUS CEMETERY—which tourists today visit by applying to the caretaker.

Adrienne died on Christmas Eve 1807 after a remarkable life of continuous self-sacrifice and devotion to husband and family. Moments before she died, she whispered her last words to Lafayette, *"Je suis toute a vous!"* (I am completely yours!). From that day on, until he died 27 years later, Lafayette wore her locket on which he had inscribed those five words. The locket is buried with him.

The Sisters of the Order of the Sacred Heart and Perpetual Adoration, who occupy the convent that Adrienne built, and who have agreed to recite the prayers around the clock eternally, offer the same prayer, one that Adrienne wrote on her deathbed. When you visit the chapel, which is a few feet away from the Lafayette grave, you will see at least two nuns kneeling in prayer, reciting the following: "Bestow upon them, O Lord, eternal tranquillity. And grant Your forgiveness unto all those who did not know how to forgive."

* * *

The Musée Grevin

Paris

The throwaway folder says that it is "the cabinet fantastique," "the palace of mirages," "the temple of Brahmin," "the enchanted forest" and "an Alhambre feast." So you plunk your admission money down at Number 10 on the Boulevard Montmartre and figure, ho-hum, another wax museum—so what else is new? What can you show a professional gaper like me that he hasn't seen before in wax figures?

Well, it's comeuppance time for one full-time gawker at least, because those Madison Avenue adjectives about the **MUSÉE GREVIN**—however much like hype they may initially strike you—simply don't convey the eye-boggling impact and brain-befuddling clout that awaits you when you step inside. Yes, the statistics show that after the Eiffel Tower and the Louvre, the Musée Grevin is the most visited tourist attraction in Paris. Demographically, the same figures indicate that over 99 percent of the people who show up are the French themselves. Most foreigners who do the tourist bit in Paris apparently don't get around to the Grevin.

Open every day of the year, and rivaling Madame Tussaud's in London, the Musée Grevin has been going strong since 1881 and has been offering a curious public many scenes of French history from Charlemagne to Napoleon, an array of stars from stage, screen, radio, sports, television and politics, and a number of other "decors of astounding reality" (again, words taken from the folder).

Almost instantly, the very first of these that you come upon is a life-like man, sound asleep on a park bench, with a copy of a Paris newspaper on his lap. The bench is right there in the middle of the main hallway, and since the wax figure occupies the far end of the long seat, you can sit down at the other end or next to him if you want to rest. Chances are some tourist will take your picture because in a photograph it would be virtually impossible to distinguish between a live figure like you and the sleeping wax figure.

Apparently, where other museums stop, the Musée Grevin craftsmen take the making of the wax impressions several steps further so that the illusion of flesh and blood and skin color is captured through a technique of ceroplastica that was used thousands of years ago in Egypt and Persia. Only when a final result emerges that is imbued with the breath of life itself does the Grevin put it on display.

But it doesn't stop with just the wax figure. The Grevin goes beyond any of its competitors by getting VIPs to donate their personal clothing or uniforms. Even Mao Tse Tung gave one of his outfits, which he sent in through the Chinese embassy.

This authenticity is also carried out in scenes like the assassination of the revolutionary, Marat. The bathtub in which the wax Marat is murdered is the very same bathtub the real Marat was sitting in when Charlotte Corday stabbed him. Another example: the original door that opened on the dungeon in which Queen Marie Antoinette was detained before being guillotined is used in the tableau that portrays her. The garments on the wax look-alike are the original ones too. Still another example: the harpsichord on which the wax Mozart-as-a-child plays is an authentic one from Mozart's time.

More often than not, the Grevin gets celebrities to pose for the models and to allow direct wax impressions of their hands to be made, as well as other parts of their bodies. People like Raquel Welch, Charles Bronson, Burt Lancaster, Charlton Heston, Catherine Deneuve, Jane Fonda, Salvador Dali, Rudolf Nureyew, Yehudi Menuhin and Bjorn Borg have given their full cooperation, among dozens of others. If anybody important is missing at the Grevin, it's usually because the administration could not get the collaboration.

Fifty-seven exhibits are available at the Grevin, and these run a wide range that shows Napoleon on a rock at the island of St. Helena; a ballroom scene including Victor Hugo, George Sand and Alexandre Dumas; the opening of the Suez Canal; Cervantes in prison imagining the adventures of Don Quixote; an audience at the Vatican with Pope John Paul II; violinist Yehudi Menuhin and cellist Mstislav Rostropovich giving a concert; Joan of Arc attending the coronation of Charles VII at Rheims; Houdini doing one of his most famous tricks (the levitation of his sleeping son resting on an elbow); and what is considered the most elaborate wax creation ever—a reception Napoleon gave for every famous French citizen of the time, depicted with great accuracy. When you walk into this big salon, you are suddenly mixing with more than 50 wax effigies, dressed fit to kill, who surround you on three sides. It doesn't take much of an imagination to feel yourself part of the gala event.

Once you've been through it all, the Musée Grevin is the

kind of attraction that makes you wax enthusiastic over what is indeed the best show in Paris.

* * *

Paris Metro

Compared to the New York City subway, the **PARIS METRO** runs a close second in the number of passengers it hauls in a year—more than 1.2 billion. But the French capital's subway system does not take a back seat to New York (or Moscow or London, for that matter) when it comes to providing "enrichment" for its straphangers. Do you know of any other subway in the world with stations that can be described as "underground museums" or "shopping centers" or "classrooms-in-culture"?

Back in the early sixties, the Paris Metro took several giant steps to "humanize its operation." After gathering thousands of suggestions from passengers, it installed soft lighting, comfy seats, live music, live dance, live theater, a live circus and exhibits.

So go underground, Mr. and Ms. Tourist. It's not only the fastest and easiest way to get from Here . . . to . . . There, but also a lot of fun in the bargain since you see a second Paris below the real city. All for the price of one ticket.

Riding the rails of the Metro each day are some 4 million people who use its 15 lines and 359 stations and get more than just a ride: they can take their pick and can listen to as many as a hundred different musicians in one station or another; they can browse in an exhibition of photographic reproductions of Rubens's paintings; they can read the works of contemporary French poets at various station shows.

Art buffs have a real field day, for there are quite a few stations where art works (or copies) are on display. For instance, at the **Franklin D. Roosevelt stop,** there is a picture gallery with Modigliani and van Gogh masterpieces behind glittering glass. Both of the **Louvre platforms** (not to any Frenchman's surprise) exhibit a copy of the Winged Victory, two statues from Ancient Egypt, the Babylonian Code of Hammurabi carved in diorite and a number of wall showcases with museum treasures. The **Varenne and St. Denis stations** also have art on display.

Here is a good tip for camera bugs: take the Metro to the Bir-Hakeim station (where the trains now go elevated instead of underground, and as you rumble over the Seine, you get what is definitely the best photographic view of the **Eiffel Tower** in all of Paris. For best results, roll down your car window part way and shoot the familiar but magnificent scene, using the window as your tripod.

The entrance hall of the **Gare St. Lazare Metro station** has an array of Art Nouveau arrangements that catch the eye, while the **Solferino station**—which has the Montmartre exit at one end and the Montparnasse exit at the other—captures the very essence of the City of Light with its decor. Mixed into the interior's atmosphere are also the inevitable subway billboards hawking everything from cat food to bras to the latest big movie.

To add a bit of nostalgia to the modernization, the Regie Autonome des Transports Parisiens (which operates the Metro, the Paris bus system and the rapid trains that serve the suburbs) reconstructed a particular station so that it would look just as it did when the Metro trains first began to run at the turn of the century.

At **La Defence station** the Metro has its most spacious shopping center where wide arrays of shops are open for business—ready-to-wear merchandise, fastfood bars, banks, quick shoe repairs, key-makers, drycleaning services, hairdressers, opticians (". . . eyes examined while you wait."), florists, automatic vending machines and tourist agencies. This particular station has a gourmet coffee bar that every morning serves what many people consider to be the most exquisite butter croissants this side of Escoffier. (By the way, at this station—and at several other ones, below and up at street level—watch out for the theft-target gypsy kids working as teams, one who accosts you for a handout while the other is entering your purse or palming your wallet.)

Less showy than the subway of Moscow and certainly more clean than the Big Apple's, the Paris Metro is without doubt the simplest for a tourist to learn. No need to know French at all. An American in Paris, armed with an easy-to-get, free Metro map, can keep in mind that once he selects the station he wants, he need only know the name of the last stop on that particular line. This tells him the direction of the train he will want to take (the word "direction" is spelled in French exactly as in English). On many of the main stations there is a large-scale electronic map—you simply push the button of the station, and, voila, a series of lights shows the precise route to follow, including changes to other lines.

Yes, mes amis, knowing about the Paris Metro gives you the inside track to Paris.

ITALY

Largest Collection of Kitsch

Lake Garda

He is today the most incredible tourist attraction to be found in Italy.

He left behind Europe's biggest collection of kitsch.

He cut off the front half of an Italian war vessel and installed it in his garden.

He made his home into a phantasmagoria of bric-a-brac, the likes of which the world has never seen and will never see duplicated again in the future.

He left behind 72 silk shirts, 57 pairs of custom-made shoes, 1,500 neckties, 10 green umbrellas and 42 bathing suits. He was the subject of an Italian postage stamp. He made love to a cavalcade of famous women and boasted of more than a thousand conquests. He was ugly and bald (from age 23) and had only one eye.

He was a painter, a dress designer, a simplified Latin version of Superman, a sometime politician, a soldier, a tyrant with everybody he dealt with, a composer of music and an opera librettist, a poet, an aviator, a novelist, a short-story writer and a playwright.

He singlehandedly seized the Adriatic port of Fiume (today part of Yugoslavia and called Rijeka) with a small band of adventurers in 1919 and ruled it for nearly a year as a self-styled dictator. He penetrated the Austro-Hungarian Adriatic defenses at Bakar with a single torpedo boat while standing on its deck with shells exploding all over. He flew his own biplane over enemy Vienna during the First World War to drop propaganda leaflets on the city amid flak and heavy resistance.

He was one of the most hated men in Italy's history—yet he had a widespread legion of ardent admirers who swore by him.

So who was "he"?

The "he" can be visited today in the small town of Gardone Riviera, an hour's drive from Verona, on the west bank of Lake Garda where stands his villa called **VITTORIALE DEGLI ITALIANI**. Though this name is not distinct enough to arrest the attention of a foreign traveler, the grounds are always full of goggling Italian tourists who flock there in convoys of tour buses and who regard the place as a kind of target the rest of the rubberneck world will someday, inevitably, set its dead aim on.

Okay, so who *was* "he"?

"He" was the man called Gabriele D'Annunzio (1863–1938), on whose museum-mausoleum villa you can now pay a call—for an admission fee of 5,000 Lire, for which you also get a red-covered guidebook in English and French.

No matter what you've heard about Gabriele D'Annunzio, good or bad, be totally prepared—as you tour his home and garden, informally known as the "Kitsch Museum"—for a succession of dazzling rooms that are in the style of a crazy dream that comes across strongly as what a junk dealer with aspirations to an antique shop of immortality would drum up.

It's all there. It's grotesque, amusing, orgiastic, in exquisitely bad taste, with necrophilia galore, exaggerated beyond imagination—seven decades of wall-to-wall, accumulated weirdness and kitsch, as befits their bombastic, unorthodox owner. Admire him or sneer at him, Gabriele D'Annunzio was a myth of a man who handed down an unbelievable bequest—a touristic site you can visit and wander around in on your own.

In D'Annunzio's house, however, a guide will help you come to grips with it all as you wend your way through a maze of 19 rooms—each room unique, with names like Dalmation Oratory, Mascheraio, World, Labyrinth, Workshop, etc.

You see the eccentric Italian's collected works of art, bizarre *objets d'epoch*, bibliographical and antiquarian rarities and curiosities, curiosities, curiosities. This crazy-quilt wealth of intriguing things would need a thick book to serve as catalog.

Here is a smattering to whet any appetite:

With the name Bagno Blu, the bathroom contains hundreds of objects—in every imaginable shade of blue—ranging from Persian bricks, Arab daggers, Chinese drinking cups, ceramic vases, and ivory art to a seven-foot-long bathtub in navy blue. D'Annunzio carried out the blue theme to the point of taking baths in water that he tinted blue.

The entrance to the study is marked by a very low doorway that forced people to kneel in order to enter—D'Annunzio's way of compelling his visitors to "bow in reverence" before meeting him. Not excluded from this ignominy was dictator Benito Mussolini himself, known to have been a most glowing rooter of D'Annunzio. Crammed to bursting, the office stands exactly as D'Annunzio left it on the day he died, March 1, 1938—atop the desk are his glasses, a pen, a pencil and several sheets of manuscript paper of a poem he had in preparation. Near his writing table is a bust of Eleonora Duse, the celebrated actress, who was one of his mistresses. Whenever he did any writing, D'Annunzio would drape a veil over it. Resting nearby is the huge shell of his pet giant tortoise.

As if the interior of his home were not enough to overwhelm you, the outdoor part of his villa is well stocked with "D'Annunziana." Taking up a large part of the grounds is the bow of the ship *Puglia*. Amid trees and other lush vegetation, it "points" toward the lake, seemingly ready to leave port. The Italian Navy often uses this land-bound half-ship to put sailors through some basic training techniques before the men move onto a real ship at sea.

Using Lake Garda as a panoramic backdrop, a magnificent Greek-style outdoor theater serves as the venue for plays given each summer. Another flamboyant building is an auditorium for concerts and stage performances, where overhead, hanging from the ceiling, is the very same plane D'Annunzio used when flying over Vienna with his pamphlets.

In a special garden building is the World War I torpedo boat he guided into action. Still another building has the **D'Annunzio Museum**, replete with art works of all kinds (heavy on nudes), reproductions of Michelangelo's works—and D'Annunzio's death mask. At the top of this remarkable garden, which he designed and built exactly to his taste, is the massive white-marble mausoleum shaped like a castle in which D'Annunzio's mortal remains rest (built and paid for by Mussolini). D'Annunzio left behind a number of garden waterfalls and fountains, the most impressive of which is a fountain in the form of a violin.

He also left behind over 70 volumes of poems, novels and dramas, nearly all of which are today considered defunct works. Among his better known writings, during his heyday as an author, were popular theater pieces like *The Child of Pleasure*, *The Triumph of Death* and *The Flame of Life* in which Eleonora Duse starred. Three of his plays have been put to music—two operas, *The Dead City* by Korngold and *Francesca da Rimini* by Zandonai, and a ballet by Debussy, *Le Martyre de Saint Sebastien*, which are occasionally performed on the Continent.

Though his reputation as a literary genius is debatable, D'Annunzio was a prolific poet, at times even a very good one. Still looked upon in some circles as one of the best books of poems in modern Italian literature, his *Alcyone* verses show an astonishing gift for rendering the healthy exuberance and youthful intensity of a boy in love with nature and women.

As you leave the "House That D'Annunzio Built"— where he died at the age of 74 from a cerebral hemorrhage that hit him at 8:00 P.M. while busy at his cluttered desk— you are bound to have all sorts of conflicting notions about him.

Very likely what best describes the villa are D'Annunzio's own words:

"Not only every one of my rooms furnished by me, not only every print studiously composed by me, but every object selected by me or collected in the various ages of my life was always a mode of expression for me, was always a manner of spiritual revelation, as any one of my poems, as any one of my dramas, as any one of my novels, as any one of my political actions, as any one of my military accomplishments. . . ."

In the final analysis this was a man who spent most of his life, kitsch as kitsch can, attempting to immortalize himself and who, in the end, turned out to be a successful failure.

*   *   *

The Pigeons of St. Mark's Square

Venice

It's plenty hard in Venice for anything to overshadow this city's song-and-storied canals and its many idiosyncratic bridges—but all the tourists who migrate to **PIAZZA SAN MARCO** like iron particles to a magnet are treated to one of the great unexpected attractions of Northern Italy—the pigeons of Piazza San Marco. This remarkable bevy of feathery show-stealers manages to hype the sales of color film by at least 1000 percent every summer because they are on stage all day long. The twice-daily special they put on makes everybody, for the time being, neglect Venice's other delights.

Though the pigeon in other cities of the world is sometimes looked upon as a creature non grata by urban authorities, in Venice the pigeon is "Somebody Big and Important." The local citizenry views him as a special kind of religious symbol and good luck charm—so the Lord help anyone who dares harm one single solitary feather on the bobbing head of a Venetian pigeon.

Unbelievable as it may sound, the cats of this city never stalk a pigeon; it is even said that mother cats apparently teach their kittens not to creep up on pigeons at St. Mark's, because in Venice there is the worst crime a tabby could commit.

Revered and beloved as they are, Venice's pigeons live a life that no other species of bird anywhere can match. Numbering about a thousand—or it 5,000?—they collectively have posed for more photos than any group of animals in history. Is there a tourist anywhere who has been to Venice and does not have at least a half dozen snapshots of the birds as they swarm about a delighted child or woman while scooping up from outstretched palms some corn kernels that are sold in bags by vendors?

About their beloved bird, known technically as *Columbia livia*, the Venetians tell two intriguing stories:

The first yarn, all documented by hard history, concerns the time when Attila the Hun and his hordes were sweeping into northeastern Italy. Because the pigeons became frightened by the invading killers, they abandoned their nests and flew off. Italians interpreted this as something extraordinary and as a sign from God that "safety is thine for thee who taketh to flight."

And, in fact, it came true for human beings. Following the warning given by the pigeons, most Italians scurried off to the many islands that dot the Adriatic lagoon and remained there in safety. This is how the Venetian city-state, which really consists of 117 islands, was founded—thanks to the much maligned bird with the smooth, compact plumage. So, now you get the picture: the pigeon here is respected and paid homage to.

The second story goes back to the Middle Ages. During Holy Week one year in the fourteenth century, the priests let loose thousands of pigeons from the facade of St. Mark's Church for the people to capture and cook at a time when there was a famine. A great many were caught and indeed cooked, but, public opinion being what it was, there was such a sentimental rah-rah for those pigeons that had eluded capture that they were put on some kind of pedestal and granted immunity from capture and harassment forever after. Pope Gregory XI even provided a special blessing.

Thus for over five centuries the descendants of those purring privileged pigeons have continued to multiply in their urban sanctuary. The only time these winged critters are ever interfered with is when a few are captured (invariably at night) and sent by crate to another city that has requested a few samples, a practice that is illegal here.

In their constant, insatiable hunger, the rasorial VIPs of Venice are probably the most well-fed free-flying birds in the world. In the summer, it's mostly the tourists who feed the birds by buying the tiny bags of corn, and then taking pictures of all the fuss and feathers that follow. The eager and friendly little guys comply by landing on your hand or on your head or your shoulder if you proffer a kernel or two. During the winter, however, the city sees to it that Signor and Signora Pigeon do not go hungry.

In 1952, Italy's largest insurance company, the Assicurazioni Generali, which has its main offices just off the square, lobbied for and got permission to undertake the daily feeding. Around 200 pounds of corn are dished out each day in two picturesque feedings no camera should miss. Unless otherwise announced, the feedings are at 9:00 A.M. sharp and at 1:00 P.M.

As the birds swoop down from their perches, the air becomes shirred with wings and in no time the pigeons are assiduously pecking the grain. The mass of fuzz forms a visible advertisement for the Assicurazioni Generali insurance company, inasmuch as the food has been poured onto the ground to spell out the initials of the firm in the giant-sized letters, A and G. Putting on their act, the birds do the scene seven days a week with flying colors.

* * *

Nora: Strangest Ghost Town Ever

Nora (Sardinia)

Now you see it, now you don't! . . .

Ghost towns don't all have the right spirit, but there's a ghost town on our Planet Three that can practice one-upmanship on all the others. So put this strange Sardinian town down as the best of the lost in the *Annotated World Dictionary of Ghost Towns*, and stay tuned for further details.

It goes like this: what you see is what you get; what you don't see is what you get, too. That's **NORA**—the only ghost town anywhere that's partly on land and partly in the sea.

If stories about the lost city of Atlantis grab you, then try your hand on the town of Nora, 22 miles southwest of

Cagliari (the walled capital metropolis of Sardinia) and visit the most Ripleyesque of all ruins. Originally built around 700 B.C., Nora is the only half-submerged ghost town in the world; actually, about a quarter of the ancient city has been gobbled up by the greedy sea. The feeling you get from it is . . . well, spooky. This once-great port city [population today: zero] is open to the public seven days a week from 8:00 A.M. to 1:00 P.M. and from 3:00 P.M. to sunset.

Of course, anybody who's a scuba-diving freak has it made. He can do his thing by descending right down into the remains of the inundated part of the city and do a tour beneath the waves. On the other hand, if you're a landlubber like most folks, then pay a call on Nora anyway, remove your shoes and socks and walk barefoot on the beach portion of the ancient city, eventually wending your way into one or two feet of water, an inch at a time, as the lost town (including the port) disappears into the Mediterranean Sea step by step. Down below in the brine, time has stopped. You are 25 centuries in the past as Nora sleeps the slumber of the millenia under its blanket of seawater.

Should the breezes die down and the Gulf of Cagliari calm itself while you are present, you can observe the most unusual underwater vegetation on the bottom. It is deserted down below, of course, and the invisible people who lie in Nora's burial grounds—the rulers and the slaves, the priests and the warriors—rest next to their strange amulets, many of which are still to be uncovered from under the salt water and sand by prying divers.

At one time Sardinia's most important center, the peninsula of Nora was pillaged and abandoned—and eventually the city disappeared from view. Not until 1952 did excavations bring it all back. Uncovered were Nora's thermal baths, its amphitheater, several temples, the mosaic floors of wealthy homes, narrow paved streets, a sewer system and a municipal plan on which every building was mapped out. At the far end of the cape stands a lighthouse and a structure built by the Pisans, a sixteenth-century tower that does *not* lean.

Nora prospered when colonized by the Phoenicians who provided an all-weather harbor along their sea-trading routes to the European mainland. Set up according to the advanced system of Phoenician urban planning, Nora was a thriving port until about the middle of the sixth century B.C. when Carthage decided to conquer the colonists of Sardinia from the south. Eventually the Carthaginians managed to unify the whole island. In 238 B.C. the Romans took control of Nora and ran things until the ancient Germanic tribe of Vandals came in during the fifth century A.D. To escape from military attacks, the population sought refuge inland—and the town declined and disappeared, to be found only centuries later, about 40 years ago, through archeological digs.

Your trip from Cagliari down to Nora is through a ruggedly beautiful region that has as a backdrop the peaks of the so-called Mountain of the Seven Brothers; the terrain that has been used by several Italian film directors for scenes in their spaghetti westerns. Hugging the coast with flypaper tenacity, the snaky road descends to the ancient town of Pula and from here a road leads to the Nora peninsula.

It was in Nora that St. Efisio (the patron saint of Sardinia) was made into a martyr by the Romans. A high-ranking officer in the army of Emperor Diocletian, Efisio was put to death because, fearlessly professing the Christian faith, he divulged "il verbo Divino" (the word of God) on the island. In Efisio's honor there is a spine-tingling festival each year that experts rank as the most grandiose, authentic folklore event in all of Europe.

Every year since 1657, from May 1 to May 4, the Sardinians undertake a four-day pilgrimage from downtown Cagliari to a chapel right outside of town. During certain years, however, the three-mile-long procession escorts the saint's statue for the full 22 miles to Nora's eleventh-century Church of Sant'Efisio.

The parade is headed by the Sardinian farmers' characteristic carts, gaily decorated and pulled by oxen. Behind them walk peasant men and women from all over the isle wearing their local costumes; members of the island's ancient militia (clad in embroidered scarlet waistcoats, black skirts and trousers of white linen); groups of horsemen

dressed in swallow-tail coats; musicians playing their bag-
pipe-like instruments (known as *luneddas*); and wagons
draped in multicolored rugs and shawls. The island's VIP
politicians precede the historic carriage that carries the
saint's effigy and is drawn by beribboned and beflowered
oxen.

To cap it all, on the evening of the fourth day, Italy's
most massive display of fireworks rocks the sky—a mammoth show against the illuminated mountains in the background. No matter when you come here, during the St.
Efiso bash or not, you know for sure that compared to
Nora, no other phantom town stands a ghost of a chance.

* * *

Pisa's Other Leaning Towers

Pisa

Since this is being written in privacy, door shut and
secretary away on vacation, no one can see me blushing. So
just move a bit closer to catch my whisper. Ready? I've been
to Pisa—the home of the famed **Leaning Tower**—at least a
dozen times. Yep, at least a dozen times. And only recently
did it come to my attention that Pisa has *more* than one
leaning tower. There I've confessed. . . .

Mind you, nobody is even suggesting you come here to
Pisa and not pay a call on the well-known attraction that
shouts "Tilt!" and ranks with St. Peter's in Vatican City and
Pompeii's volcanic ruins as one of Italy's most-visited
places. But when you've done *the* Leaning Tower, try to
find a half hour or so to pay a call on Pisa's *other* leaning
tower. No tourist ever seems to hear about that one, yet all
the locals in Pisa know about it and just seem to have kept it
among themselves. Don't ask me why.

But here's even more news, which sent me reeling while
I was on the hunt for the "other" leaning tower. Pisa
actually has *three* (count 'em) leaning towers. Now that has

to give this estimable city some kind of monopoly. Here-with some details:

Sharing, if you please, second place in Pisa's leaning tower beauty parade is the one to be found alongside the **CHURCH OF SAN MICHELE DEGLI SCALZI** on the main northern route leaving the city, said route having the same name as the church. It would not be possible to walk to the San Michele crooked belltower from *you-know-where*, and no public transportation goes in that direction. So take a taxi, and take along your camera for proof to the folks back home, because, understandably, they might be skeptical. At least, I was, when I asked a Pisan traffic cop what was the quickest way to the Leaning Tower, and he asked me, "Which one do you want to visit?" That's what started it all. That's how some stories are born.

The Church of San Michele degli Scalzi was built at the end of the twelfth century by a group of Benedictine monks who did not wear shoes or socks—hence the use of the word, *Scalzi*, which means barefoot in Italian. The campanile, built in the early thirteenth century, rests on a strong base of stone supported by a foundation of bricks. But because the soil underneath the stone has given way, the San Michele belltower has swayed off center over the years.

The tilt is not so dangerously pronounced as Big Dad-dy's in the center of town, and the lean is not increasing year by year the way the fabled papa's is. Like its architec-tural celebrity father, however, the San Michele tower bows to the right when you face the church. Interestingly enough, nobody associated with the church, nor any of the city's public officials (including a gaggle of guides asked) knows how much of a tilt the tilt is. Finally, let it be said that San Michele's leaning tower cannot boast of any of the artistic grandeur that Numero Uno possesses. Both the tower and the church were damaged during the Second World War and by the flooding of the nearby Arno River in 1947.

As for Pisa's third leaning tower—it is about ten minutes walking distance from the main attraction, along the Via Santa Maria. The twelfth-century church's name is **SAN**

NICCOLA, and its off-kilter tower is sandwiched between the church itself and an old apartment house next door.

Located at the corner where Via Trento crosses Via Santa Maria and becomes Via San Niccola, Pisa's third lopsided tower comes into focus only when you position yourself so that your eye can run along the flank of either the church itself or the apartment house. You can climb to the top by way of a spiral staircase, but don't do it when the bell is about to ring, otherwise you might lose an eardrum.

How it ever happened that a tower—shored up on both sides by buildings that are erect—has a tilt that seems to defy the rules of physics is a question nobody associated with the church could provide a ready answer for. As a matter of fact, the first priest I summoned (a newcomer to the cloth, in his twenties) wasn't even aware that his church had a leaning tower. Public officials merely shrugged their shoulders and gave me the impression that only a "crazy tourist" would even ask. So, as afar as an unpracticed eye could determine, I'd say that the San Niccola tower bends over about a foot and a half.

There you have it. Three leaning towers of Pisa. All you used to get was one!

* * *

Now You Can Visit the Isle of Monte Cristo

Isle of Monte Cristo

Any travel zealot who has boasted about having been "everywhere" can't rightly say he's ever been to the mysterious, previously inaccessible and strictly prohibited ISLE OF MONTE CRISTO. Because Alexandre Dumas himself never visited here, however, doesn't mean you can't. Now's your chance. . . .

Since the Isle of Monte Cristo—where Edmund Dantes, the fictional hero-swordsman of Dumas's *The Count of Mon-*

te Cristo, spent x-number of years in a prison from which he made his historic escape—has been declared a nature preserve by the Italian government, boat excursions to this archipelago near Elba are now being made on a daily basis for tourists with a romantic and/or fictional bent. Boats leave from the nearby islands of **Giglio** and **Elba** (at its pier at Porto Azzurro). If you don't mind traveling on a fishing vessel (you may choose to hire a private boat), they too are now allowed to dock at Cala Maestra, one of the many coves around Monte Cristo's rugged coastline.

Thirty-eight miles off the Tuscany coast and just a tiny dot of land measuring about six square miles and with a perimeter of nine miles, Monte Cristo is roundish in shape and quite mountainous. Its highest peak tapes in at slightly more than 2,000 feet. Most of Monte Cristo is without vegetation and is so rocky that Italians have not thought it worthwhile settling. During the nineteenth century, it was used as a kind of Devil's Island prison.

Fabled in fiction and legend both, Monte Cristo, which in the past has also been called Oglasa, Artemisia and the Island of Jove, has defied human habitation for upwards of 20 centuries. Over the years, groups of hardy maritime pioneers from abroad have tried to establish colonies there but failed each time. Though Carthaginians, Greeks, Romans, Arabs, Spaniards and Genoese have sought to conquer this watery chunk of Tyrrhenian real estate, Monte Cristo has always hunched up a cold shoulder.

Centuries ago, a senator of the Roman Empire built a summer villa on Monte Cristo, but according to an historical account, he fled in desperation from the huge rats that dominated the rocky bump in the water. Pirates later invaded and carted away most of the plush lodge.

As recently as 1852, Monte Cristo got into the hands of an Englishman named George Taylor. He spent a fortune fixing up the insular rock for colonization, but after eight years of heartbreak, Taylor gave up when a band of seafaring vandals set fire to his place. For 12 years after that nobody visited Monte Cristo.

In 1884, a certain Marquis Carlo Ginori-Lisci stocked it with wild game to use as his private hunting ground. The nobleman, however, gave it to Italy's King Victor Emanuel III at the end of the First World War to use as a royal retreat. Warned of the island's ancient curse and its reputation for "hating people," the king nevertheless built himself a lavish, 26-room palace facing the only bay, Cala Corfu, as a hideaway to putter over his stamp collection. As Italy went down in defeat during World War II, the monarch abdicated and fled to Egypt where he eventually died in exile in 1947.

Thereafter, a construction engineer by the name of Dino Vitale maneuvered to lease Monte Cristo for 99 years from the government—throwing all superstition to the Mediterranean winds—and mine it for its touristic potential. With the help of trained dogs, the first thing Vitale did was to eradicate the rat population on the world-famous fleck of earth.

After spending a tidy sum to refurbish the castle, he suffered a series of heart attacks, one of which brought on his death. Vitale willed the deed back to the state. But in his will, Vitale—who had managed to acquire the title of a Count and in effect became the latter-day "Count of Monte Cristo"—left behind an ominous warning to the effect that state officials would have a real battle fighting the curse of Monte Cristo.

Has the curse materialized? Well, apparently, such is not the case. Tourists who land today are allowed on Monte Cristo's fine beach on the cove, but cannot visit the royal villa because it serves as the custodial house for the three persons who live permanently on the island—the superintendent and his family. Although there are no footpaths on the island and the rocky sections far inland are a bit tricky, you can do some exploration hiking if you are sure of your footing, or you can go in for a swim during the ferry's two-hour stay.

What tourists see, besides the beach at Cala Maestra, is an array of exotic plants and trees, but these don't really belong to Monte Cristo, for they were imported and planted by Victor Emanuel III to make his retreat look nicer from the outside. Even though none of the action in Dumas's classic novel took place here, Italy's black-sheep island of Monte Cristo is a household word. No matter what blows are aimed at the stark gray hunk of volcanic rock, it will never go down for the count.

*   *   *

Shh, All About Elba, Shh. . .

Island of Elba

It's a secret. So nothing, absolutely nothing about **ELBA** is supposed to be said to anyone. The some 30,000 people who live here just don't want any publicity about their isolated chunk of geography facing the Tuscan coast of Italy six miles away. Since the island of Elba does not promote itself, it really hasn't been discovered yet by the tourist trade. It will be, however.

This pinch of salt on the sea is aloof from, and disinterested in, the rest of the world. It is a place of great quiet, where the romantic landscape is a Sunday painting done by a master, where there are few automobiles and a lot of stray chickens, where people still sit in the shade of gigantic trees waiting for tomorrow—or the day after tomorrow. Here the accent is on peace. Any complaints?

Napoleon Bonaparte once referred to Elba as "my isle of rest," and when you visit this seagirt hideaway, you get the feeling that Father Time has been canceled out by Mother nature. As your tiny steamer paddles its way here from the Italian mainland, most visitors become aware they are approaching an insular sanctuary stocked with scenic bonuses. True. Elba has dazzling white beaches, wooded valleys, high cliffs and a port of arrival (Portoferraio) that looks like a stage setting for a verismo opera.

Portoferraio, after your 90-minute boat ride due west from the coastal town of Piombino, serves as your handshake to an island civilization that is edging its way into the eighteenth century. Looking like a toy Naples, Portoferraio thrusts forth its shuttered, cream-fronted houses that curve around the horseshoe harbor, which in one stroke of the brush sweeps Elba from blue sea to blue sky.

But about all these things no one is supposed to say boo. Elba's folks know that utopia is a place where if too many people visit, it will no longer be utopia. Ergo, if too many people come to Elba, it will no longer be Elba.

Once a popular target for pirates, the island of Elba (known as "the island of sea horses") is part of the vanished continent of Tyrrhenia, which sank into the sea 70 million years ago, leaving other maritime vestiges like Sardinia and Corsica. Pierced with eerie sea-caves, Elba's steep and rocky coastlines make it an H_2O-heaven for a small contingent of skindivers who practically have it all to themselves.

One "tourist" who discovered Elba a long time ago was Emperor Napoleon I. He got here in May 1814 during his first exile, and the island was made into a tiny state for him. France's fallen sovereign ruled here for a little over ten months with 100 grenadiers and a naval force consisting of one brig. On his 86 square miles of kingdom, Napoleon lavished his administrative genius that had previously dominated a huge empire. He developed Elba's iron mines, built roads, improved agriculture, built up a fishing industry and modernized the capital hamlet of Portoferraio. Brooding over the sight of his native Corsica lying on the horizon, Napoleon enjoyed nothing more than wandering over the island or sailing around it on his brig. He was truly Elba's first tourist.

He will forever remain number one here. For the islanders have lifted Napoleon to the level of a legend. The flag he designed, which has three golden bees on a red stripe with a white background, is held in the highest reverence. Elba's inhabitants claim it has brought good luck to their right little island. That explains the letter *N* which you see everywhere.

The ubiquitous *N* is also all over **Napoleon's summer lodge**. He chose a country house set in Elba's silent hills where evergreens, oaks and terraced vineyards abound. The villa is a high-priority must-visit. As easily done as it is said, any Portoferraio taxicab will get you there in no time flat.

The place contains Napoleon's personal library, including the 70 well-thumbed volumes of Voltaire's works on display, not to mention various Napoleonic mementos including a plaster mask of his face taken when he died on St. Helena. In one memorable room, which has a small octagonal pond in the center of the floor with a jet of water playing into it, Napoleon left his autograph on the wall. He scribbled in Latin the following: *Ubicumque Felix Napoleon* (Happy Napoleon wheresoever he may be).

No matter where you are on the isle, that letter *N* greets you, telling you that Elba is the Napoleon of islands—to the *N*th degree.

*   *   *

The Galleria in Milan

Milan

Nothing so dominates any city in Europe as the Galleria does Milan, Italy's second-largest but least-visited tourist city. The Galleria is not the kind of place you step into, give a quick glance and then walk out. Heavens, no! Rather, it is a place to stroll through and take life easy, to watch patterns of people swirling around you. It's the place where everyone is an actor and, at the same time, a spectator.

Inside the impressive architectural structure with its heaven-high glass-and-steel cupola rising to 164 feet in height, it is like a mammoth cocktail party happening all day long. No matter what the time of day and usually until very late at night, whatever season—be it radiant and sunny, hot and suffocating, wet and foggy or cool and clear—the Galleria bustles with Milanesi just being themselves. And at least half of them are engaged in that most popular Italian pastime, humanity watching.

Doubtless the finest arcade and easily the largest one in the world (there is no auto traffic), the Galleria is a promenade lined with shops and restaurants and cafés and propaganda displays of all kinds. Everybody meets everybody else in the Galleria, especially since much of the year sees Milan immersed in the discomforts of adverse weather— and Italians don't like to stay home anyway.

Officially named the VICTOR EMANUEL II GALLERY, Milan's "drawing room" has met the specific needs of this city for well over a hundred years. (Although there is one almost like it in Naples, that one is mostly filled with noise and doesn't really dominate the city.)

With its four major arms in the form of a cross, of which the longest is 640 feet in length, the cavernous Galleria is where you go for window shopping, aimless strolling, promenading, and morning coffee, afternoon coffee and evening coffee. You can buy a suit, get a shave, have a letter typed, book a plane or boat ticket, pick up bolts of silk, rent an umbrella, engage in a business transaction in the center floor, meet your friends club-room-style, buy books or newspapers, bid on paintings, acquire life insurance, take a bath or shower, browse in bookstores or look at the magazines, get to meet members of the opposite sex, buy wonderful Italian ice cream and have anything from a snack to a feast. But mostly you can slow down and unwind *alla Milanese*, with the tangy odor in your nostrils of freshly made Italian coffee, the semiofficial smell of this amazing, active arcade.

The history of the social salon of Milan goes back to March 7, 1865, when King Victor Emanuel II laid the first cornerstone. The area occupied today by the complex structures and buildings forming the Galleria was at that time a maze of narrow streets and old houses in great need of more functional and esthetic planning. In 1859, the King had decreed that a lottery be authorized for the collection of money to finance a glass-covered passage leading from the square in front of **La Scala Opera House** and from the square in front of Milan's impressively huge cathedral, the **Duomo** (third largest church in the world).

Of the many projects submitted, the one accepted was by Giuseppe Mengoni, who directed a British firm in the construction that took about seven years to complete. The irony was that a few days before the inauguration, cruel fate killed Mengoni. While inspecting some work from a scaffolding, he slipped and fell to his death, not far from the four pavement mosaics that represent Europe, Africa, Asia and North America. Buried underneath the spot where his body landed, Mengoni is not forgotten by the Milanesi today who revere him for giving their city a show-offy architectural wonder, one that is harmoniously integrated into the city's overall appearance.

Besides Mengoni's untimely death, there have been other disasters in the gallery. On the night of August 15, 1943, a devastating air attack left the Galleria in rubble and ashes. The roof was almost totally destroyed, the northeast building demolished, the facades torn, the impressive floor mosaics damaged, the main arch completely collapsed and most of the flanking palaces badly burned—not to mention that the remaining structural skeleton threatened to fall at any moment.

If anybody ever thought that the Milanesi would impassively accept the charred ruins of their city's pride, he did not reckon with the resiliency of these hard-working people. As soon as World War II ended, reconstruction of the monumental symbol of Milan's hospitality was a priority. And when all the work had been done, the Galleria was back in business.

Should you want to do the kind of tourism that involves serious kaleidoscopic people watching, then park yourself at one of the domino-dotted table arrangements (tantamount to being in the open air), sit back with an espresso and become, like the Milanesi, a gallery slave.

* * *

Bam, Bam, Bam—Those Sicilian Puppets

Palermo

The heroes of the cinema, television and opera all take a backseat here to another array of "name stars"—Sicily's heroic folk puppets. There is perhaps nothing in Europe quite like a performance of Sicilian puppetry. So consider yourself truly cheated when you visit the biggest of the Mediterranean islands and don't treat yourself to a stage presentation of *i pupi siciliani*.

This ancient tradition is very much alive today with permanent theaters in **Cefalù, Messina, Acireale** and **Palermo** for the hardy animated dolls who carry out episodes from an era when simple courage and steadfast virtue were the first and foremost values that counted. When you go, a good tip is to sit way in the back, because part of a Sicilian puppet show is watching how the audience behaves and reacts to the principal characters on stage as the story unfolds.

Never mind that you don't understand Sicilian dialect; you'll be able to follow the plot and know who the good guys and the bad guys are, as they assault each other with clubs and swords and a dialogue that mixes raucous invective with righteous speeches.

Mind you, the good guys don't always win, and the bad guys don't always lose, but that is not the point to many of the some 600 different traditional plots. They are not written down, and they pass orally from one generation of puppeteers to the next. The main themes of every one of the stories are honor, total respect for the family, chivalry and a man's word—the code by which Sicilians live, even today, and these cherished values are manifest in every tale.

As far as the audiences are concerned, it does not matter how many times they have seen the same episodes over and over again. Besides booing and cheering, the people in the seats react physically to each one of the puppet characters—the villains get chips of wood, dried figs or rolled balls of paper thrown at them. The heroes get flowers or coins lobbed at them—in addition to hearty words of encouragement and joyous sobbing. To a foreigner watching this, it's almost unbelievable how seriously the spectators (of all ages) take it all and get themselves so emotionally involved and worked up. That's why you should sit in the back.

Up front what do you see? Unlike marionettes that are

manipulated by strings, the *pupi* here are controlled by a solid metal rod that projects from the head, with another rod that runs to the sword arm. There are some strings, however, for the second arm and the shield, but the legs swing freely. The puppet is controlled by a man standing on a platform above and out of view who also supplies the spoken words.

Most of the puppets are knights in shining armor and plumed helmets—with detachable heads, arms and legs that are often lopped off during the combat (and later, backstage, are reassembled for the next performance). Standing about three feet in height, the puppets weigh almost 45 pounds apiece. The heads are usually made of solid mahogany, walnut or beech; almost a necessity because they take a fierce pounding during each show. The life span of one of these solid dolls is about four years before it has to be replaced by another one—which takes about ten days to make by hand.

The most popular plots are based on the Charlemagne saga, whose heroes are Orlando, Ruggero, Rinaldo and Astolfo and whose heroines are Angelica, Isabella and Bradmante—the detested meanies are Gano di Magonza, Serpentino, Falsarone and Bulugante, all of whom are enemies of Charlemagne. Other plays come from Ariosto's *Orlando Furioso* and the Crusader sequences from Tasso's *Jerusalem Liberated*, while still other story lines come from the Bible, the lives of the saints and fairy tales.

Sicily's all-time famous puppeteer was Mariano Pennisi, a descendant of a renowned family of *pupari*. Although unable to read or write, he knew from memory the dialogue of each one of the standard 600 stories. A superb teacher, he taught at least a dozen men his craft—one of whom was an orphaned child he found in the ruins of an earthquake in 1908 and adopted as his own son. That child's name is Emanuele Macri, and he is generally considered the best-known Sicilian puppet master today. Like others in his specialized field, he has taught his son Salvatore the art. One nice thing about attending a Sicilian puppet show, you always have a good time—and there are just a few strings attached.

* * *

Villa of the Odd Spinsters

Battaglia Terme

There are an umpity-ump number of castles all over Europe, give or take a few dozen villas that could be called castles in a pinch, but nowhere in *Ye Olde Catalogue of Castles* will you find anything to match the strange **VILLA DEL CATAJO** some 35 miles from Venice. It looks like a Tibetan lamasery and has its own unique wall that reminds people of the Great Wall of China, ministyle. Not many tourists ever come here—yet the rectangular mass of masonry, which is so unlike any other castle, brings on open-mouthed gazes and complete wonderment.

Created over a three-year period, from 1570 through 1572, by a Venetian general whose family bequeathed it to Austria's Archduke Ferdinand, the Villa del Catajo is owned today by two quixotic spinsters—Giannina and Rosetta Dalla Francesca—who keep their 350-room, architecturally abnormal building closed to the public most of the time. The colossal castle, which has earned for itself the name of "Xanadu in Veneto," is open from time to time on a whimsical basis, simply because the incommunicado sisters suddenly decide to let people go in without any previous notice.

You take potluck about getting in when you come here, but if you locate the mustachioed, friendly gardener (who's not averse to a friendly tip), he'll give you a friendly tour, if his duo of boss-ladies is not inside. Whether you go in or not, just looking at the commodious château from the outside is an experience.

When General Pio Enea Obizzi, who invented the howitzer, began building what is today called by the local residents "the house of the odd spinsters," he used Marco Polo's *Far East Journal* as his inspiration, for he wanted a Mongol palace that would shape up as some kind of Kubla Khan mansion. Capricious and stately, given to flights of fancy and alluring architectural intricacies, the castle was intended to rival all of the some 2,000 villas strewn around the Brenta Canal and just about everywhere in Italy's palace-pocked Veneto region.

General Obizzi picked the highest hill he could find in the Veneto, reaching an altitude of 2,000 feet above sea level, and it turned out to be near an obscure spa town that provides mudbath and chloride-sulphate water treatments for the alleviation of arthritis and rheumatism. Battaglia Terme might be hard to find on most maps, though it is a mere giant-step from Venice on the road toward Lombardy after passing through Padua. Since the town only has five tiny hotels, which are mostly booked out to patients for weeks at a time, you could make a visit to the castle as a day tripper by auto or by rented taxicab, since no buses come to this remote, semi-isolated corner.

On its sugarloaf hill of volcanic origin, surrounded by fig trees, the castle is said to have supplied the inspiration for Samuel Taylor Coleridge to write his immortal "Kubla Khan" poem and parts of the "Rime of the Ancient Mariner" when he came to this part of Italy.

As luck would have it, when my wife and my daughter accompanied me to the Villa del Catajo, it turned out to be a day, hoorah, that the gate to the grounds was open. We did not see the eccentric sisters, but, after all, our mission was the castle.

The approach to Catajo sets the stage: a muscular Hercules and an alert Cerberus, whose three defying tongues stick out at you, guard the entrance. Up above the top of the gatehouse, there are other flamboyant sculptures—each more weird than the other—looking down on you with threats. All callers now pass quickly under a powerful grating and into an oblong court.

The enclosure is devoted to topiary trimmed to form a geometrical pattern that includes 20 broad leafy drums. On the other side, an artificial grotto accommodates the **Fountain of the Elephant**, which is an intricate group of animals and drinking companions who are quaffing themselves drunk and toasting the "Triumph of Bacchus." Pelted with flowers by female wine bibbers and bedecked with ivy, Bacchus and Silenus (his male nurse, also drunk) ride on the back of a trumpeting elephant.

Goat-footed votaries swing bunches of grapes as Indian panthers draw the victorious wine god's chariot. Near this moist miscellany is an imposing flight of steps with a balustrade, each step set at a tilted angle and leading to a roof terrace where you get a marvelous view of the purple hillsides below.

Catajo's courtyards are as vacant as are the stables and the large carp pond. There is a deer park (with no deer anymore), and wild grass and bushes have obliterated the four-path intersections that in various odd nooks, hide chipped cupids and embarrassed nymphs.

Some of the regal apartments you visit recount the story of General Obizzi in frescoes. The rooms are rife with gilded mirrors, unusual-looking clocks, inherited preciosa and antique Venetian furniture—not to mention a library thick with dust that has an enormous array of books, albums, letters, maps, a collection of 14,600 coins and medals and a layout of cancelled stamps that goes back to the late nineteenth century, which includes rarities from the Kingdom of the Two Sicilies. Though most of the rooms are unlocked, the castle still has its own tightly locked secret room, **La Camera Segreta**, whose contents are suspected to be forbidden art works that go back several centuries.

As a matter of fact, the time you spend in the Villa del Catajo raises a number of questions that have no answers. But then what tourist needs answers when the questions are such a big draw?

* * *

The Trulli of Alberobello

Alberobello

They used to say that only the most intrepid travelers ever ventured into the region of Apulia stretching along the Adriatic shore in the heel of the Italian boot. That this is undeserved becomes quickly evident to any tourist who comes here to the deep south for a touch of the Arabian Nights.

As you approach **ALBEROBELLO**, between the port cities of **Brindisi** and **Bari**, in a green-tinted landscape dotted with vineyards and olive groves, you see what looms like an Oz created by a master wizard—hundreds upon hundreds of houses with conical tiled roofs pointing skyward. These are the *trulli*.

The Italian government has classified Alberobello as a state monument, which gives the strange town the rating of a national park. Seen from a distance, the *trulli* make you think of the circular huts of straw shown in movies about darkest Africa, but the *trulli* are constructed of stone. Comprising something entirely different in tourism, Alberobello's colorful beehives are made of washed limestone slats, expertly stacked together without cement.

The beginnings of the *trulli* and the origin of the word (which rhymes with Julie) are unknown, but there is no doubt about why stone was used in the construction of these oddball farmhouses. There is no timber in this area, but there is a superabundance of field stones, which the diligent residents have to move anyway in order to farm. This also explains why there are only stone fences here.

Since Italian reference books provide only a squib of information on the *trulli*, a curious visitor has to fall back on what the local folks say. Legend has it here that the *trulli* first came into being in the fifteenth century when this part of Italy was ruled by the Spaniards. There are two accepted local explanations:

One story has it that a duke living in another town once levied a tax on Alberobello's farmers on the basis of the amount of flat roof surface their houses had. Responding to this unfair assessment, the canny farmers built their houses in the *trulli* design, which has no flat roof surface at all.

The other story, more widely accepted here, is that the local duke, knowing that the Spanish king in Naples would raise his taxes if his region looked too prosperous, ordered the peasantry to build homes using only native stone and no mortar. Then, when the King's tax inspectors came to look around, the farmers could quickly demolish the houses and scatter the slabs in the field, making it look as if the stony land was difficult to cultivate.

Whatever their origins, the *trulli* are not to be seen anywhere else in Italy. Understandably, the people who live in them are quite proud of their unusual homes, and many of the black-garbed wives sit outside their humble domiciles with doorways open to invite passing visitors in for a look. With some of the walls five feet thick and with windows often the size of a sheet of typing paper, you come to realize why the interiors are so cool, even on days of hot, glaring sun.

What always draws the attention of outsiders are the ornamentations on top of the cones. Yes, they have special meaning. A roof that ends in a point or a sphere symbol indicates that a male child was born in the room under that particular cone. A flat-type disc or plate-like fixture on the top means the birth of a girl in the room below. Painted white decorations on some of the roofs are hex signs to ward off bad luck.

As one of the most bizarre of Italian towns, thanks to the *trulli*, Alberobello has nearly 2,000 of these circular homes—which is why it is haunted today by artists and has become a magnet for Italian tourists (foreigners seem to have not yet discovered the place). Because the *trulli* are truly unique, Alberobello's Dali-esque landscape makes it one of Italy's greatest eccentri-cities.

*   *   *

The Island of Glass

Isle of Murano (Venice)

The silence is almost total, and you get the decided impression that even the waters of the canal refuse to ripple. At first glance, you might think you've come to a ghost island because everything seems asleep. Not so.

This is tourist country, all right. And if, when you arrive, you do not see any visiting firemen, they are all inside watching an activity that involves nearly every one of MURANO'S 7,000 men, women and children—the great and honorable craft of making glass.

Observing a team at work here is something to write home about in capital letters. There has to be perfect backfield coordination as the molten glass passes from man to man since a fumble is fatal. Without a wasted motion, the artisans and their acrobatic assistants take a lump of fire-hot gluey glass out of a methane furnace that reaches a temperature of 2,000 degrees Fahrenheit and nimbly pass it through a series of stages. They transform the incandescent blob—thanks to a blowing pipe, a pair of metal pincers and a bucket of water—into a perfect, fragile piece of art.

The master glassblower is the star of the squad. He's good. Plenty good. He's big league all the way. Since he's the quarterback of the team, his sidekicks carry out his every bidding. Capable of executing the most intricate and delicate of designs and shapes, he has the skill to combine a sure eye, an exact sense of timing and a breath and hand control that smack of being pure fiction.

To attain the high status of "master," genus Homo vitreus has to start his career and apprenticeship at the age of 13, so that by the time he is 25, his technique has reached maturity, and he can execute the most complex of designs with 100 percent uniformity.

Venice's glass industry is located mostly on the island of Murano, which embraces an area of less than a square mile. It became "the island of glass" as far back as the year 1291 when a law was passed ordering all glass furnaces moved from the Lagoon City to nearby Murano. This safety measure was taken to protect Venice's world-leading glass works from spies who wanted to steal the secrets of glassblowing.

So secret were these formulas that the Grand Council of Venice, composed of ten master glassblowers, would only allow the information to be handed down by word of mouth from father to son. It was against the law to put any of the formulas down in writing. Some of the island's success, however, can be credited to the type of sand on the

Murano coast and the soda content of the ashes from Murano seaweed.

For five centuries, the law required all glass workers to be kept prisoner during their entire lives on Murano. No man was allowed to leave the island except by rare permit, and the penalty for absenting oneself without a document was the ultimate—death by dagger. A runaway glassblower in those days was tracked down by Venice's paid secret hit men, no matter where he fled to in Europe.

Murano's improved methods of making glass are generally credited to Angelo Beroviero who, in 1463, invented crystal. The secrets of his color and crystal formulas were eventually pilfered by one of his assistants, a dwarf who demanded the master's daughter in marriage as payment for his silence. Even so, the dwarf one day set up a furnace of his own and became the greatest rival of his father-in-law.

In some countries Murano glass has even been used as a medium of exchange, especially the beads, since they were convenient to carry. Window glass was invented during the second half of the sixteenth century—which was the golden age of the Muranesi glass magicians—so Venice was the first city in the world to enjoy this luxury.

Venice exports millions of dollars worth of glassware annually, with the United States its best customer. The Murano glass items range in price from very little to very dear. You can buy tiny glass horses with flowy tails for a few dollars or a set of champagne glasses for $350 apiece.

As you stare at the masters of Murano, displaying their virtuosity of vitreosity, one thing becomes crystal clear—these boys are certainly worth their weight in glass.

* * *

Italy's Hotel for Kiddies

Aprica

The latest wrinkle for the smallfry fraternity is one of the most unusual hotels in the world, a hotel for children only—where anyone over the age of 14 is not permitted to sign the register. So give one cheer for the kiddie crowd! . . .

Located in the hideaway mountain of Aprica—one of the few snow resorts where you can ski the whole year round—the **KINDERHEIM BIANCANEVE** (Snow White Hotel) has accommodations for 40 guests, starting with the age of 4. Operated by a trained man-and-wife team, the kid inn, as you might have guessed, is geared to Mr. Little Himself/Miss Little Herself, with all the furniture scaled down to size.

"Nearly all of our clients," explains codirector Laura Negri, a child psychologist and a former schoolteacher (who hastens to explain that the hotel's guests are never referred to as children but as clients), "come from families of people who don't have time to go on vacation or who are on vacation themselves and prefer not to drag their children along. Young people can be notoriously bad travelers at every age up to about 14. So the parents who realize this like to board them with us where they know our clients will be content and will be well taken care of. We have a staff of 13 trained and experienced personnel.

"We also give them intensive coaching in adult sports like tennis (popular in the summer months) and skiing (popular when the weather is cold), besides taking them in limited groups on daily hikes up into the nearly mountains and forests where Mother Nature has provided Aprica and its environs with more nature than you might find anywhere in creation. It's astounding what we have up there within a half-hour's walk."

The half-pint hospice is located in a newly constructed Swiss-style chalet with complete playground facilities and sport courts on its grounds. As for sunshine-drenched Aprica—which has been called Italy's most beautiful small town, but which, ironically, is hardly known to the outside world—it is planted magnificently on top of a high plateau, 3,874 feet above sea level, in the wild, unspoiled heart of the Alps, just below the Swiss border and north of **Lake Como** in the province of Sondrio.

By comparison with most other first-class hotels, the

Snow White Hotel is relatively inexpensive for three substantial meals a day, Italian style, lodging and professional instruction in various sports—not to mention a wide variety of other games and activities. Naturally enough, hotel reservations are sometimes difficult to obtain during the high tourist-season months. For bookings one can write the Snow White Hotel at 55 Via Italia, 23031 Aprica (Sondrio), Italy, or telephone 0342/746.521.

Since the staff is multilingual, language is no problem at the Snow White Hotel (the English translation of Kinderheim Biancaneve, an odd combination of German and Italian because the owners could find no suitable word in Italian). As for the children, who come from many countries, they manage somehow to communicate with each other when they play, whether they speak the same language or not. One interesting phenomena for those kids who reach the Snow White not knowing any Italian is that they leave after a week or two speaking purty good colloquial Italian, even if they can't conjugate a verb or parse a sentence.

The Snow White can be called a "one-star" hotel because of its director, 56-year-old Umberto Negri, who was one of Italy's star skiers and who is now one of its best ski instructors. He specializes in training professional ski teams for various competitions and is on the government payroll to do precisely that for those squads representing Italy in the Olympics or in European competitions.

But Umberto's first love is children—and they love him in spades. Since the Snow White opened in 1974, several of Umberto's diminutive clients have come back as grown-ups to join his staff. Jestingly, he is known as the "Pied Piper of Aprica" because he has a magic way of getting the tiny people to follow him wherever he goes or to do whatever he does. Most of the boys and girls at the Snow White don't want to leave when their booking is up—"but we're so used to this 'problem' that we know how to handle it skillfully," smiles the handsome Italian who could easily pass for a movie star.

Aprica is an astonishing Alpine setting that is the nearest thing to God. The kids in this mountainous heaven all agree that Aprica is the Inn place to be.

* * *

The Little Men

Brescia

Bring your magnifying glass.

The "Little Men" may never become big shots around here, but they certainly loom large and may well turn out to be the Boot's eye-deal attraction of the travel season. Altogether there are over 40,000 of the Little Men and they've been around for some 4,000 years—waiting for you to drop by and pay a howdy visit.

Why such a fuss over the Little Men—and who indeed are they?

The best way to find out about these diminutive characters is to come here to the **Val Camonica lowlands**, 40 miles north of Brescia. You'll get answers and see for yourself. Bring your specs.

Literally marching out of Italy's prehistoric past, the Little Men are carvings that were chiseled on the polished surfaces of 920 ice-age stones by the unknown Camuni Tribes who, before the dawn of history, spread across the region near Lake Iseo. After the Gauls and the Romans took over 18 centuries later, the mysterious Camuni people disappeared forever, never again to be traced until 1909 when their strange engravings, the only kind existing anywhere in the world, were found by hunters and scientists.

Although the scratchings, hidden under moss, were believed at first to have been done by kids, archeologists later determined that the eerie carvings had been made by bone knives and flint pieces, something kids just would not do. Thus were the Camuni traces finally found, with an assist from the Little Men.

Most of these etchings are now officially part of a national park just outside **Capo di Ponte** called **Parco Nazionale delle Incisioni Rupestri** (Rock Carvings National Park). The wee figurines, mostly line drawings with a circle for a head, a single line for the body and two each for the arms and legs, are all in the new park.

Available is a free folder with a detailed map to lead visitors around the paths that have the stones with the Little Men. Not all of the ancient pictures, by the way, represent men; some of them are animals and tools. Other designs, looking like paddles, comprise the Camuni version of a labyrinth—which, according to a scholarly book by Prof. Emanuele Anati, are likely meant to be a fertility symbol.

Other experts from Germany and France hold to the view that the carvings were not intended to represent letters or words. Probably more decorative in principle, they may have also recorded or represented events of the epoch, since many of the mini-males are shown handling weapons or engaging in military activities.

"We believe the designs were at one time colored, but over the centuries they were exposed to all kinds of harsh weather, and the colors used have been worn away," said Prof. Mirabella Roberti, an officer of the Lombardy Superintendency of Antiquities, who set up the park and prepared the detailed map tourists are given on entering.

The biggest single stone in the park is the one at a place called **Naquane**. Bearing 870 figurines, its entire surface includes warriors, goats, dogs, dancers, hunters and ritual motions. Note especially the wrinkles made by the glacial movements on the stone that the ancient Camuni (a branch of the so-called Ligurian race) used as background props for their tiny bipeds.

Because some tourists in the past have tried to make plaster casts of the Naquane boulder, severe warnings are posted everywhere to the effect that guards in the park have orders to arrest anyone who even so much as puts a finger to any stone.

Besides the Capo di Ponte park, other parts of the valley—from the top of Lake Iseo at Pisogne to as far as Edolo—are full of these ant-like Homo sapiens. In the town of **Crape**, where there are actually 16 large stones with the prehistoric stick-figures, one shows a fish being caught in a cage. Your folder describes this as "the only one of its kind known anywhere."

The Little Men have a way of making a big impression on you. They will capture the fancy of every tourist who takes the time to browse among them. But don't forget your goggles, Gulliver.

*   *   *

The Strange Domiciles of Matera

Matera

An asterisk is a little fuzzy mark on a timetable that probably means that the train doesn't leave on the day you want to go. But as far as **MATERA** is concerned, asterisks and any other punctuation thingamajigs that bollix up your travel plans should be ignored. Lo, the message doth be simple: get thee to Matera, O tourists smitten by the travel bug.

At first blush, Matera sounds like a place a long way off from nowhere. It is. It is located in Italy's southern Basilicata region where the Boot widens before turning down into the heel. Not many tourists go there. Veritably a supermarket of surprises, but little known to the guidebooks, Matera is no stranger to all of Italy's schoolkids who know it as *I Sassi di Matera* from their geography books and the Italian Encyclopedia.

Over 40 years ago, Ripley said in his "Believe It Or Not" cartoon that in Matera (an ancient town of 40,000 people) you find that sidewalks are formed by the roofs of houses. True. He could have explained it a bit further by saying that there is nothing in Italy or in Europe or in the world that quite matches *i sassi*—which are terraced cave dwellings covering both sides of a ravine as though spat out from an earthquake.

The strange domiciles rise in terraces at all angles, in all sizes, in many styles and from all periods. Instead of streets and roads, *i sassi* are pocked by narrow passages and roughly hewn, uneven steps leading up or down. Many of the entrances do not have front doors per se but trapdoors and a ladder.

Overlooking a ravine, *i sassi*—which in Italian means

"the stones"—are a short distance from where the Adriatic and Ionian seas kiss and hug, a spot on the map that still has the town crier making his rounds ratta-tat-tatting his drum in authoritative rolls and rumbles to announce important news and sundry municipal decrees.

Unlike most cities, which are ashamed of their slums, Matera has set up several observation terraces that offer every visitor the "most strange experience" (as the local tourist folder understates it) of looking at houses chiseled chaotically into a massive karstic stone that faces a wild gorge. There is even a scary panoramic Street of the Stones that has been cut from the rock like the grotto dwellings that line it. It skirts the unruly ravine and gives most visitors the heebie-jeebies, since there is no railing.

But don't let that deter you from getting a good perspective of *i sassi*. Throw caution to the breezes and go down into and among the oddball labyrinthine abodes, in which at one time better than half of Matera's population lived. Since, inevitably, you will be approached by one of Matera's freelance boy-guides (known colloquially as *i ciceroni*), accept his offer to take you around the dark, eerie arches, up and down gloomy stairways and into the abandoned dank lodgings. Now you can see for yourself how many streets are formed by the roofs of houses whose lower stories are drilled out of the rock.

You'll feel better about being safely guided through the musty maze and eventually to the **Church of Santa Maria in Idris**, one of the few churches in the world entirely chopped out of a huge rock. This took place way back in the year 1268. Here reigns Matera's patron saint, the Brown Madonna—who is not brown at all but colored pink and cream. Once a year the Brown Madonna is mounted on a cart drawn by mules and after circling the town, it goes back into the church. But the cart then is broken apart by the crowds, and every person manages to get a small piece that is "guaranteeeeeeeed" to give you good fortune for the upcoming year. Be a good joe and buy such a splinter from your little guide. That's his pay.

History buffs will want to know that during the tenth century shepherds began carving homes from the lime-

stone rock along the edges of the promontories, Sasso
Barisono to the north and Sasso Caveoso to the south.
Every conceivable nook and angle of the monolith was
gouged to create domiciles until the population rose to a
full 20,000 in the eighteenth century. Then *i sassi* began to
deteriorate, or so government authorities believed, and the
dwellings had to be abandoned by law.

One of Italy's most famous poets, Giovanni Pascoli, was
enchanted by *i sassi* and referred to them as a "veil of
melancholy." But perhaps even more struck by *i sassi* was
Italy's great novelist, Carlo Levi, author of *Christ Stopped at
Eboli*. His famous novel is said to have induced the state to
pass a bill in 1987 setting aside approximately $74.5 million
to put new life into *i sassi*. And to advertise them.

Carlo Levi's own phrase for *i sassi* is the best ad of all:
"They are like a schoolboy's idea of Dante's Inferno."

*   *   *

The Cardinal's Toys at Tivoli

Tivoli

Clinging to a shelf on the Apennine foothills 20 miles
from the Eternal City, the town of Tivoli is so old that
Rome by comparison is but a young whippersnapper. Ever
since the year one, Tivoli has been a target for VIPs who
could meet the expense of living here. But it was a certain
big shot who arrived in September 1550 whose most unusual "toys" made Tivoli what it is today—an nth-power
tourist draw.

He was Cardinal Ippolito d'Este, the son of Lucrezia
Borgia, who came here at the age of 41 after he had failed
in his bid to become pope. Retired to the governorship of
Tivoli with his political career at an end, Cardinal d'Este
had plenty of time on his hands for the rest of his long life
to play with his so-called toys—thereby giving the world a
fantabulous garden of fountains of which there are probably few equals.

The fountains at **VILLA D'ESTE** (the cardinal's toys) cannot really be described by thesaurus gee-gosh phraseology—nor can they, for that matter, even be photographed properly. By all rights, you are supposed to walk among them and get the total stun-effect of the network of watery jewels that adorn various levels of the garden. It is truly a dress parade for H_2O.

Perhaps even more remarkable is the sixteenth-century hydraulic know-how that went into the project, a job that would give today's civil engineers cause to pause for comment. The cardinal was his own designer, and his plans were not exactly what you'd call simple, since they were on the scale of the Hoover Dam. He diverted the Aniene River in such a way that it flowed uphill (yes) and then thundered down a slope in a most ingenious and fanciful aquatic setup that used no pumps at all—just gravity and the thrust of the river itself.

The cardinal's most striking water toy at the Villa d'Este is the **Organ Fountain**. Designed to play an entire motet based on the force of air driven by water through the pipes, the Organ Fountain required a waterfall all its own. Although the dancing liquid still splashes in various directions, the mechanism for the music doesn't work today— and its secret unfortunately has been lost. At approximately noontime almost every day, a spectacular rainbow forms over the Organ Fountain's spray. This is a sight worth your planning for.

At the **Oval Fountain** nearby is another fabulous toy, where a pathway is concealed in back of the cascading water so that tourists can stroll behind it. It's guaranteed to cool you off without dampening you or your enthusiasm for artistic jet sprays. Also overwhelming is the **Avenue of the Hundred Fountains**, which is three tiers of fountains running the entire length of a long terrace.

Originally, some of the fountains performed mechanical feats. One such was the Fountain of the Owl and Birds, which in the Cardinal's time had metal birds that chirped and trilled hydraulically. An owl used to pop out and hoot, whereupon the other creatures would fall silent and then erupt into a panicky twitter. Alas and alack, this fountain does not function anymore either and the birds are all gone—but the water still splashes around sans feathery accompaniment.

One gimmick fountain that does still work is called the **Girandola**. It is contrived to make sound effects that imitate a cannon and exploding rockets. Curiously enough, many tourists don't realize this, but if they would stop and listen carefully to the gushing noises, they would sporadically hear the fireworks. It's uncanny!

Cardinal d'Este died an embittered old man. Apart from his disappointment at not having become the next pope, his fountains became the subject of considerable criticism at the time he was illegally diverting all that water into his toys. Today, if he could only see his controversial water-magic under night illumination, he would be jarred indeed at the floodlit glory and by the immortality he achieved with his own watergate.

* * *

Rome's Nearby Ghost Town

Ostia

As perhaps the most freakish ghost town in all Europe—a people-less survivor of the Roman Empire—OSTIA ANTICA is better preserved than the famous Pompeii, but largely unknown because it didn't have a dramatic, storybook finish. Wander the deserted streets of Ostia Antica, which at the time of Christ served as Rome's first colony and as its main seaport, and you get the feeling that the inhabitants are all away on vacation and that the dead city is waiting for them to come back. Yup, it's all kinda fearsome.

A mere 15 miles away from the Italian capital, Ostia Antica is a short taxi drive from downtown Rome or a half-hour ride on the Rome subway. The experts say that Ostia, which has been dead a millennium and a half, gives the serious tourist a more penetrating insight into the life of the ancient middle-class Roman citizen than does Pompeii or Herculaneum.

Ostia was founded in the year 335 B.C. on a site where the mighty Tiber River once met the Mediterranean. As Rome's chief outlet to the sea, Ostia not only served as a defense fortress for the Roman government but prospered as a commercial center of some 100,000 inhabitants. Then, after the slow buildup of sand gradually moved Ostia away from the sea, the city began to decline and was abandoned during the fourth century A.D.

The absence of commerce and an invasion by malaria forced residents to duck out. One of Ostia's last written records was put down by St. Augustine, who stopped here in the late fourth century on his way to Africa. His mother died in an Ostia hotel, and his notation of her death cites that Ostia had already taken on some of the aspects of a moribund metropolis.

After that, the abandoned city sank into the ground and lay entombed for over 1,500 years. The only persons who wondered about the odd-shaped dunes that covered the spooky city were shepherds who occasionally scooped away some dirt and stared in bewilderment. In Ostia today you get a marvelous picture of how ancient Roman men and women lived day by day, where they went to shop, where they gathered to argue, where they worshipped, ate, drank and slept. It's all there, preserved for the twentieth-century visitor. Roam about Ostia's melancholy buildings—the silence is broken only by the whispering of the wind—and you begin to sense the ageless charm of this museum that has only the sky for its roof.

Along the main street, called Decumanus Maximus, stop at the intersection of Via della Fontana where the fountain is. Here stands the tavern of Fortunatus whose paved floor bears the inscription: *Dicit Fortunatus: vinum craterae quot sitis bibe.* (Fortunatus says: drink your fill of the crater wine.)

There is much to see in Ostia—a Christian basilica that has been stripped of its decorations and marble, the dungeon-like rooms of a gladiator school, the Baths of the Seven Wise Men, a temple dedicated to Jupiter, Juno and

Minerva, a public latrine with 20 seat holes cut into a solid
marble slab, a firemen's barracks, House of Cupid and
Psyche, huge warehouses that stored imported goods, or-
nately carved marble columns and Ostia's biggest leftover—a 5,000-seat amphitheater that was built by Caesar
Augustus and expanded in 200 A.D.

By sitting on a top tier, you can fantasize about this
archeologist's dream as you look down on the stage and
also look over most of the spectacular 200-acre excavation.
Better still, make a point of coming here during a summer
evening when an Italian actors' troupe puts on dramatic
plays.

Not far from the amphitheater are the Baths of Neptune. The pavement has a mosaic of Neptune in a chariot
drawn by four aggressive seahorses and surrounded by a
coterie of his water fans. Another pavement, in a nearby
warehouse (which bears the unlikely name of Horrea
Epagathian et Epaphroditiana), displays a mammoth swas-
tika, a symbol the Nazis later borrowed.

In addition to running water, the ancient Ostians had
indirect heating—an unusual convenience for a city of that
epoch. They were also old hands at urban planning, their
streets having been shrewdly laid out for efficient traffic
movement. Just outside the baths, the citizens set up li-
braries and a board for new bulletins to keep folks informed.

No spot in Ostia Antica more vividly conveys the sense
of the city's heydey than Big Corporation Square (in Italian, the Piazzale delle Corporazioni), a sort of Wall Street
that today is sadly decrepit. The small temple in the middle
and the pine trees help revive its personality somewhat.
Around the edges are to be seen the outlines of small shops
that were once the scene of fierce haggling and bargaining
over prices and merchandise.

During the some 750 years of its existence, Ostia had no
temperamental volcano or press agent to drum up tourists
eager to make a pilgrimage into the past. With Pompeii
hogging center stage, Ostia never had a ghost of a chance.

* * *

Statue of Pauline Napoleon Bonaparte

Rome

The news is now out that the little sister of a big celebrity in the history books is finding fame on her own in a prominent Rome museum that is racking up statistics to show that our heroine is drawing more and more of Rome's tourist hordes—and she deserves it.

The topic is the half-naked beauty who pensively reclines on her featherbed in Rome's stately **BORGHESE MUSEUM**, beckoning all visitors who enter the side hall. Supergirl is Napoleon's youngest and favorite sister, Princess Pauline Bonaparte, who has been immortalized in marble by sculptor Antonio Canova in a state of *puris naturalibus*— a life-sized statue of the undraped princess.

Transformed into a breathing beauty with living softness, thanks to Canova's touches of genius, Pauline's innocent gaze and the delicate abandon of her poise and pose compete for attention in a lineup of the museum's great names that include Raphael, Titian, Bernini, Caravaggio, Rubens and El Greco.

Although the supine figure has often been described as the most beautiful piece of nude sculpture ever created, Pauline was for a long time the storm center of criticism. Among other things her enemies rapped her for showing bad taste and for being pornographic. Even the Nazis didn't like her, and when they occupied Rome during the Second World War, they forthwith covered her from top to toe with a cloth.

Not for the first time, either. Before the turn of the century, Pauline stayed "prudently secreted from the knowledge of the vulgar" until 1092 when the Italian government bought the Borghese art collection for museum purposes and removed the bedsheet that had concealed her in the basement.

The history of the showy statue goes back to 1809 when Pauline, in her early twenties, went to the studio of Italy's great neoclassic sculptor, whose magic hands had a way of turning marble into "living" human beings. Explaining to Canova that she had a provocative art work in mind, she revealed it was a full-length study of herself garbed as "Venus Triumphant." She said she wanted to be depicted lying on a couch while holding a love-symbol apple between the thumb and forefinger of her left hand. (It should be mentioned in passing that Pauline was a lefty.)

Quite apprehensive about portraying the kid sister of the powerful Napoleon in such a risqué position, Canova tried to talk her into a Diana pose instead, on the grounds that it would create much less of a stir. To do Pauline in the posture she wanted was sure to bring Canova considerable flak from the emperor and possible incarceration for insulting the royal house, etc. Pauline insisted and insisted. So Canova gave in, and was he ever surprised when she refused to have a professional model stand in for her during the long sittings. She had no qualms about posing barefoot from the neck down in front of a man—so Canova assumed a professional stance and put his dextrous chisel to work.

From strictly a sculptor's point of view, Pauline had certain bodily defects that had to be cosmeticized: for one thing, she did not have the right kind of bosom or the proper legs. Since her ears were also quite big with no rims to them, Canova—the complete gentleman and total artist—corrected these to Pauline's utter delight.

When the work of art first went on exhibit, there exploded, as expected, a dilly of a fuss. Pauline's husband, Prince Camillo Borghese, and his staid Roman family flipped their royal wigs at the too-too-real statue that left nothing to the imagination. No sooner had Pauline gone back to France than the family hid the marble "monstrosity" in the cellar, preferring to put it out of sight rather than to destroy a piece of marble that had cost so much

money—its artistic value not having been taken into con-
sideration.

Today all the world pays homage to Canova's masterpiece that graces the main building of Rome's leafy-oasis
Borghese Park. As you come to admire Pauline in all her
frozen marble splendor, it might be interesting to recall
that the making of that statue gave rise to an anecdote that
has since launched a thousand quips.

One day while work was in progress, a friend asked
Pauline if she didn't feel a bit uncomfortable without any
clothes in front of the illustrious sculptor. Forthwith came
her reply, which has since gone down in history:

"Why should I?" she said. "There's a stove in the studio,
no?"

*   *   *

Campione—Italian Enclave in Switzerland

Campione d'Italia

No, your map has not made an error about this tiny
oasis of peace and natural beauty. Completely encircled by
Switzerland, CAMPIONE is an enclave belonging to Italy—
thus an island surrounded by land, virtually like a bubble
in a pane of glass.

Call it a topographical error.

Campione is a dandy example of some gee-geography.
Planted on the southeast shore of Switzerland's Lake
Lugano, this tiny morsel of Italian soil measuring two
square miles was once described by Goethe as "a little
Italian boy in Swiss costume." Not a bad way of putting it,
but it doesn't tell you why in tarnation such a topsy-turvy
situation like this ever came about. How did Switzerland
ever allow a bite-size piece of Italy to occupy Swiss soil?
That is question number one every tourists asks when he
pays a call.

According to historian Giovanni Cenzato, Campione's oddball history goes back to the seventh century A.D. A rich landowner by the name of Lord Totone gave what is now Campione to the St. Ambrosian Monks of Milan. It became a fief of the Roman Empire, and through the Middle Ages it managed to maintain its independence because nobody ever gave it much thought. When the new Kingdom of Italy came about in 1870, Campione was naturally included. That's the way the maps have been printed ever since, with nary a boo or a correction by Switzerland.

Today, what is daily living like for the some 1,200 Italian citizens living in the enclave? It goes like this: For instance, if they want to buy an item on the Italian mainland, they must pay customs duty at the Swiss border. So most of Campione's residents don't do much shopping in Italy; they go to the Swiss town of Lugano, and when they get back to Campione with their acquisitions, Italian Government reps do not exact any duty.

Although the tiny territory is politically Italian, there is no real border between Campione and Switzerland. The currency used in Campione is not Italian but Swiss, as are the postal and telephone systems. To go into Campione you do not need an Italian visa, but a Swiss one, whenever the law is applied—which is hardly ever.

The job of patrolling Campione falls to the Italian state police, the *carabinieri*. Since bringing guns into Switzerland is against the law, one quite naturally wonders how Italy's cops get their firearms through Switzerland into Campione. Well, it's complicated.

Campione's police force consists of a cadre of ten men who are shipped in from Milan once a week. They do not travel by land from Italy into Switzerland, however, because Swiss law strictly requires that the guns the Italians are transporting be confiscated. But, ah, there is a convenient loophole in the rules that allows the *carabinieri* to take a boat at the Italian end of Lake Lugano.

As soon as this boat reaches the invisible line where Italy ends and Switzerland begins, the boat stops and the *carabinieri* surrender their weapons to the Swiss border patrol. Then the Italian boat, which is technically "under arrest," is allowed to proceed under Swiss escort to the landing pier at Campione, at which time the escort squad gives the Italian police their guns back because they are now on Italian soil. The Swiss do not have the legal right to disarm citizens of Italy in Italy. What makes the whole thing even more amusing is that Campione's police force has not fired a shot in over a hundred years.

Besides its paradoxes, peculiarities and picture-postcard pleasantness, which includes a mile-long esplanade on the lake, Campione has still another attraction—a totally luxury-outfitted casino where you can gamble only with Swiss money. Said casino is owned by an Italian company that has to turn over 73 percent of its net profits to the government of Italy (the Swiss get not a cent!).

This same casino, which first opened its doors in 1923, was the setting of one of the most incredible gambling occurrences in history. It happened in the summer of 1963, and the event is still talked about today—with a special name of its own, "L'impossibile."

It was a Wednesday evening in mid-July, shortly before midnight, when players at the roulette table were left wide-eyed in disbelief. The wheel stopped five times in a row at number 21 red. The mathematical odds for something like this occurring run into the trillions. So would you like to make a bet as to which number is now a favorite among all gamblers here?

Though Swiss VIPs take a dim view of Campione's casino, they don't want to make waves with Italy. Casino or no casino, Switzerland would never try to gobble up this orphan chunk of Italy. Rather than take such a gamble, they are playing their cards right.

AUSTRIA

Puchberg's Nutty Engine

Puchberg am Schneeberg

It puffs and sneezes and c-c-coughs. It groans and moans and wh-wh-wheezes. It jerks and r-r-rattles. It waddles and trembles and sh-sh-shakes.

To discover "it" for yourself, you have to make a trip to **Puchberg** and its high-flung **Snow Mountain**. A 90-minute drive from downtown Vienna takes you to the quaint, old-fashioned cog railway that has been doing its thing since before the turn of the century. Perhaps the country's oddest tourist novelty, it draws thousands of Austrians each summer to Snow Mountain, partly for the mountain and partly for the train ride itself. The nutty engine is shaped with a slant that makes it look as if it's busted, and it has eye-arresting moving parts on its flanks that give the impression it could never possibly function. But it does.

The engine pulls two cars, each seating 50 people on long wooden benches, and runs uphill (chug-puff) with a speed of three miles an hour, grabbing each iron tooth built into the tracks one at a time with a short jerk.

You board the so-called **SCHNEEBERG EXPRESS** (Snow Mountain Express) in the tiny town of Puchberg, which is connected to Vienna by both the main railroad line south of the capital and by a superhighway. Bear in mind that reservations for the cog railroad are an absolute *must*, especially on weekends when it seems all of Vienna wants to ride up to the Schneeberg.

Although the oldtime train has been plowing the beloved mountain since 1897 and freights tourists to what is one of the highest rail stations in Europe, standard guidebooks don't give play to Schneeberg. Halfway up, there is a plumbing stop at a wooden shack of a café where you can get snacks, including Snow Mountain's famous prune-filled bun. It's also a good time to snap some nifty pictures and meet up with those adventurous, calorie-burning hikers who either trudge up and ride back down or ride up and then walk to the bottom.

The ride to the Hochschneeberg Station takes passengers past mountainsides replete with wildflowers and a genus of dwarf pine tree that gives off a special perfume, but then you pass the level of altitude where trees no longer can grow. As you enter the first of two tunnels with your train reaching its maximum slant—an incredible 200%—you are obliged to close all windows, inasmuch as the smoke from the engine fills up the tunnel faster than your train can ascend. When the train finally reaches its last stop at Hochschneeberg (altitude 5,900 feet), you find that while hugging the side of a mountain, you have climbed 4,000 feet in an hour and a half on just six miles of track. At the top of Snow Mountain you now get another reward—a massive plateau with rolling hills and dips, presenting an orb-gripping panorama.

What attracts the Viennese in great numbers each week are the well-marked hiking trails leading eventually to one inn or another up there. Altogether, there are 14 recommended hikes; some of these, however, do require a professional guide who lends a sturdy arm when needed and keeps you away from tricky footings.

My mountaintop escort was Hans Gross, who is the Schneeberg's government-approved guide. He also manages the area's official mountain-climbing school. As a trainer for Austria's Olympic ski teams, he also runs adult and children's ski schools. Hans Gross's fame is not that he could be a double for film star Gene Kelly (he *is* a dead ringer, though) but that he is reputed to know personally every rock and wild plant atop the Schneeberg. He's done it for nearly 15 years and even earned his spurs by having been caught in an avalanche that took him all the way down a mountainside, from which he miraculously escaped with nary a bruise.

Many VIPs and celebrities have taken a ride on the Schneeberg Express, but perhaps none more important than Austria's Emperor Franz Josef who made two trips early this century. He had his own special living-room car, aboard which he dined on cauliflower soup, salmon, braised beef with vegetables, fattened Styrian chicken, fruit salad, apple strudel and coffee. This very same dinner is offered today in most of Puchberg's better hotel-restaurants—like at the **Kneipp Kur Hotel** (which specializes in water-cure treatments for patients).

You may also order the imperial dinner in the only hotel that perches on top of Snow Mountain. Rustic and old-fashioned in every sense of the word, the **Berghaus Hochschneeberg Pachter** is run most efficiently today by Dieter and Veronika Holzer who know what old-fashioned Austrian hospitality is all about. What this mountain-peak treasure of an oldtime inn lacks in the way of modern-day hotel facilities (bottled water instead of potable running water) is certainly made up for with a superior cuisine that ranks among the best in Austria (try their exquisite poppyseed cake). And let's not forget the hotel's Friday night get-togethers with food/drink/live music/dancing and merriment hyping up the atmosphere.

Standing about 100 yards from the hotel are the sky-high railroad platform and the tiny stone chapel built in honor of the cherished Empress Elizabeth (better known all over the world as Sissy), who was stabbed to death in 1898 by a crazed assassin.

Down below, Puchberg itself (population 3,000) has more than 20 modern hotels and pensions with over a thousand beds. Puchberg is the kind of Austrian town that would make an ideal stage-setting for any operetta—complete with a park lake in the center of town that is stocked with swans, plied by rentable rowboats and flanked by weeping willow trees. Patrolling this lake is a tremendous outsized swan who serves as some kind of unofficial reception committee—when he spreads out his massive wings, he looks like a white jumbo jet.

Small as Puchberg may be, it holds the distinction of housing the world's only **Marzipan Museum**, and whether you like the taste of marzipan or not, this is one museum that comes at your nostrils strong with its exquisite aroma and at your eyes with its incredible marzipan artwork.

The man—and the artist—who created this private museum is a Hungarian immigrant, one Karl Szabo, who also runs a fashionable and popular lakeside café and bakery-pastry shop. Using only marzipan and chocolate, Herr Szabo has sculpted more than 150 extraordinary displays.

Among the exhibits the marzipan-master has fashioned is a full-sized reproduction of Marilyn Monroe (seated on a chair) and a replica of the oldtimer Schneeberg railway engine. Then there are such appealing works as Disney's Sleeping Beauty Castle, Snow White and the seven dwarfs, the Muppets, chairs made of what looks like Gobelin lace, a violin atop a Mozart score, one of Christopher Columbus's sailboats, several chessboards with all the pieces, maps of Hungary and Austria, a giant statue of Peter Rabbit made out of chocolate and a scene of a bunny marriage done in white chocolate.

As Puchberg's mayor, Michael Knabl, puts it: "The Marzipan Museum is not only the best smelling and sweetest museum in the world, it's good enough to eat."

* * *

Eye-Boggling Nauders

Nauders

Well off the beaten path, dubbed "the corner of three countries," and known as "the lock and key to the backdoors of Austria, Italy and Switzerland," this glorious suntrap of the Tyrol becomes a picture-book sports resort in winter and the butterfly capital of the world in summer. There are over 800 (count 'em!) butterfly breeds here that paint the high meadows and lush pastures that dominate **NAUDERS** (elevation: 4,500 feet) and make it the worthiest detour yet.

But that's not all. When you hie your way to Nauders, by using the main highway from Italy, you are in for a treat unusual, worth an eye-boggling half-hour stop. Less than three miles from the border, under an artificial lake in the

Venosta Valley, lies the swallowed-up village of **Alt Graun** (also known as Curon). The only evidence of the sunken hamlet is its church spire sticking up from the lazy waters in what may well be one of the most weird, but fascinating sights to be found in the heartland of the Continent—truly photography fodder. Take advantage of this rare spectacle and park yourself on the elevated terrace of a café facing it; enjoy a slow dish of Italian ice cream and keep the Kodak klicking before going on to mix with the butterflies just over the border.

These carefree daytime insects that entomologists put into the division *Rhopalocera* of the order *Lepidoptera* number in the millions here. Some locals even make jokes about Nauders and tell you, tongue-in-cheek, that there are more butterflies around than insects, according to the latest census. By the same token, there are also more scientists in town than people. Once you get away from the crooked, meandering streets of Nauders, you begin to walk on the area's carpet of flowers that thrive below the timberline and you are in butterfly domain. By the way, capturing butterflies and plucking flowers are illegal here.

Eventually, however, all roads lead to that unusual point on the three-way frontier where Austria meets Italy meets Switzerland, in what is called in German *Die Dreiländereck*. It's best to go with a guided group or hire a native who will take you there, as the hike is mostly uphill and a bit rugged in places. The walk back and forth will take up the better part of your day. On your way up you will encounter three shimmering lakes mysteriously hidden in a mountain complex; they are called the **Black Lake**, the **Green Lake** and the **Gold Lake** because these are the colors the waters reflect.

There are no border police up there, and you can step into any one of the countries in a matter of seconds—and, if you want, even straddle three countries at the same time. But up there you are rewarded with what may well be the most majestic panorama anywhere—with views of the Inn Valley all the way down to Innsbruck and up to the Tyrol's Ortler summit of 12,800 feet, which is permanently armored in glistening snow. Up there life is good and simple; you are a zillion miles away from the crazy world; everyone gulps in a chestful of invigorating clean air; and it's just plain gotta be a wow-something that God created for Himself and His heavenly pals.

Nauders goes back to the year 15 B.C. when Roman General Octavianus (later he became Emperor Augustus) ordered his soldiers to attack and decimate the Rhaetian inhabitants of the area. The Romans built a military road that went through Nauders (long before any kind of road was built through the Brenner Pass). Later Octavianus's son, Emperor Claudius, improved and finished the project in 46 A.D. Although the Romans never really wiped out the Rhaetians completely, many of the legionnaires eventually settled there, and today the language spoken in the region is the *lingua rustica* which is known as Romansch and which is Switzerland's fourth official language after German, French and Italian.

So much for the hard history. The natives have several other versions—and one of them is the saga of Laurin the Dwarf King and his mythical mountain dominion. The early Rhaetians put up a constant military resistance against him and other alien marauders, but when Laurin's midget troops captured a Gothic princess who was the favorite of Theodoric, the Ostrogoth chieftain, all hell broke loose in the mountains. The Goths trapped Laurin in his hideout, which was camouflaged by thousands of gorgeous roses, and put him to death.

The roses are still very much around today—but however abundant and delightfully visible they are, they necessarily take a backseat to the butterflies-are-free landscape. Yes, if nothing else, Nauders is one town you can say lives up to its reputation—with flying colors.

* * *

Paracelsus Statue in Salzburg

Salzburg

This city's 3-M image—Mozart, music and magic—just never gets tut-tutted by any tourist. When you come here, you see it all, you hear it all, you do it all. Such is the Salzburg formula for every visitor. The formula has one slight gap, however, and that gap is a madcap genius called Theophrastus Bombastus von Hohenheim. With a handle that looks like the bottom line of an eyechart, Theophrastus Bombastus von Hohenheim was the real-life Renaissance figure who inspired the fictional Frankenstein monster.

Not one of the city's tourist-office folders or any of the guidebooks ever bothers to mention this grave of the strange man or that he became renowned for more than the cures of the highly reputed Salzburg waters. Although he is buried in a tomb in the courtyard of Salzburg's **St. Sebastian Church** on Linzer Gasse, just a few paces away from the Mozart family's grave, the thousands of tourists who pay their respects to the Mozart gravesite every year hardly ever give a glance toward the tombstone of "the forgotten man of Salzburg" who won a place for himself in every encyclopedia extant. Ironically, even a statue of him in the city's main park goes unnoticed. How sad! . . .

Better known all over the world by the nom de plume of Paracelsus, this remarkable man, born in Switzerland in 1490, spent many years of his life in Austria, and his last days in Salzburg at the invitation of the Archbishop. He died in 1541 under some questionable circumstances. His enemies (and there were many) claimed he died during a drunken spree, but another prevailing opinion asserts he was pushed down a steep incline by thugs in the employ of jealous physicians who would not accept his way-out theories for treating diseases. One reason for this disdain was that he had no university medical degree.

Paracelsus, who remained permanently deformed from a boyhood case of rickets, spent his life in eccentric behavior, often garbing himself in the clothes of a beggar and at all times carrying a giant sword, which he even took to bed with him. Obese, beardless and bald, Paracelsus remained offensively arrogant throughout his career, overcharging rich people for his medical treatments and, more often than not, ministering to the poor without accepting money. Emphasizing direct experience and renouncing book learning, Paracelsus often engaged in public book burnings of standard medical tomes, yet he was the first to identify silicosis and tuberculosis as occupational hazards and is credited with being the first medical man to recognize the congenital form of syphilis. A believer in homeopathic plant remedies, he was also the first man to engage in the use of chemicals internally, at a time when chemicals had only been used externally.

Paracelsus won great renown for himself—along with contempt—in various cities of Europe where he lectured and practiced. Though his exaggerated egotism brought on disfavor from the intellectuals of his time, he had a great influence on his own and succeeding centuries. Apart from subscribing to many of the fantastic philosophies of his day, the sixteenth-century freelance doctor advocated the use of specific remedies for specific diseases that were not acceptable to the medical community, and he introduced such new medicines as opium, arsenic, mercury, lead and copper sulphate, as well as popularizing mineral baths, tinctures and alcoholic extracts.

Fighting all odds and defying his colleagues all the way, Paracelsus compiled a volume called *One Hundred and Fourteen Experiments and Cures* in which he cited a number of grisly experiments he had done with human corpses. Centuries ahead of his time, Paracelsus was the first man to believe that animal tissue, if properly processed, could replace dead human tissue or trigger the growth of new tissue in human beings.

Another of his seemingly far-fetched experiments involved the injection of a concentrated distillate made of animal brain cells into a "freshly dead" human brain. One night, Paracelsus reported, a corpse in his lab stirred, emitted a hoarse groan and twitched its arms and legs for fully a minute. On the basis of this occurrence, Paracelsus said he was convinced his experiment showed it was "possible to resurrect and synthesize life itself."

The English translation of the Paracelsus book came into the hands of Mary Wollstonecraft Shelley, wife of the poet Percy Bysshe Shelley. In 1818, Mrs. Shelley published *Frankenstein*, generally considered to be one of the best of the early terror novels, and there is good reason to believe that the mad scientist in the book who created a live monster from pieces of human bodies was patterned after Paracelsus.

Paracelsus has been dead for over 450 years, but he's managed to come back to life and stay alive, albeit in an eccentric way—a way that would have certainly pleased him. Anyway, give a close look to the Salzburg statue and observe the slightly ironic curl of his upper lip. Theophrastus Bombastus von Hohenheim is having his last laugh—and everybody knows that laughter is the best medicine. . . .

* * *

Vienna's Smash-Hit Quirky Statues

Vienna

It is often said that travelers who come to Vienna expect to see people waltzing in the streets to Johann Strauss tunes. But any tourist who during his stay here visits the PRATER—the outdoor living room of the Viennese—where the emphasis is on fun-damental things and which is the most original product of the Viennese mentality, will get the real "feel" of the Danube capital because it is Vienna's natural stage.

Immortalized in verse, in story and in music, the Prater's 1,750 acres lie on an island formed by the mainstream of the Danube River and its canal, all within the city limits. Since 1766 the Prater has allowed the Viennese to give full rein to their inborn talents for the zest of life. Paint it all colors—but paint it green!

As a spot for observing local folk customs, the Prater has no match in any other city of Europe. Unto itself it is unique, and therefore belongs in every traveler's bag of treks. The Prater's most distinguished landmark hits the horizon at an impressive 210 feet—the largest ferris wheel in the world. Built by a British engineer in 1897, this

Riesenrad (as the Viennese call it) topped the movie celebrity list when it served as the scene for the unforgettable chase sequence between Orson Welles and Joseph Cotten in Carol Reed's 1949 spy-thriller, *The Third Man*. From the 15 spacious cars, passengers get a nifty eyeful of the Danube, the embracing city and especially the 125-acre amusement park down below, which offers some of the most gimmicky rides ever conceived, several going back 100 years.

Which brings us now to the quirky statues. After I did a double-double-take, and then looked at them again, I decided to throw my trusty thesaurus into the Danube.

As if there wasn't enough to do in the Prater's luna park, the city commissioned a sculptor to create some "picturesque statues" to brighten up a few of its busy walkways and gave the artist 100 percent free rein to exercise her imagination. So two years ago, sans fanfare or publicity hype, the painted aluminum statues made their debut. And the fun-public went gaga over the some 300 forms that changed the Prater—and maybe the world somewhat.

Tracked down in her atelier in Vienna's 8th District, the sculptor does not strike you as an escaped creature from the 11th planet or one of Jupiter's moons. She is Christa Müller, fortyish, petite and slim. She tells you that these brightly painted statues that have become the rage of Vienna took her all of three years to make and that she is presently preparing several dozen new quirky ones for the Prater. The unveiling is due in two years.

One statue in the Prater's **Calafati Square** is *so* popular with the public that they interact with it, photograph themselves with it, climb all over it, try to figure it out and talk, talk, talk about it. This complicated series of figures, intertwined with a pair of fountains, shows two arms holding a baby's milk bottle from which a steady stream of drinkable water flows. Close to it, a baby-faced adult male and another man wearing a blue hat and orange shoes look as though they are trying to get a drink. Lying on her back is a woman, water flowing from the baby bottle onto her face while her foot holds a sort of soccer ball with red and black dots on it. Stuck out from everywhere are mocking faces, legs, and a mishmash of arms—all this being scrutinized by a face peering through a horse's saddle.

To add to the merry confusion, the main part of the fountain fans into an arch, with water bursting forth from a green bottle. About six feet high, the arch represents a faceless man and woman holding each other, while the upper part sprouts a pocket with five fingers sticking out (no thumb), above which is a collection of look-alike male faces. One man's arm reaches out of his neck with a green glove. Then there's a hand holding a circus mask. Another arm clutches a woman whose glowing red face is in the crook of an elbow. Altogether, seven faces mix into a nutty juxtaposition.

As you walk under the arch, you see a clown's face in a striped shirt and a woman in mesh stockings; a pair of vivid red shoes is holding up a cane, with yet another arm coming from behind her ear, with two more arms holding a green bottle from which a steady supply of water bubbles out—this is where real people can drink.

Another woman, an integral part of this complex statue, is a Marilyn Monroe type wearing a low-cut sarong and modestly covering up her left breast with a flashy open fan that she holds with a mesh glove. The man nearby has two faces on his legs, one of which is upside down. A series of six heavily rouged red lips with protruding upper teeth somewhat uglifies the whole picture. Bizarre? No. It's pure fun—and you can wet your whistle, too.

There's more, plenty more—but first some more about who and why.

Christa Müller is no stranger to the Viennese. She first splashed into the public eye during the 1984 Vienna Festival when 300 of her zaniest life-size papier-maché dolls cavorted in every imaginable form of whimsy, from the utterly way-out to the preposterously absurd. Everywhere in downtown Vienna Müller's puppets were doing their thing, while scores of gaping tourists gasped at what had invaded the Danube capital. Could such things be? Everybody was delightfully thunderstruck—for example, by a Superman doll crashing through the tinted glass facade of a multistory office building. Also by four men on high scaffolding painting the side of the Albertina art building and another taking a nap. And by a mountain climber in full gear clambering out of a hole in the sidewalk of the pedestrian zone. In every direction that camera-wielding tourists looked (click), puppets in the doll-scape extravaganza (click-click) were acting out a lunacy (click-click-click).

Because of all the public commotion Müller's statues caused, requests from other cities flooded in hot and heavy, begging to borrow, rent or buy the hot dolls at any cost. Thanks to this unprecedented behavior, Vienna shed once and for all its sometime image as the most old-fashioned capital of Europe.

Until discovered by the minister of culture, sculptor Müller's way-way-out art works gathered dust in her atelier. Now all has changed. And the Prater has become her public art gallery, the better for visitors to see for themselves these incredible "masterpieces of non-nonsensical nonsense," as one of Vienna's toughest art critics described them. The bottom line is that these faces of fantasy, interwoven with arms and legs in contorted and twisted jumbles, delight the crowds roaming by—a treat for kids from the age seventy on down.

In the Prater's other main square, which has no name but is at the junction of Leichtweg and Jantschweg, stands another spread of weirdo statuary that draws people like a magnet. One with the automobile theme dominates. All over this yellow human creature on all fours are painted roads with toy autos racing all over them, and on top of his back stands a four-window house with a crooked red roof, from which a heavy column of smoke pours downward to form a face meeting up with something akin to a turtle and becoming a head whose eyes also look like the house windows. Speeding up his tie is an auto, and on the right sleeve is another automobile ready to zoom up the tie, too. The back flank of the house looks, disturbingly, like a flaming-red fireplace that has a human nose.

Müller says that the one statue that draws the most comment through letters, direct questions, and from TV cameramen is that of a very tall baby boy in his yellow

terry-cloth togs holding the hand of his three-foot-tall father (all dressed up in a blue suit and wearing glasses), as
the toddler leads "Big Daddy" to one of the kiddie rides up
ahead.

Herr Doktor Freud, yoo-hoo, where are you? . . .

* * *

Vienna Clock Museum

Vienna

This city's peerless **Clock Museum** can be a horological
hideaway (if you have a lot of time on your hands), but you
don't have to be a clock-watcher to kill a few hours there.
Any traveler who hits Vienna should do the **Spanish Riding School**, the **Schönbrunn Palace and Gardens** and a
few of Vienna's other tourist staples, but you'd better go to
the Clock Museum for the best time of all.

Five minutes from **St. Stephen's Cathedral**—the sym-
bolic beacon of Vienna—stands a small secluded square
called Schulhof into which bleed four tiny alleys whose
names even very few Viennese know. On the corner of one
of these alleys is the Clock Museum. You enter a wooden
door to an old house, walk up one flight of stairs and there
you are.

Concentrated in fifteen rooms on three floors, the half-
century-old museum houses over 900 timepieces, some of
which are indeed curiosities that turn back the clock. There
is, for instance, a priceless astronomic grandfather clock
built over 200 years ago that still runs and shows with
accuracy all the celestial dates, including the partial and
total eclipses of the sun and moon.

This odd museum contains primitive Gothic iron clocks
from the thirteenth century, others in wood and bronze
from the Renaissance period, clocks that have "smiles" on
their faces, ladies' painted enamel pin watches, night-lamp
clocks and one wall timepiece that actually plays the harp
(in tune).

Included in the showcases are some of the most picturesque pocket watches ever contrived—one in the shape and
color of a partly ripe apple, another that looks like a pear
and still another in the form of a violin. Other oddball
timepieces include one from France constructed in the
image of a wheelbarrow and one built to fit into a real
thimble. There are also two pocket watches for blind people, designed so that the hands can be felt without changing their specific positions. Another curiosity is a pocket
sundial, with compass attached.

Easily the most unusual clock of all, however, is the one
that kept time by burning oil through a wick. The oil,
colored blue, stayed in a suspended globe that has the
hours painted vertically on the surface. As the wick
burned, the oil level went down indicating the hour.

A collection of hourglasses in one of the rooms features
an unusual "three-hourglass," dating from the year 1664.
Some of these sand-timers did duty at sports tournaments
and political conferences, while others were used in shops
to determine the number of hours worked so salaries could
be calculated. This room also has some water clocks, known
as far back as antiquity.

A mammoth tower clock from St. Stephen's Cathedral
has also found its final resting place here. First installed in
1700, it did service until 1861 when the tower steeple was
changed totally. The man who had to strike this clock on
the hour was helped by "watchmen's watches" that rang a
bell each hour to remind the watchman of his duties. These
were perhaps the first alarm clocks ever.

Standing in all sizes and shapes, many of these tickers
are still running and keep fairly accurate time, partly because of the present-day care they get and partly because
they were built with the greatest skill during the heyday of
the Vienna clockmakers, who, from 1650 to 1850, made
their creations with love coming out of their fingers.

The Clock Museum was founded in 1917 when the city
of Vienna took over a collection of some 2,000 clocks
belonging to Professor Rudolf Kaftan. He carried on as
director of the museum until his death in 1961 at the age of
90. During his lifetime search for the world's scarcest time-

keeping specimens, Professor Kaftan never succeeded in finding a clock on which face an *IV* was printed instead of the usual IIII—even though Roman numeral *IIII* is not correct for the number 4 and *IV* is. Moreover, the Clock Museum can offer no explanation why *IV* is never used on the faces of clocks.

Then there is the matter of cuckoo clocks—you won't see one on display that cuckoos. There's a valid reason for this. The cuckoos had to be silenced because every hour on the hour the racket was just terrible.

* * *

The Kahlenberg Bride

Vienna

Tourists to this celebrated Danube metropolis almost never get to one of the most touching sites ever—behind which is the tragic story of the **KAHLENBERG BRIDE**.

On top of the **KAHLENBERG HILL**, truly hidden in the embrace of friendly trees, lies a tiny cemetery—which happens to be the highest cemetery in Central Europe and that holds the graves of fewer than a dozen people. It is at one of these graves, which goes back over 175 years, where the tombstone recounts one of the most sorrowful stories told in Vienna. The gravestone has the following inscription:

HERE LIES
KAROLINE TRAUNWIESER
BORN ON 8 DECEMBER 1794
PASSED AWAY IN HER PRIME ON
8 MARCH 1815

On the side flank of the stone, written in German, the story of Karoline Traunwieser is related. It goes like this:

Born on the Kahlenberg, Karoline led a carefree childhood playing with her little village friends. When she grew up, Karoline blossomed into a beautiful young woman and, soon falling in love, was betrothed to a handsome young man of good family. But it was the year 1812, their country was at war, and her young fiancé was called to the colors.

After the historic Battle of Leipzig, like so many thousands of mothers, wives and sweethearts, Karoline sweated out the return of her beloved. Day after day she waited at the top of a picturesque winding path that they had always used in their days of courtship, wearing her best flowery dress. Every time a deer or small animal rustled through the undergrowth, she took to fancying that her loved one was hastening home.

None of the neighbors had the heart to tell her that the handsome young lover would never be returning to make her his wife. For he was one of the countless soldiers who had fallen on the field at the Battle of Leipzig. Though eventually given the bitter news, Karoline simply refused to belive it, continued to wear her best dress and returned to wait on the path, their path, each day.

One cold morning—it was nearly spring—the pathetic form of Karoline, dressed in her flimsy bridal costume, was found on the pathway. During her overnight vigil, she had frozen to death, still clutching a small bunch of forget-me-nots, while waiting patiently for the lover who would never return.

The news of her hapless death stirred the whole city and brought a huge crowd of Viennese to her burial in the little cemetery on the Kahlenberg heights. And forever after, Karoline Traunwieser was known as the Kahlenberg Bride.

The Kahlenberg hill—which is visited by dozens of tourist-laden buses every day during the warm months—provides from a height of 1,585 feet what is probably the most astonishingly spectacular panoramic scene available of Vienna, the Danube River, the extensive vineyards of Grinzing and the easterly spur of the Vienna Woods. Up there is a restaurant, run by monks, that serves authentic Austrian dishes, and in the summer, when the garden is set with tables, diners also feast on the view below.

Not far downhill is **Leopoldsberg** (1,388 feet), which has a modern hotel, with a good restaurant and café with a terrace in front that overlooks the Danube. A few feet away is the historic little church, **Leopoldskirche** (run by Polish priests), where there is a fascinating relief map of Vienna as it was in 1683. It's from this church that you begin your walk downhill to the grave site of the Kahlenberg Bride.

The tiny cemetery can also be reached on foot from down below in the Heurigen-wine section of Grinzing by walking into the **Vienna Woods** (page 165) along an unsurfaced, winding path uphill, which during weekdays is almost deserted. Before you depart Grinzing, however, do ask for directions. Remote and peaceful beyond description, your walk through the Vienna Woods at this point will take about a half hour.

Ever so few tourists, by the way, bother going on a hike in the friendly forest, famed in song and story. If you plan to walk to the Kahlenberg Bride, why not also plan to spend at least a whole morning or an entire afternoon (if not the full day) strolling in the Vienna Woods as Beethoven and Schubert did all the time. These two composers, among others, based some of their works on the sounds they loved there.

One of Beethoven's favorite sounds, which he caressed into the Sixth Symphony, was that of the cuckoo. You'll definitely hear this bird call for yourself—but remember that the Austrian cuckoos are birds of another feather, unlike their wooden Swiss cousins in captivity. They don't cuckoo every hour on the hour.

*   *   *

The Pummerin: Vienna's Big Bell

Vienna

The sound of music in this musical capital of the world is not necessarily Beethoven or Brahms nor the bap/boom of the downtown disco joints here. What is music to every Viennese's ears, especially on the day of an important event or New Year's Eve, is a most unusual sound effect, one that comes out of the top of **St. Stephen's Cathedral**. It is a city-wide, deep PU-MORRR-EEEN that makes nearly every building in the center of town vibrate, registering something like five points on the Richter Scale.

The Viennese call their beloved big bell **DIE PUMMERIN**, which is not a German word at all but an onomatopoeic dialect word to suggest what the sound sounds like. Actually, there are no words in any language to quite convey how the Pummerin dong reverberates. You simply have to hear it for yourself—and never mind your thesaurus. And as far as seeing the Pummerin, which is one of Vienna's best tourist attractions, well you can't look at it walking toward St. Stephen's or from any vantage point on the sidewalk. You've got to take an elevator to the top of the tower to get close to one of the world's most unusual big gongs.

Although it is not the biggest bell in the world—nor does it have the kind of crucial significance that the Liberty Bell in Philadelphia has for Americans, or Big Ben for the English—the Pummerin nevertheless has a track record few bells can match, even apart from its special sonority that no bell, past or present, can match. It is without doubt the only bell in the world that fell from its lofty perch, crashed to the ground into a hundred pieces, only to be brought back to life again and reinstalled where it came from. Name me one bell, Mister, that can one-up the Pummerin on that score. . . .

The fabulous history of the Pummerin goes back to the Second Turkish Siege of 1683 when Viennese troops successfully beat back the invaders and the Turks left behind hundreds of cannons. Proud of their achievement, the Viennese decided to melt down the heavy guns and cast an enormous bell, which would tell the world every time it rang out how the vaunted Turkish army got its lumps. The epoch's greatest bellmaker, one Johann Achamer, was called in to do the job.

Achamer came up with a bell that was adorned with the images of St. Joseph, the Virgin Mary and St. Leopold bearing the coats of arms of the Holy Roman Empire, Austria, Bohemia and Hungary. Weighing 22.5 metric tons and sporting a diameter of 10 feet, the bell was hung in the steeple and consecrated in December 1711. It rang for the first time on January 26, 1712, when the young Emperor Karl VI (the father of Empress Maria Theresa) returned to Vienna from his coronation in Frankfurt am Main. Because of its unique resonant tone, almost immediately it was named Die Pummerin.

Over the centuries, the old Pummerin rang out only on special occasions—but on Easter Sunday 1937, it gave its last bong, for the Church did not endorse Hitler's presence in Austria and on April 12, 1945, after some heavy gunfire from the retreating German batteries, the area surrounding St. Stephen's went up in flames. Since there was no water for the city's fire brigades, embers showered onto the cathedral and the entire roof eventually burned out. The conflagration spread to the interior of the church, burned the wooden construction in the belfry, and the Pummerin crashed to the ground in a shatter. No sadder day could have existed for the Viennese as their cherished, history-laden big bell lay in shards.

But all was not lost. It didn't take the postwar federal government long to decide that while St. Stephen's Cathedral was being reconstructed, a new Pummerin would be cast from the bits and pieces of the old one. Not all of the old Turkish cannon metal was to be found, however, since some souvenir hunters had taken home portable hunks and splinters, but most of it went back into the new bell—which at 21.4 metric tons was a bit lighter than the old one. As for the sound of the old Pummerin and the new one, well there are many Viennese who claim the previous sound was "different"—but everybody here agrees that the sound is the kind you will not hear from any other bell in the world.

The new Pummerin was fashioned under the supervision of an expert, Karl Geisz. The new adornments also differ: there are now the heads of six Turks on its top, with three bas-reliefs showing Mary, a scene from the 1684 Turkish war and a depiction of the 1945 fire. Most tourists, unfortunately, will never get a chance to hear the Pummerin, unless they're around at New Year's Eve when thousands of Viennese gather just to hear it ring in the

fledgling year at midnight. Both radio and TV also carry
the beloved sound to all parts of the country. This is one
bell that is gong-ho for Austria.

* * *

The Vienna Woods

Vienna

There is a certain purity about the VIENNA WOODS—the
same Vienna Woods of the old songs and stories—for its
trees are never touched by the ax or saw of the building
contractors and its breadth of nature is the breath of life.
When that rare visitor, the tourist, comes to the Vienna
Woods, he is greeted by total silence, except for the chirp-
ing of birds—the call of the cuckoo especially—and the
rustling of leaves. Hmmm, *is* this tourist country?

It's tourist country, all right! It's only a short trolley ride
from the center of the city (take tram number 38 to the last
stop and ask someone to point you in the right direction
uphill). And before you know it, you have embarked on the
least-touristed of Vienna's multiattractions. Give yourself a
casual two-hour stroll or a healthy four-hour hike in Vienna's chlorophyl oasis, and the Viennese will guarantee that
for every arithmetic minute clocked in their beloved Wienerwald, you reap geometric hourly rewards later on.

Although the Viennese themselves literally invade the
cozy hillocks of the Wienerwald mostly on weekends,
whenever you go—weekdays are best—you somehow get
the feeling the place is deserted . . . well, practically deserted. "Where is everybody?" is the first question that
comes to mind. The truth is that everybody *is* there; the
throngs have simply been swallowed up by the vastness of
trees, meadows, vineyards and hiking paths that are well-
marked for you in various keyed stripes of color on the
trees.

In still another respect you are never alone in the Vienna Woods, a thousand or so feet above the city, for it has

been an inspiration for composers and artists since way back. The walks and lanes once used by Beethoven, Schubert, Johann Strauss, Hugo Wolf and Gustav Mahler are the same today as they were in their times—quiet and peaceful and undisturbed by city concrete and traffic, free and away from the tensions and pressures of the world.

Rain or shine, Beethoven is known to have taken daily walks in the Wienerwald, absorbing the wonders of nature and exuding his impressions and feelings in his works. In his Sixth Symphony (the *Pastoral*), Beethoven captured many of his favorite Wienerwald sounds, and indeed all of his nine symphonies have something of his beloved woods in them. Franz Schubert was another titan composer, more lyrical perhaps, who filled his music with the Wienerwald's tinkling brooks, sporting trout, happy butterflies, the colorful carpets of wild flowers and Mother Nature's other miraculous creations. Then, too, Johann Strauss immortalized and eulogized the foresty enclave with dozens of his waltzes, but especially with his *Tales From The Vienna Woods*.

Spreading over an area of nearly 500 square miles, the protected green belt that surrounds the capital of Austria is best visited with a 163-page *Wienerwald Atlas* that sells in all bookstores here. Although nobody could possibly explore the entire vast cushion of flora and footpaths in the Vienna Woods in one lifetime, many Viennese give it a real try. In the Wienerwald, a visitor is never more than one hike-hour away from an inn or *Gasthaus* that will serve Austrian dishes, Austrian wine and Austrian desserts (try one of the pastries that include berries freshly picked in the Wienerwald).

Portions of the Vienna Woods are inside the Vienna city limits, and one of the highest and most spectacular points within the city is **Leopoldsberg** (cherished here as the easternmost Alp) from which you get a marvelous bird's-eye view of the rooftops of Vienna and the Danube River ribboning through the city. With or without binoculars you can make out Vienna's landmarks, like the spired **St. Stephen's Cathedral** (page 158) and the world's biggest ferris wheel, the Riesenrad, in the **Prater** (page 154) amusement park.

Another's hour's hike, slightly uphill, will take you to the **Kahlenberg Inn** where Mozart wrote **The Magic Flute**, and where you can enjoy a panorama of Vienna while dining in the garden. Not far down below are the towns of **Grinzing** and **Sievering** which are noted for their "new wines" (namely the wines of the current harvest, called *Heuriger* wines by the locals). The Heuriger restaurants that dispense these wines are mostly self-service, with some of the best lip-licking specialties (garlicky sausages, roast smoked pork, thick slices of rye bread with a paprika-orangey cheese-spread called *Liptauer*). In the Heuriger inns you can absorb in every way the true Viennese mood, or *Gemütlichkeit*.

But the hike's the thing in the Wienerwald. The marked trails will lead you to who-knows-where. Sure, you could get "lost" in the Vienna Woods on your first foray—but so what? As any Viennese knows, you will find your way and also find yourself.

*   *   *

The Sidewalk Painters

Vienna

The sidewalk is their canvas. . . .

You usually find them on hands and knees working with colored chalk and reproducing an old master like the *Mona Lisa* or a work by Rembrandt or Raphael. The sidewalks of Vienna's central district provide an al fresco studio—with an admiring, attentive audience, no less—for a new type of itinerant master painter. A tourist delight, his "works of art" fascinate everybody who passes by.

These Leonardos of the pavement chalk up a winner every time. Their sidewalk paintings, done expertly with classroom chalk, are treated with great respect by pedestrians—very few people actually step on them while a work is in progress. How can you, if the artist seems to be capturing, let's say, the mysterious eyes of the Mona Lisa and her famous enigmatic smile almost the way da Vinci did.

"Yes, I know that my portrait is not going to last very long because it is subject to the weather, especially the rain, but I wouldn't want the painting made permanent by somebody putting varnish over it or someone removing the sidewalk slabs and hanging them on a museum wall. I consider myself a public entertainer, and I enjoy having 20 or 30 people watch me as I do my thing. And if they appreciate my talent and the pleasure I give and then throw a coin into my hat, well, that's the name of the game. Simply put, I need the money to get by. . . ."

Those are the words of Phil from Australia (he won't tell people his last name). He and his wife Patty have been touring all of Europe's major cities for the past year or so, and with his handful of colored chalk and pavement paintings, which bring in about $40 a day in contributions, they are meeting their expenses as they move with their few belongings and chalk from one big city to another to practice their art of fine art.

A little further down the street is another painting in progress—a Caravaggio called *The Vocation of St. Matthew*, being done by a Polish refugee, Ignacy Gorcyzn. This 38-year-old comes from Czestochowa. He abandoned Poland a few years ago with fake papers, and while waiting with hope against hope to emigrate to the United States or Canada, he is using his training as a graphic designer to do sidewalk art to keep his modest savings intact.

Ignacy was scrubbing out the faces in the Caravaggio because they were too big, he said in half German and half English. "Caravaggio would not like," he adds. "Working outside is like working in a free studio. I have come to like it. With all these people looking at me, it gives me big energy. I do not make too much money, but I keep alive. The materials cost big. So I make my own pastels. I mix colored powder with glue and water. My next painting, when I finish this, is one by Guido Reni, because the Viennese like him."

Ignacy cooperates with another Polish artist who doesn't have as much artistic talent as he does. When Ignacy has to leave his unfinished painting for a few hours, his partner takes over. He pretends to be working on the incomplete drawing so that admirers throw their coins into a cardboard box. Ignacy's sidekick (who wants his anonymity respected) has a serious face and wears spectacles that make him look more like a university professor than the usual street artist. Which is what he was. . . .

While putting the finishing touches to Corot's *Girl With An Amulet* at a roofed tram station along the Ring Strasse, 43-year-old Karl Koran estimated, conservatively, that in the ten years he has been working the sidewalks, he's executed more than 2,000 paintings. Ordinarily, it takes him two hours to do one painting when the weather is warm, but during the winter months when his fingers are stiff, a painting can eat up some five hours of work.

Koran, a former freelance commercial artist who lent his talents to ad agencies for some 15 years, decided one day to chuck that career in favor of making his living out on the street all year long, weather or no weather. Partial to Italian painters, he says his all-time favorite is Pompeo Batoni (1708–1787), a neoclassic artist from Lucca whom he pushes a lot.

"I do his stuff from memory, rarely using a photograph of any works. Sometimes I may change an aspect or a small detail of a painting because that's what I feel like doing. For instance, in this Corot I'm finishing up, you'll notice that the amulet around the girl's neck is not exactly the same amulet Corot put on her. And I've done the painting under this shed while people come and go or wait for the next tram. Here the rain can't get at it, so it should last about three days before shoe leather and boots wear it off," explains Koran, a native Austrian from the nearby town of Krems along the Danube River.

Though Vienna's statutes do not permit "defacing" sidewalks, the police never bother the artists, nor for that matter has a city biggie ever ordered a painting to be hosed away. So chalk one up for the law. . . .

SWITZERLAND

The Cat Museum

Riehen bei Basel

Sooner or later it had to happen. The cat is out of the bag. Now that the cat has statistically surpassed the dog as man's first-choice household pet, the world today has its first cat museum—stocking more than 10,000 feline-related items any tourist would need more than nine lives to look at.

This is one place where genus *Felis domestica* gets long-overdue honors, for the range of items takes you all the way from an ancient cat mummy to cat sheet music to cat jewelry to cat postage stamps to cat cult objects in every imaginable cat-egory. This doesn't exclude some ceramic cats that are so realistic you expect them to give out with a welcoming howdy meow, but, fear not, because there's also a live show—the curator's own six cats who roam among the exhibits and brush up against visitors like official hosts.

Known in German as the KATZEN MUSEUM, an entire villa and its expansive grounds provide the purr-fect venue for kitty. Although the museum is open only on Sundays between 10:00 A.M. and noon and from 2:00 to 5:00 P.M., curator Rosemarie Kürsteiner-Müller will unlock the gate at almost any other time if you simply make a telephone appointment with her by calling 061/67.26.94. A letter to her villa-museum (at Baselstrasse 101, CH-4125 Riehen bei Basel, Switzerland) will also bring results. From downtown Basel, the museum itself can be reached easily by tram number 6 with a ten-minute ride.

"The cat in history and as a good friend and companion of man goes back to 3,500 B.C. when it first became domesticated," explains Mrs. Müller. "In fact, one of our exhibits is a 3,000-year-old Egyptian cat mummy—which gives you a clue as to how ancient Egypt viewed this marvelous creature of God. No other household pet, not even the dog, brings so much warmth and joy to its owner because of its varied personality and ways."

It was this high esteem for the cuddly meowers that catapulted Mrs. Müller and her husband into starting up the world's first cat museum on an ever-growing collection of cat lore that they had begun 15 years earlier in connection with their careers as antique dealers. They threw open the portals to their museum in June 1982 amid considerable European TV coverage, and as a result catfanciers all over the Continent have, in one way or another, contributed new items to the collection.

A feline buff in his own right, husband Tilo is a recognized artist, and during his spare time has created over 50 Persian-cat statues in clay and cement. All of these are in different poses and are scattered throughout the English-style garden that embraces the villa-museum. One of these stony cats, standing 4.5 feet high, sits on a marble pedestal and is the first to greet all visitors. It is a stately black statue of an Egyptian cat queen and it is the exhibit that gets the most camera attention. Whenever large groups of visitors or schoolchildren on field trips are on the grounds, this statue is invariably the centerpiece of the group photographs.

Besides the astounding array of cat items, the museum also keeps what may well be the largest collection of books on puss-in-boots in the world. With thousands of articles on the subject, the library is open to serious scholars and scientists doing research on the popular domestic four-footer. Having read every one of the hundreds of books on the shelves, Mrs. Müller answers questions over the telephone whenever they come in and on Sundays during visiting hours when she also pitches in as a guide.

Her delightful spiel includes the story of how cats helped the Persian Army defeat the Egyptians around 500 B.C. According to Arab history books, the Persians had just about lost the war and were already planning a retreat when the commanding general got a bright idea. Remembering that Egyptians considered doing harm to a cat sacrilegious, he had each of the soldiers carry a cat under one arm while armed with a sword in the other to attack the enemy lines on the battlefield. The superstitious Egyptians would not and did not fire a single arrow, so the Persians scored a solid, bloodless victory.

The museum is systematically laid out to cover the following subjects: cats in the distant past, cats in the recent past, cats as seen by painters and sculptors, cats in music, cat postage stamps, cat kitsch, cats in mythology, in literature, in art, in fairy tales, in photography, in fire departments, in advertising, in films, in politics, in cross-breeding, in the circus world, cat heroes, cat dangers, cat appreciation, cat curiosities and oddities and cat toys (for kiddies and kitties).

Specifically, some of the unusual individual items include a cat skeleton, some cat teapots and cat ashtrays, the cat Napoleon and his French Army, two cats on their hind legs (one playing the violin and another clashing cymbals) singing a Merry Christmas to all, some cats seated at a table having tea, many unique pieces of cat jewelry, cat clocks, cat "piggy" banks and a cat deck of cards. And in one kitty-corner of the museum, the extremely popular section on cat kitsch often brings on laughter.

So move over, Fido. Basel's meow museum has everything you could possibly want to see on the long-whiskered mousers. In fact, the entire cat-alog. . . .

*   *   *

The Richest Street in the World

Zurich

Whether or not money is the route to all evil, money-Money-MONEY knows where to go in Switzerland: all such roads lead to the **BAHNHOF-STRASSE**, the richest street in the world. This makes it a blockbuster of a tourist destination and is therefore the natural habitat of—dare I say it?—the Gnomes of Zurich.

Okay, one sight you probably won't see on the Bahnhof-Strasse, during working hours, is a real Swiss banker himself. Of this species of silent Homo sapiens pecuniarius, Voltaire is supposed to have once said: "If a Swiss banker jumps out of a window, follow him, for there is money to be made on the way down!"

Contrary to expectations, the "Queen of the World's Main Streets" is, in fact, relatively short in length, altogether no more than a half-mile long, running from the main railroad terminal from whence it got its name) to Lake Zurich's shore. Automobiles are not allowed on the Bahnhof-Strasse, since the artery is mainly a pedestrian mall. Electric trolley cars, however, still rumble along it smoothly and sanely—without a taint of pollution.

Tourists emerging from the train station may not be instantaneously grabbed by the Wall Street of Europe. But as you get into it, it's like touching Aladdin's lamp. Suddenly the department stores, pastry shops, taverns, cafeterias and supermarkets are rubbing shoulders with the furriers, jewellers, perfumeries and the chic watch and dress boutiques. Throw in the posh movie houses and the posher hotels and you have beautiful music—all that do-re-mi and Swiss yodeling about all those bank notes.

To the tune of billions of dollars, the Bahnhof-Strasse can boast of real-estate values probably not matchable anywhere, for land here is worth considerably more than on New York's Fifth Avenue. That's because all of Switzerland's major banks and most of the secondary and private ones keep their main buildings or headquarters on the Bahnhof-Strasse. Can any other avenue on earth dare to compete?

From the train station it is only about a 15-minute stroll to the end of the Bahnhof-Strasse, although it usually takes several hours to do the stretch on foot because the attractions will make you tarry. As you walk up the street going toward the lake, the big bank buildings eventually loom, practically one after another. Here is the milieu of the oil sheiks, the maximillionaires, the heads of foreign states and other VIPs who deal in six- and seven-figure transactions.

Less endowed mortals like you and me, however, are not denied access to these banks, which are certainly the most influential in the world. First of all, if you're a mere tourist, there is no charge for looking. But if you have any kind of business, however, small—even if it's merely to change some dollars into Swiss francs (or vice-versa)—step inside and find out how quickly you're made to feel like Mr. Important Himself. The Swiss lay out the red carpet for everybody. Now you will come to know why the Bahnhof-Strasse best demonstrates the Helvetian affection for democracy in action and makes capital out of it.

Strollers along the Bahnhof-Strasse can read the latest stock-market quotations on closed-circuit television screens in the windows of the banks. Judging from the lingering gawkers, this must be the most popular show in town.

A money show you can't afford to miss (free admission) is the public gallery of the Zurich Stock Exchange (open from 9:45 A.M. to noon) that hands out a free folder explaining in simple English what the "what" is all about. And while you're in the middle of all this money bit, don't forget to pop in at the Monetarium, another free exhibit, that is on permanent display in the Swiss Credit Bank; a collection of gold coins, old and new—some of which are available for purchase.

Here's a fascinating tip: clustered along the avenue where money talks with a most miraculous tongue are many of Switzerland's private family banks that go back generations. Since Swiss law bars them from any kind of advertising or even from displaying so much as a sign in the window inviting deposits, the private banks make their presence known with a small metal plate (like that of a doctor) stating only a name.

Your safari along the Bahnhof-Strasse will show you that the Swiss are into money and what makes the world go round. The name of the game is "Real Life Monopoly." Here you don't only get your money's worth, and you can bank on that.

* * *

Summer Glacier

Les Diablerets

Hey mister—psst! Looking for something really cool? Something a bit different in the way of tourism? Something like jogging on a glacier or walking on it—in the middle of summer? Yeah, in the middle of summer. . . .

On my office wall there's a list of eight must-do's in Europe, and it is now all checked off. For years I have had a nutty obsession with going for a walk on a glacier in the middle of summer. But when I asked in Italy, they laughed. When I asked in France, they laughed. They also laughed in Sweden and everywhere behind the now-rusted, woebegone iron curtain. Ha Ha was always the No No answer.

But they didn't laugh in Switzerland! In fact, they asked me, "Which one?"

My "which one" turned out to be **LES DIABLERETS**, which is the Helvetian republic's own choice as *the* Summer Glacier for Tourists. They even have a snow-bus up there, for lazy hikers who would rather ride the full length of Sir Glacier Himself. It doesn't have wheels but runs instead on a pair of army-tank tractor tires. The snow-bus is heated inside, snugly holds seven passengers at a time and makes the round-trip in 45 minutes—with a stop at one end of the glacier at a wooden shack hut called Yeti Palace, at an altitude of 9,384 feet. I took my trip on a hot day in August last year and made the mistake of going with only a light sweater. The weather up there is some 40 degrees colder than below, so don't pay attention to the warm summer climes down on the bottom, and do take along something heavier—either an anorak, a ski suit or a thick blanket. If you do go up with just a simple wrap, then a ride in the snow-bus is de rigueur, after which you should follow up

with a piping hot bowl of soup and/or a swig of schnaps
once you get back to the mountain plateau inn that skiers
use all year long.

Yes, you can even take a shot at summer skiing up there.
It's fantabulous, since the landscape is as grandiose as *le
Glacier des Diablerets*, which rests on a mountain shelf that is
about 9,843 feet high. The white stuff all around you is
called "the eternal snow" because it hasn't melted for centuries. And that's the snow you walk or ride on. So come up
and see it sometime—and enjoy a bumpity-bump-bump
ride on the one and only *bus des neiges*. The fare is low and
when you climb aboard this unique, monster-like carrier,
the most original means of transportation in Europe, you
catch a tremendous view of 20 peaks that are over 13,124
feet high.

As your vehicle plows its way safely across the icy
plateau, you reach the glacier's famous hut where a hot
drink is served while you peer over a sturdy iron rail for
the ultimate view of the Top of Switzerland. With one 180-
degree-turn of your head you get a breathtaking panorama of the highest summits in the Alps. The two snow-buses
run daily every 45 minutes or so and are on duty only
during July, August and September.

Reachable from **Geneva** by rail in just two hours and 30
minutes, Les Diablerets is plunked almost midway between
Gstaad and **Aigle**. For motorists there is a road from Aigle
or from Gstaad over the Pillon Pass. Away from the tussle
and bustle of the cities, Les Diablerets in the heart of the
Vaudois Alps is a genuine alpine community that leads the
double life of a farming village and of an up-and-coming
tourist resort.

With a widespread network of telecabins, ski lifts and
skating rinks (that also accommodate hockey and curling
fanatics), Les Diablerets boasts origins that go back to the
Middle Ages and has managed to maintain an authentic
aura from this era. By connecting up with other resorts,
Les Diablerets offers 75 miles of well-kept ski runs with 50
ski lifts. During the summer, Switzerland's World Cup and
Olympic ski team uses Les Diablerets to practice. The place
even offers torchlight skiing at night with expert ski-guides

on hand to lead the way. For more information, summer or winter, the office of tourism can be written to at CH-1865 Les Diablerets, or bookings can be made over the phone by calling 025/53.13.58 (Telex: 456 173 OTD CH).

One final thing about your hike or ride on the summer glacier: the Swiss government allows you to "steal" some of the glacier snow. This is what I did. As was to be expected, however, my souvenir snow-in-a-jar has taken on another image as the water slowly evaporates.

But my memory of that summer glacier is forever frozen in time.

*　　*　　*

Gornergrat's 4,000 Club

Zermatt

To become a member of the 4,000 Club—no, not the elite 400, but a *higher* society—simply take a ride on the **GORNERGRAT RAILWAY** from **Zermatt** (Switzerland's southernmost ski resort) to the **Gornergrat**, the mountain that is your ringside seat facing the circular stage of the "four thousanders." Twenty-four peaks that measure over the 4,000-meter mark (more than 13,000 feet) are visible in one sweep of the eye, but the mighty **Matterhorn** takes the lead role in this icecapade of four-thousanders—even if it is 515 feet shorter than its tallest brother—because it stands alone, free, unique and extraordinarily photogenic as the world's most talked-about mountain.

You already get your initial dosage of the big "M" down in Zermatt when you first arrive by train. No matter where you are in the town, that crooked-nose horn is sniffing the horizon. And you are warned that he who doesn't catch the twisted snout as it emerges against the sky in the early hours of dawn, first blushing pink and then turning gold, misses what may be the most spectacular pageant in the Alps.

When visitors get off the train, they are greeted in the

square by horses and sleighs (or carriages in the summer) and mini electric vehicles to transport them and their baggage to the hotels—no gasoline exhaust. That's right. In its rucksack of charms, Zermatt's biggest plus is what it does *not* have, namely auto traffic. Anybody who comes here by car has to park it in Täsch, the next town and six kilometers distant (3.5 miles). Everybody's happy that way.

To get to the Gornergrat, leave the center of Zermatt (the best time is the early morning, and dress warmly with comfy shoes, no matter what season of the year) and board the bright red double-cars of the Gornergrat Railway (inaugurated in 1898), which runs all year round for skiers, hikers and sun worshippers.

Chugging its way upward, easily carrying 5,000 people in a day, the electric cog train rises 5,000 feet in 40 minutes, providing through picture windows a brand new landscape at every turn of your head. It twists and turns along the curving tracks against a backdrop of snow and ice and valley below, with the Matterhorn in a different position at each blink of your eye and that of your camera's.

Tourists soon discover that the best and simplest way to conquer the Matterhorn is to see it and fall in love with it, not to climb it—unless, of course, they are tempted by the yarns of how "easy" it is. Which is true. . . . But the graves of would-be climbers in the church cemetery give testimony as to how dangerous the mount is and how tricky-changeable its "own" weather can be, despite the sunshine everywhere else.

The Matterhorn has taken many lives in the past century, about 15 deaths a season on unguided climbs (emphasis on the *un*!). Without a guide and experience or ropes, you just do not walk up those 14,689 feet. If, however, vanquishing the Matterhorn is your goal, you're advised to hire a guide for a trial hike on the Gornergrat; pass that test and you'll be allowed to try for the big one.

At the end of the line, destination Gornergrat achieved at 10,285 feet, walk up to the broad terrace jutting out from the **Hotel Kulm**, which not only accommodates tourists with a café-restaurant (in addition to serving up the Matterhorn on a platter, so to speak), but also provides space for two observatories. From these, groups of astrono-mers and scientists from all over the world find the air ideal for their day and night studies of the heavens because it is free of the dust and vapor-saturated atmospheric layers of the plains.

The Gornergrat, the "little" upstart which stands right in front of big brother Matt, is idyllically located. Why? Well, not one mountain dares ever to throw a shadow on this geological titan, that's why. As one of the most beloved observation points in the entire Alps, it offers you yet another high-riser, its cable car, which is a sort of a "contin-uation" of the Gornergrat line up to the Stockhorn. There, at 11,240 feet, exists the world of glaciers.

Try trekking around the alpine pastures on the wide ridges and have a good look at fully one-third of Europe's tallest ice and rock giants. Among them is Switzerland's highest, the **Monte Rosa Dufourspitze** at 15,204 feet (sec-ond only to Mont Blanc), named after Helvetia's first gen-eral. These peaks are planted against the bluest sky ever, which is why it is said that the paint pots were mixed here when the color blue was created.

When you decide to descend (cars run about every 45 minutes), there is a big surprise ahead, compliments of the cog railway. Get off at Station Rotenboden and in a few minutes the trail takes you to the **Riffelberg Lake** where the Matterhorn makes with an icy stare at its own reflec-tion, sphinxlike, in the water. To fully appreciate this phe-nomenon of the entire mountain looking at itself in the mirror-lake, you have to get there during the morning hours. (You can also disembark at the next stop, at Station Riffelberg, but the hike is longer.)

The heartbeat of the Alps, Zermatt has much to boast about—of the 38 four-thousanders located in Switzerland, all of 29 can be seen from different points in the Zermatt area. The biggest underground funicular (really an alpine metro) whisks up to the **Sunnega terrace** at 7,500 feet in a few minutes, and if one wishes, from there by cable car another 3,000 feet. Small wonder that, with such a string of records, Zermatt is the biggest summer alpine ski area.

Set up like an arena, Zermatt is surrounded by glaciers

and towering mountains, protected from wind and rain, with weather so good that the proverbial topic is a bore here. In fact, the clouds seen hovering on the horizon over the mountain chains drop their rain only before or on the ridges, leaving Zermatt, the center, dry.

Strolling along Zermatt's main street, away from all the shops, toward the Matterhorn, you come upon the old part of the town of a century ago—rows of leaning log cabins built on stilts (so cattle could sleep in the warmth below) and underpinned by flat round stones to keep out rats. Most of the present 3,700 permanent residents are descendants of the original dwellers of these huts.

By the way, all the land encircling the town legally belongs to Zermatt, and that includes the Alps—but only three faces of the Matterhorn. The fourth, or south face, is Italian. But whichever side you look at, it's the Horn that Matters.

*   *   *

Hotel to End All Hotels

Degersheim

Reserving a room at a hotel ordinarily requires no Houdini skill or sleight of hand, but checking in at the **MAGIC CASINO HOTEL** here beats anything yet in the history of hoteldom. It modestly classifies itself as "the most original hotel of Switzerland," but in fact earns the ultimate designation, "the most original *magic* hotel anywhere." More about the Houdini stuff and even *magic museums* later. . . .

For starters, guests have a choice of 20 rooms, each totally different from the other; each done up in a decor that pushes an original theme—like the Western Saloon Room, the China Room, the One-Armed Bandit (Las Vegas) Room, the Coca-Cola Room, the Pinball Room, the *Saturday Evening Post* Room, the Louis XV Room, the duplex Wedding Suite and the Hollywood Room.

If you book the Hollywood Room, be prepared to spend the night with statues of James Dean and Marilyn Monroe (the latter was sculpted from the famous nude pinup poster). Signing the register for the One-Armed Bandit (Las Vegas) Room, means you can play any one of the half dozen coin machines that line the room. But taking the *Saturday Evening Post* Room could give you some entertaining reading matter—articles or short stories printed in the *Post* during the 1930s and that now appear as slick wallpaper. In the Coca-Cola Room, your pillows and bedsheets bear the blown-up familiar trade label of the American softdrink, while the telephone is the exact shape of the familiar bottle.

Upon entering the Western Saloon Room, which is laid out as a kind of hangout you've seen in dozens of Westerns, you push open the swinging halfdoors and, bang, you are confronted with an armed life-size-replica cowboy who is ready to shoot, *High Noon* style, provided you don't shoot him first with the rifle hanging on the wall. The Erotic Room with its sexy waterbed and mirror on the ceiling is high on imagination and . . . er, beyond description. The upstairs/downstairs Wedding Suite (stylized for honeymooners) has a winding stairway that takes you from the living room, which has a kitchen/bar, up to the bedroom where stands what is probably the biggest canopy-covered brass bed in captivity. Since the Magic Casino Hotel—open the year round except for July—is a relatively new enterprise, all the rooms, no matter what the theme, are equipped with color TV, radios, telephones and modern bathrooms.

Part of a much bigger layout, the hotel management runs an evening dinner revue in which magic and magicians are interspersed with the songs and dances of chorus girls, emcees and comics in a lavish theater that highlights the world's largest self-playing dance organ. During dinner two roving magicians will come to your table to do a couple of mystifying tricks right under your eyeballs before the stage show starts up. The gala event offers a five-course meal, a 90-minute stage pageant, dancing until 1:30 A.M. and a concert by the Taj Mahal dance organ.

This imposing organ with the grandiose name survives today as the largest, most ornate automatic musical instrument on earth. Measuring nearly 26 feet in width and 20 feet in height, its decorative front features a delicately carved statue of a larger-than-life goddess emerging from a bath with a robed angel blowing a trumpet. The overall architecture of the Taj Mahal is that of a castle with domed minarets, supported by elaborately carved columns. Blazing with 1,000 lights, it comes alive with 700 organ pipes, a xylophone, drums, castanets and a huge temple bell—a mammoth music maker that dishes up pieces ranging from the "Beer Barrel Polka" and the "Tennessee Waltz" to "My Wild Irish Rose," "When The Saints Come Marching In" and "Dixie."

By arriving early and/or staying over for a few hours the next morning, you'll have time to inspect the now-you-see-it-now-you-don't Magic Casino complex itself. Lo and behold, many different (but connected) museums feature special aspects of the world of magic for you to walk through in an unforgettable fun-filled hour. A special guide will take you around and explain things in English or you can do it alone.

What comes over to you most strongly in each of the museums is the nostalgic spell that covers specialties like Automobilia, Cinema, oldtime Amusement Arcades, Automated Dolls and Puppets, Famous Freaks of Yesteryear and Ventriloquism. Quite a few of the 3,000 exhibits work when you press a button while hidden loudspeakers provide sound and explanations (in German).

Who is the mastermind behind Degersheim's Magic Casino? His name is Retonio Breitenmoser and he made his living for 20 years as a professional magician and ventriloquist.

"My idea," Retonio says, "was to bring people into the realm of magic by providing them with a colorful, dazzling and unforgettable voyage into the world of dreams and illusions."

To enchant his customers and fans with the only vaudeville extravaganza in Europe, he hired another professional wizard and ventriloquist from France, the personable

Jean-Michel Cathery, now art director of the stage show and its host and emcee (he also takes a turn at doing some spellbinding sorcery at your dinner table).

Home for the oddball hotel is Degersheim, a picturesque farming town of some 3,000 people about a half-hour auto or train ride southwest of St. Gallen near the Austrian and Liechtenstein borders—not far from **Appenzell** which Switzerland pushes as its most typical Swiss village. For bookings in the Magic Hotel and/or its Dinner Spectacle Revue (held on Wednesdays, Fridays and Saturdays), either write to the hotel at 9113 Degersheim or telephone 071/54.24.54.

Owner Breitenmoser admits that getting his unique project pulled out of his hat was a tricky proposition, but today his one-only hotel, museums and dinner show are jackpot winners. With many surprises up its sleeve, the Magic Casino conjures up its own style of black magic.

* * *

The Sunrise on Mount Rigi

Rigi

Don't be fooled by the sign around here—*Rigi hell*—that doesn't mean what you think it means. It's German for "Rigi clear," and that means it's safe to go to the top of **MOUNT RIGI**, the celebrity mountain of Switzerland, in a country where three-fifths of the land is mountainous. The most touristed peak in Europe, better known as the Queen of the Mountains, draws more visitors than any other anywhere in the world, over a million a year, because it has something extra special to offer guests.

The sunrise. . . .

Sunrises come and go, every day in the week all year long. But if you're standing on the pinnacle of the Rigi (5,906 feet high), you get the message of the Alps: there is no other sunrise on the whole globe that can beat the sunrise at the Rigi.

When Mark Twain attempted to catch that first morning glow here in 1878, it took him three days to get to the summit, according to his own funny account in *A Tramp Abroad*, but that was because he elected to climb it and not take the new-fangled train. Because of the **Arth-Rigi Cog Railway**, in 1871 the Rigi became one of the very easiest mountains in Switzerland to conquer.

The cog railway is an historic attraction in itself. As the first mountain train in all of Europe (still using 95 percent of its original track), the Arth-Rigi line provides, with Swiss precision, a safe climb in slow-motion and treats you to panoramic sights best described as sheer delight and awe-inspiring—all in an old-fashioned observation car. Offering a nostalgic excursion along the side of the VIP mountain, the train also goes back in time since the views have not changed in some 200 years that men and women have tramped on Rigi's flanks.

What makes the Rigi sunrise unique among sunrises is that from the zenith you take in the dozens of towns and all of nine lakes down below—at the same time seeing mountains all around you in a 360-degree sweep. It often happens that at dawn clouds form a blanket down below, so that what you see up there looks like water all around you with the peaks of all the mountains poking through. One negative note is that the Rigi can get cranky on certain days. You may get up for the sunrise and be disappointed to find the whole sky is clouded up or covered over in fog. Therefore, it's advisable to play to stay two days at one of the 14 hotels dotting the area, for then you are sure not to miss it. And if you're in luck, you will have seen it twice, not to mention the bonus of the Rigi sunset.

Although getting to the apex for nature's Show of Shows is now easy, not so easy is the whole bit of getting up at 5:30 A.M. Awakened by the blares of the eight-foot-long alphorns outside your hotel, you'll not be alone, if that's any consolation, because countless millions of people have also done it since the seventeenth century. That includes luminaries like Sir Walter Scott, James Fenimore Cooper, Felix Mendelssohn, Goethe, Alexandre Dumas, Victor Hugo and Czar Alexander.

Unlike the aforementioned who made the trip by cog railway, when Mark Twain did it the hard way, he went on foot from the bottom with a guide, and his humor is such that he wrote that he overslept and saw the Rigi sun*set* (itself spectacular indeed) and "mistook" it for the Rigi sunrise.

Coming at you strong—besides the stiff winds—is the total silence up there, except for the bells hanging on the necks of the grazing cows. The cowbell concerto goes on most of the day and much of the night, except during the snowy wintry months when the animals are kept in barns. If nothing else, however, the cowbells remind you that you've left the hustle and bustle of the world for a while. The Rigi air is so pure and cool (bring wraps and sweaters even in summer) that when you hit the sack, early like everybody else, the fresh alpine ozone will perform its morpheus magic and you snoozzzze. . . .

For a day's diversion on the Rigi, you can go down on the mountain on foot to **Vitznau**, **Weggis** or **Arth-Goldau**. At the blue lake below, you can even take an excursion boat to **Lucerne**, if you're booked for longer and are not a ski-freak. Keep your eye on your watch, however, and remember that the cog railway lists 10:00 P.M. as the last trip up, a ride that takes about 35 minutes.

However you deal with the Rigi and its lure, you'll be at a loss for words. Perhaps Mendelssohn described its grandeur best when he made a striking musical comparison. He said: "The Rigi. It's as if the overture were repeated at the end of the opera."

*   *   *

The Swiss Stone-Throwing Meet

Unspunnen

Any tourist who comes here when the men start throwing stones will think the Swiss have rocks in their heads.

Every 12 years in early September, the musclemen of

the region come to this tiny Bern canton for a stone-throwing contest that has been going strong since 1805. The last one took place in 1981 and the next will be on September 4 and 5, 1993. The particular stone in question weighs 183 pounds, and the hardy Swiss who take turns pitching the bulky boulder have a choice of using one hand or two. So far, in over 185 years, no contestant has ever competed with a single paw, but that is understandable because stone throwing, Swiss style, is not a sport just anyone can play.

Staged on the last two days of Switzerland's week-long **COSTUME AND ALPINE FESTIVAL**, the contest draws thousands from all over. Considerable betting goes on, and the odds are pretty high that the all-time record throw, which stands at 11 feet 2 inches, will never be surpassed. Some Swiss oldtimers, however, stubbornly refuse to this day to accept that historic cluck as a true indicator because they say a stiff wind was blowing.

Hurling the celebrated Brobdingnagian pebble calls for a special array of foot and body movements that contestants have perfected over the years, just like shot-putters and discus-throwers. But there is one limitation: the rules say that the stone-bouncer may not utter a single groan from the moment he places his hands on the defying rock.

To prepare himself for the big he-vent, Herr Strong Arms spends practically a half year before the contest priming himself with heavier weights. Thus, by the time of the show-off throw-off, the 183-pound cinder seems cream-puffy by comparison. That is why Hercules seems to be able to hurl the igneous missile through the air with the greatest of ease.

Attending the long-distance toss is something no foreign traveler in Switzerland should miss because of the contest's infrequency. A spine-tingling excitement grips Unspunnen as husky herdsmen from the distant mountainsides come lumbering into town, flexing their egos. The prize for the winner is a gold medal and an afternoon date at the outdoor banquet with the pinup girl of his choice. Six local queens are named for the honor of being chosen by our robust hero, and not infrequently has it happened that the damsel selected by the triumphant he-man ends up with a marriage proposal.

Picture the proceedings: a hulk of a bruiser, either stripped to the waist or wearing underwear that shows plenty of beef, bends down to pick up the stone (which has the dates 1805 and 1905 carved into it—to mark the first century of the game), raises it over his head and then with nary a snort heaves it into space. As it makes an arc through space and thuds to the earth, three judges amble out with their tapes and make separate measurements. They confer. Then they announce the distance. Applause. Cheers.

Once the winner has been determined (each competitor may have three tries), pandemonium breaks out. The losers lift Mr. Has-What-It-Takes onto their shoulders, and with everyone shoving to touch and congratulate him, he is borne to the lineup of local beauties who wait in blushing anticipation as he eyes them carefully before making the momentous selection—not without a lot of kibitzing from the sidelines and from the losers themselves. Most of the adversaries have already given their macho glances to the array of belles long before the first throw, but in the posttournament dither the winner makes with his best histrionics in the choosing. His decision also throws a lot of weight.

The Unspunnen festival draws some 5,000 participants from all over Switzerland's various mountain regions, which means that plenty goes on day and night. There are flag twirlers, melody-making cowbell ringers, skillful bullwhip crackers and costumed mountaineers (dirndls are a must for the women) doing their thing against the backdrop of flower-bedecked cows in the forested heights, with the snow-covered **Jungfrau** mountain majestically presiding over it all.

Another event that always attracts massive crowds is **Schwingen**. One of the oldest alpine games, this is a wrestling match with some 200 contenders grappling in four huge sawdust circles. One more highlight is the Saturday

afternoon folkdance marathon in which over 1,000 country folk in full costume from all of Switzerland's language
areas demonstrate their skill in dance and music on a
virtually nonstop basis.

The site of the festival on the grounds of the Unspun-
nen meadow is between the **Lake of Briens** and the **Lake of
Thun**, affording a good view of the famed 13,653-foot
Jungfrau peak that boasts the highest point reached by a
railroad. Tiny Unspunnen is less than two miles from
Interlaken—literally, one might say, a stone's throw away.

* * *

Glacier Garden

Lucerne

Now, what tourist in his right mind would hie himself all
the way to Switzerland to visit a place whose principal
attraction is no longer around? But this is precisely the case
in Lucerne where thousands of visitors come every year to
take a look at what isn't anymore.

When discovered over a hundred years ago, "it" created
a maxi sensation, and today any visitor who pays a call on
the charming lake shores of Lucerne will sooner or later
wend his way to the tourist attraction that isn't.

So what is the mystery all about?

Well, let's start from the beginning. Back in 1872 a 30-
year-old manager of a Lucerne bank, one Joseph Wilhelm
Amrein-Troller, decided to earn some extra pocketmoney
by raising grapes and making wine as a sideline. He bought
a piece of meadowland near Lucerne's famous **Lion Monument** in order to build a wine cellar in the rock.

While Amrein-Troller was having the earth blasted and
carted off, a friend of his—Dr. Franz Josef Kaufmann, a
geologist and teacher at the cantonal school—passed by
one morning on his way to work. The day was November 2,
1872, a memorable date in Swiss history, for that was the
day "it" was discovered.

Dr. Kaufmann's practiced geological eye spotted a bowl-like recess in the molasse sandstone that had already been partly destroyed by the explosive charges. Recognizing the importance of the discovery, the geologist prevailed upon his banker friend to stop the blasting and call in the authorities.

The wine cellar was never finished. But, Switzerland had on its territory a secret from the ice age. That first pothole led to the uncovering of the entire Lucerne Glacier which had done its thing for centuries on end and then melted, leaving behind a chunk of terrain that reminds you of Oz, even without the wizard around.

What has been brought to light here among the rock and moraine debris can without exaggeration be termed a minor natural miracle. In addition to the splendid potholes, further evidence of ice-age glaciation is provided by the visible glacier scratches and the boulders dragged down from the Alps. These same sandstone rocks reveal seashell ripple marks and the imprint of the fan palm leaf, all testifying to a subtropical palm-fringed ocean in the neighborhood of Lucerne some 20 million years ago.

Given the name of **GLETSCHER-GARTEN** (Glacier Garden) when it was opened to the public in May 1873, the curious round holes in the fantastic rock formation are so-called glacier mills, hollowed out by waterfalls plunging from a crevasse of the huge ice-age river. In time, a total of 11 of these glacial phenomena came to light, and now the outdoor park of spectacular natural wonders has been enhanced with an adjoining museum.

The stone badge from a bygone era shows that Switzerland was once, incongruously, a subtropical country with a large ocean covering most of it. The ocean is no longer there, nor are the subtropical trappings, but when you visit Lucerne's Glacier Garden, you have paid admission for an offbeat look-see at Earth during a great change in the face of our planet.

Nor will you be alone either. So far, nearly eight million people have been attracted to the strange enclosure; last year, a record number of over 160,000 visitors checked in. The unique lure is open from mid-March to the end of

April, from May 15 to the end of September and from October 16 to the end of November.

Altogether there are 43 different things you're supposed to see in Gletscher-Garten, so that you get a full inside view of "the clock of Earth's history." Is there a more wonderful way to spend time?

PORTUGAL

Market of Women Thieves

Lisbon

Here's the word: Do what all shop-oholics do when visiting this breezy Portuguese capital. Hie off to the **MARKET OF WOMEN THIEVES**. Already some 300 years old, it gives every sign of continuing full blast for at least another three centuries. That's because—as all sharp, ship-shape shop-oholics know—it's a dandy place to pick up bargains, but also a place to keep alert for *the sting*. Of course, that's up to the consumer with street-smarts, who is aware of the buy-word here: b-e-w-a-r-e.

No, you're not going to find women thieves, or men thieves, out to steal you blind. The Market of Women Thieves (known here as the *Feira da Ladra*) is a kind of flea market with plenty of history behind it. It got its name from the days when goods snatched up the *sovaqueiras* of yesterday—the distaff professional robbers of the seventeenth century who used to hide stolen objects in their armpits or under their ample breasts—were peddled through stalls then located in Lisbon's central Rossio Square.

There are several books on the subject of those cute 'n' clever crooks, indeed a fascinating page in Lisbon's history, but all of the books are in Portuguese, alas. Meanwhile, the so-called *sovaqueiras* have long since taken a powder, but the oddball name for the hustle-bustle Tuesday and Saturday market still sticks. Some wags like to say that if you're not careful what you're buying, the saleslady could turn out to be one of those "women thieves." Not true, not true.

A popular anecdote about the Market of Women Thieves—to which there is more than a semblance of truth—has to do with an underground group planning a

military coup to overthrow the government. The uniforms
for the would-be coup leaders were acquired at the market,
all foolishly on the same Saturday morning. Smelling a rat
because of the simultaneous purchases, the police kept a
suspicious radar eye on the buyers and zeroed in on them
just in time to snuff the planned uprising.

Since 1882 the market has been doing business on the
hilly site of the **Campo de Santa Clara** in the eastern sector
of Lisbon. Behind Santa Clara rises the **pantheon of St.
Vincent** where the bodies of the Kings of Portugal lie.
There are also in the same neighborhood the haunted
ruins of the **Santa Engracia Church** and the ancient palaces where Portugal's military establishment has set up its
headquarters.

From the market itself, the tricky winding streets lead
downhill to the **Tagus**. Is there any sight more arresting
than that of the pastel-colored, cosmopolitan seaport city
seen in the evening from the left bank of the busy river? O,
luminous Lisbon, your winding uphill cobblestoned streets
and centuries-old gray walls towering high above the
Tagus and your painted houses (in pink, in forest green, in
sky blue), you so teem with life and perpetual motion. How
do I love thee, let me count the by-ways. . . .

But, save this part of Lisbon for when you leave the
market. This is one market that has its share of werbedeebs
and other assorted junk, but it also offers a wide assortment of local goods that should not be passed over lightly.
Let's start with cork. You can pick up some nifty cork
coasters, dolls, boxes, buckets, wine-bottle holders—almost
everything imaginable Lisbon has in cork—even writing
paper with envelopes.

The market displays handwoven skirts (with gold and
silver thread), handwoven carpets, hand-embroidered
blouses, stylish jewelry and silverware, gold-and-silver Portuguese filigree work, artistic statuettes, pottery (most of it
brilliantly colored) and a large selection of antique glazed
earthenware bowls that come in from **Coimbra**, where
they've been making these since the thirteenth century.

And don't miss another kind of item that comes from
the state border police. Whenever people refuse to pay

duty on certain goods, the customs authorities confiscate these things, and by law have to put them on sale at the market. That's usually reserved for Saturdays. Be warned that to get in on some of these particular surprise buys, you have to go early in the morning, because Lisbon's pros start out before daybreak to buy up and whisk away the good stuff. Run largely by armed policewomen, the government stalls practice a no-nonsense hard policy of first-come-first-served. Understandably, at these stands you just don't do any bargaining with the lady cops; you pay the asking price—or you don't get the item.

A visit to the market is not complete unless you give a recommended peek to the adjunct mart where the fish-wives hold forth. The *varinas*, as they are called, have a history that goes back centuries to the Portugal of yesteryear. Bring videocameras because it is a sight (and a sound) you can't capture in a frame with a single click.

Barefoot in summer, wearing short black bunchy skirts and aprons, with gold hoops in their ears, and carrying baskets of fish on their heads, they call to you with their special weird-sounding hoots as they swish along in elegant strides. Some of these *varinas* are what showbiz is all about. After they've sold their day's fish, they nevertheless continue with their blatant, shouting songs—empty baskets still balanced on their heads—for the tourist trade, of course.

Yes, let's both say it at the same time—they're now fishing around for tips.

SPAIN

Franco's Colossus

Madrid

Ranking with the pyramids of Egypt is an astonishing memorial 30 miles north of Madrid, a $100-million sepulcher for the 150,000 men who fell fighting with Generalissimo Franco during the Spanish Civil War. Also known by its nickname, Franco's Colossus, EL VALLE DE LOS CAÍDOS (The Valley of the Fallen) must be placed among the modern wonders of world.

Spain's gigantic mausoleum rises on a granite-faced mountain in a huge, rock-strewn plain. Because it tends to reduce him to the size of the mere man that he is, the Valley of the Fallen, with its breathtaking underground cathedral and mammoth crucifix, casts a spell over any visitor. The colossus is just a few miles away from the fabulous **El Escorial**, the ancient burial place of Spanish royalty.

Standing in awesome command over the area is an enormous cross, over 500 feet high and 150 feet wide. Chiseled from a single piece of stone, the cross is more than a third as high as the Empire State Building, and its top can be reached by an elevator. Galleries have been hollowed in the arms and small chapels are at each end.

At the base of the imposing crucifix are huge statues of the four Evangelists. An elevator trip is recommended to the landing at the base of these mighty figures, where you get a better perspective of just how big they really are—not to mention a splendiferous panorama of the region and a rare view of Madrid.

To construct the subterranean church, more than a quarter-million yards of granite had to be blasted and scooped out of the mountainside. Although it is not as large as St. Peter's Basilica in Rome, the cathedral still

194

ranks as one of the largest churches in the world—and certainly the largest underground. A long network of tunnels branches out from the church, leading to six ossuaries—immense underground chambers that hold the bodies of the Civil War dead.

Not to be overlooked amid all aspects of the sprawling magnitude is one of the highlights of the interior—the "Sistine Chapel of Northern Art." This collection of eight massive pieces of wall tapestry, woven in gold, silver, silk and wool, depict each incident in a series illustrating the apocalypse of St. John. Dating from the year 1540, they hang on the wall spaces of the great nave where, with the imaginative treatment given them by an unknown artist, they combine into one harmonious whole.

Another attraction is the bronze door. Opening into two Norman arches with rusticated interiors and simple oblong designs, the door describes in relief panels the 15 mysteries of the Rosary, and along the lower frieze are illustrated texts from the Apostles. Atop the doorway is the recumbent form of Christ, his head slightly raised by Mary who gazes with sadness at her Son's face.

Along each of the flanks to the entrance of the monument, a series of buildings houses a cloister and a monastery on one side and a hostel and a study center for social studies on the other. Enclosed by an eye-catching arcade, they are built of granite with slate roofs and conform to the mammoth scale of the rest of the valley. Behind the cathedral mountain spreads a spacious residence for the priests and laymen who minister to the church and grounds.

Credit for choosing the site for the astounding memorial goes to Franco himself. He had long been intrigued with the top of the rocky gorge on which stood a cone-shaped crag of bare rock surrounded on three sides by a mountain.

On the open end (which is the approach by auto if you come from Madrid or from El Escorial) stretches a wide valley in all its grandiose beauty. A few yards from the entrance to the valley, on both sides of the road, two pairs of monolithic columns known as the Juanelos, (carved in the sixteenth century) stand like sentinels.

This whole setup impressed Franco no end, and in April 1940 he decreed that work begin on a momument "in memory of all those who lived up to their ideals in the name of Spain for which they laid down their lives." The work lasted for nearly 20 years, during which time nothing was ever published in Spain about the project and very little abroad.

In spite of its grandeur, the Valley of the Fallen has come in for some criticism. Some Spaniards are of the belief that Franco built it as a tomb for himself.

*   *   *

Las Ramblas

Barcelona

There's a quip used in this largest port city of the Mediterranean that goes something like this: "Whether you go to heaven or hell, you have to pass through Barcelona and walk along the Ramblas."

True or not, it is true that everybody wants to go to heaven, but not everybody wants to walk along **LAS RAMBLAS**, Barcelona's legendary daytime-and-nighttime pedestrian mall that was once the bed of a mountain torrent. The ebb and flow along this incredible street, less than a mile in length, makes the Ramblas a perpetual-motion machine. No matter how many pictures you may have seen of the Ramblas, nothing can prepare you for the actual sight—there's just nothing quite like it.

Changing names several times, the tree-lined Ramblas starts with the statue of Christopher Columbus at the old harbor and moves on past the sex shops and velvety bar zone to the food-market stands and their sales matrons, every one of whom has her own unique hairdo, certain to keep your trusty Nikon working overtime. Some people argue that the Ramblas may be the "Hairdo Capital" of the world.

Bisected by the pedestrian mall, Las Ramblas is a series of very broad avenues on which thousands of citizens and tourists alike slowly pace back and forth, virtually 24 hours around the clock. It is a pavement that every one of the nearly 2 million Barcelonians has helped to walk into a smooth shine. When not glued to their café chairs, people along the Ramblas buy tropical birds, fish, puppy dogs, a monkey or a guinea pig, and flowers, flowers, flowers. You can even have your shoes shined by a Spanish señor wearing a silk hat. Every kind of business is to be found on the Ramblas.

On both sides of the thoroughfare there are stores, cafés, theaters and a rich vein of bookshops, bordered with houses of every size and style. And whenever you spot a tight crowd, it could be a hot political discussion with everyone emoting in smooth rhetoric, or it could be an overheated exchange over a recent soccer match. Or over a bullfight. But no matter. The arguments have no conclusions.

Since the Ramblas never ceases to be full of pulsating life, try the street at three in the morning, for it will still be thronged with folks eating, drinking and talking. Before dawn there is no better people-watching place than on the Ramblas, partly because every form of humanity is there and partly because the straights, the crooks and everything-in-between are there.

With dawn lifting an eyelid, the kiosks soon begin to unshutter and get busy selling newspapers and magazines from all over the world. And at 6:30 A.M. there is scarcely time to sweep the pavement before the cafés open and the market comes to life. Spanish playwright Federico Garcia Lorca once described the Ramblas as: ". . . the only street in the world which I would never wish to end."

Along the Ramblas you find Barcelona's famed, seven-tiered opera house (the **Liceo**, built in 1847) and the **Poliorama**, where a distinguished theater company holds forth every night across the street from the **Hotel Continental**—whose quarters begin on the third floor and whose roof hosted George Orwell for one night. Whenever you're afoot on the Ramblas, it is always a good idea to keep your hand consciously on your wallet or your purse securely strapped to your body.

If you're in Barcelona on a Sunday, then Las Ramblas

may offer a special treat supreme, Catalonian style. Sometime around midday, Barcelonians come on their own to take part in a mysterious dance called the *sardana*. When it doesn't take place on the Ramblas, then try the nearby **Catalan Gothic Cathedral Square** just before 11:00 A.M.

What is the *sardana*? Well, people join hands, form a circle and break into long and short steps, counting silently to themselves as a band of rustic flutes, a bugle, a small calfskin drum and a soprano guitar provide the eerie music. Probably there are no living Barcelonians over the age of 17½ who have not at some time danced the *sardana*, which dates from the Middle Ages. You're always welcome to join in—but you need a hand-holding partner of the opposite sex, as it is not considered polite to sever the chain of males-females-males-females. The stately dance is a spontaneous rhythmic hoofing of simple steps, and even folks with two left feet do it acceptably.

Fancifully, the Ramblas provides a multiplicity of Barcelona atmosphere in one knockout blow. If you start the Ramblas at the "top," at **Plaza Catalunya**, then work your way down to the port area where stands the **monument to Columbus** (who is known as Cristobal Colón in Spain). Standing near the shipyards, the Columbus column is 200 feet high with a bronze statue of the Italian explorer perched on the top of a balanced globe with his arms stretching out and his finger pointing—in the "wrong" direction. It was from this port that Columbus set sail on his historic voyage, and dozens of sculptors employed to tell that story tell it in graphic detail on the base. An elevator will take you all the way to the top, from which point you get a spectacular panorama of the Ramblas and the harbor where Columbus's three ships—the Pinta, the Niña and the Santa Maria—were built for him.

No visitor ever leaves this city without going aboard the replica of the Santa Maria lying in the harbor. This caravel, of course, is not Chris's original ship, but a superb reproduction that tells you a lot about the "mad mariner" and his crew. Once on it, you naturally ask yourself if you would have set sail on an unknown ocean in a ship of that size.

Since the Ramblas is both a daytime street and an all-night street and therefore the heart and soul of the city (which is playing host to the 1992 Olympics), you may not be able to do it all in one 24-hour period. Try the Ramblas, therefore, on a half-and-half basis. Do the morning/ afternoon tour first on one day—and then come back the next day for part two. After a dosage of the Ramblas, you may find yourself agreeing with the natives here, who, down to the last man and woman, say it best: "Not to want to live in Barcelona and walk the Ramblas frequently is like not wanting to live at all!"

* * *

Gibraltar's Friendly Apes

Gibraltar

The Rock! The name is legend.

The Rock of Gibraltar does not deserve to be used by travelers as a kind of stepping-stone to somewhere else— nor as a place to stare at through binoculars. No! Tarry a few hours, or better still, even a few days, and you will get a royal greeting from what may be the world's most unusual reception committee. I'm talking about the golden-brown macaque monkeys, popularly referred to as the "apes of Gibraltar."

As the only simians still roaming wild in Europe, Gibraltar's beloved mascots live among the gun emplacements in two separate packs atop the windy limestone heights of the Rock (altitude: 1,400 feet). Friendly and playful by nature, the no-tail monkeys love and adore tourists, not so much for the dollars they feed into Gibraltar's economy but for what visitors feed them—chocolates, candies, nuts, fruits and even ice cream cones. For a half banana, you will always find one furry feller who'll give you a handshake or pose with you for camera shots. I kid you not.

The apes make such a hit with people that one New York Tourist has for many years been sending them packages of peanuts. Several universities have dispatched research teams to Gibraltar to find out more about the monkeys, a type of social animal that lives in family and community units. Weighing around 60 pounds at maturity, most of them survive to about the age of 15—a life of carefree existence found nowhere else. No scientist as yet has been able to find out what happens to an ape when he dies, since no one has ever found a body or a skeleton in their some thousand years on the Rock.

Numbering about 40 today, the Barbary apes can be reached by cable car up the west slope, a rather scary ride that nevertheless offers a stunning panorama of the bay and the Spanish town of Algeciras. But if you wait until 4:00 P.M., the apes come down from the heights to a lower perch (reachable by taxi) for their daily feeding (provided by the British Army with an allowance of 15 pence per head per day), and that's when you can say hello and/or shake hands with some of them. This is the afternoon period when they are fed their usual ration of bananas (which have vitamin pills hidden in them), oatmeal, sweet potatoes and green vegetables. This supplements the wild berries, roots, seeds and insects that the monkeys hunt down themselves.

Be warned, however, that the apes—pals of man though they are—are easily upset by quick movements or sudden loud noises. They also have some bad manners. If they see something they want, they're not timid about pilfering it—just ask somebody who has tried to feed them peanuts one at a time, only to have the bag rudely snatched away.

There's one monkey in the pack, a female, who is prone to stealing mirrors and taking them up to the top where she will spend time admiring herself in the looking glass before smashing it to pieces. During the height of the tourist season, when some 300,000 people come in, the bushy-haired creatures have been known to filch milady's purse or to run off with somebody's camera. Again, I kid you not.

But also be warned that anyone who molests a Gibraltar ape faces a prison term or a fine, for the *Macaca sylvana* species (their Linnaean nomenclature) enjoys the protection of the British government through a special keeper, a sergeant-at-arms, whose responsibility it is to see that the delightful, daffy denizens of the Rock are nurtured and kept in good health. This latter responsibility includes having to give the apes some whisky when they are coming down with a cold—a most delicate maneuver, since the frolicsome animals are not corralled so easily.

Even Winston Churchill, though beset in 1944 with crises on all fronts, had to do with the apes. While on his way to the Tehran Conference, Winnie stopped at the bastion to see how the frisky quadrupeds were getting along. Shocked to hear that their numbers had dwindled to below ten, he let it be known that the survival of the apes of Gibraltar was a matter of keenest personal concern to the prime minister and that their number was thereafter to be kept above 24.

It's said in Gibraltar, among its colony of 30,000 people (most of whom are British subjects), that if the apes ever disappear, then the British must also go away. Thus, whenever a baby ape is born and adds to the regimental strength, the army records the birth with a flourish as part of the glory of the British Empire.

The Barbary ape is so held in esteem by British officialdom that when the first decimal coin—in the denomination of 25 new pence—was put out in 1971, it contained a portrait of Queen Elizabeth II and on the obverse side Gibraltar's monkey. Explained the Royal Mint: "The Barbary ape is so well known to thousands of visitors to the Rock that it is the obvious choice of design for Gibraltar's first Crown coin since decimalization."

The pampered primates are the joy of all tourists. So when you come here for a visit, get ready for some monkey business.

BELGIUM

The Beguines of Bruges

Bruges

Most tourists who come to Bruges—which is more of a mood than a city—don't know that they can pay a call on a beguine by visiting the beguinage here. This is a peculiarly Flemish institution, which is a walled enclave (a sort of tiny city within a city) that is inhabited by an old order of Catholic semimonastic women whose doors are open to the public during the daylight hours. A visit to a beguinage is an unforgettable tourist sidebar—but first some definitions and clarifications.

A beguine is a cross between a nun and a laywoman. Though she takes vows that involve poverty and obedience, she keeps all her personal possessions, supports herself by doing needlework, nursing or teaching, and engages in multiple charitable works—besides which, she is free to marry at any time.

Visitors of any religious persuasion are always welcome to Bruges's "anonymous settlement of the Middle Ages," which is called OUR LADY OF THE VINE and is within walking distance from the center of this small moated Belgian city of the golden past close to the North Sea. The mother superior or a clerk in her office will make arrangements for you to meet some of the beguines and show you around the quiet community, but any such arrangements should be made well before 6:30 P.M.

If you stay for lunch at the beguinage—for which you are not expected to pay or make a contribution—chances are you will be given a bowl of rice pudding, known as Begijn-rice, which has been served from as far back as the twelfth century by the beguines to guests and to themselves. Extremely delicious and different from all other

rice puddings, Begijn-rice is made with a secret recipe that
the sister-superior cook hands down to the next before she
dies.

"Our women are all self-supporting and lead a Christian
life in the full sense of the word," explains the septua-
genarian grande dame who wears the typical beguine
habit—a black dress and a white linen hood. "Each woman
serves God and people at the same time, which means we
often do work that nobody else wants to do and for little or
no money. We help old people, poor children, working
mothers, and we clean homes. We work on farms and in
infirmaries, schools and churches. In short, we never
shrink from hard manual labor, and we never leave the
world. The average beguine services anywhere from ten to
twenty needy persons."

Covering some 15 acres, Bruges's unusual convent settlement is an array of neo-Gothic buildings with towerlets,
turrets, narrow windows and gables. With a main entrance
that looks like the gate of a fortified city, the beguinage has
its own "village green" planted with tall trees and surrounded by houses, or huts, that provide the private apartments for the women. Most of the some 200 beguines are
in their fifties or sixties, and since young women today
prefer not to join the order, the beguinage appears des-
tined to become obsolete.

Although the history of the beguines is wrapped in
mystery and confusion, some facts about them are known.
In the year 1317, after the pope issued a bull denouncing
them as heretics, the persecutions began. Many were ex-
pelled by the Catholic church and several beguinages were
disbanded, including all of the ones in Germany and
France.

The bishop of Cologne personally threw several dozen
rope-bound beguines into the Rhine River to drown, and
for a long time after that the word *beguine* was synonomous
with *heretic*. Part of the Vatican's campaign against the
beguines was that as a collective group they sheltered be-
lievers of the Cathar religion that encouraged women to be
priests.

When the Reformation came to Europe, the beguines

suffered even more blows and were suppressed in all Protestant countries. Though there were nearly 2,000 beguines
according to official figures in 1825, the number dropped
to 1,200 in 1910, at which time there were only ten beguinages, all of them in Belgium and Holland. Despite
some 800 years of persecution and tumultuous history,
there still remain a half dozen beguinages in various towns
in the Netherlands, and today the women are no longer
harassed by church or government authorities.

"It is not clear even to us how the beguine movement
started. We believe that in 1180 a highborn woman of
Arras, known as Begue, turned over her worldly property
to a hospice at Liege to bring together a voluntary community of piously inclined women who were motivated by
those virtues exemplified by the first Christians, and who
wanted to do God's work in the spirit of self-sacrifice without becoming nuns," the grande dame says.

They started off on a sour note but are today making
beautiful music for God and mankind. This was the beginning of the beguine. . . .

* * *

Strange Art Museum of Wiertz

Brussels

When he died in 1865 at the age of 59, the highly touted
Belgian painter, Antoine Joseph Wiertz, was swept under
the carpet. End of story.

Well, not exactly. At great expense to itself, Belgium
keeps a museum of his complete works—certainly one of
the very few painters in history whose entire output is
preserved in one building devoted exclusively to him. Your
visit to the **WIERTZ MUSEUM** at 62 Rue Vautier will be more
than a visit—it will be a happening.

Who was Antoine Joseph Wiertz? And just why would a
whole museum be dedicated to this one painter? Wiertz
was a man obsessed by Rubens, and he set out to prove to

posterity that he alone was Rubens's artistic equal and heir, and that he [Wiertz] matched Michelangelo and Raphael. Some people agreed with him and others thought he was a madman. A few even claim he was 100 years, nay 200 years, ahead of his time, while explaining that he was a genius who did some wrong things right.

Long before his heated fame withered, Wiertz suggested to his government that it build him a large studio where he could live and work. In return, he would leave the state all of his works, on the additional condition that after his death his house and its contents be converted into a museum that would be open to the public six days a week. Because he had admirers everywhere in Belgium, the government accepted this proposal and Wiertz kept his word: he never offered a single one of his paintings for sale. No one was ever quite sure what his source of income was, though he did receive several large art prizes early in his career, one of which enabled him to study in Rome.

Built to Wiertz's own specifications, the building has an immense studio flooded with light that comes through a massive skylight overhead. It serves as the main salon of the Wiertz Museum today and houses all of the eccentric artist's gigantic paintings, some of which are bound to bowl you over. Many of them require a ladder for better appreciation and closer study. The Wiertz Museum is open every day between 10:00 and 4:00, except Mondays.

But size is not what Wiertz is all about. Many of his works are on a theatrical scale—macabre, erotic, phantasmal and horrendously barbaric in content. When Wiertz's incredible works were put on display for the first time in a Paris show, the critics crucified him. Bewildered and enraged, Wiertz returned to Brussels, poured himself into his paintings at a furious pace, hardly ever ventured outside his home after that, and deliberately had nothing to do with people for the rest of his life.

Totally individualistic and fiercely independent, Wiertz produced many paintings that turned people off, especially the majority of Victorian art buffs. His canvas entitled *L'inhumation Prescipitee* (Premature Burial) presents a man clawing himself out of a coffin with a terrified look on a face that shows one eye and part of his head. The distorted mouth is apparently crying out that he is not dead and asking why he has been buried.

Some visitors have been known to faint over this weird painting, as they have for some other Wiertz creations—like the one in which a woman, crazed by poverty, has slaughtered her baby and just thrown one of its legs into a boiling pot of soup. Another, *La Belle Rosine*, shows a beautiful woman staring at herself in a mirror that reflects her skull. Then there's one that depicts a man committing suicide in front of his wife and son.

Dominating the main salon is Wiertz's huge masterpiece, *Greeks and the Trojans Fight Over the Body of Patroclus*. This explicit canvas may well be the biggest square painting in the world, rivaling some that Tintoretto produced in Venice. To examine all the gruesome details of this particular Wiertz could take the better part of an hour.

Nearby, not very far from Wiertz's black-bronze death mask, is an equally enormous canvas portraying the scene of Ulysses and the Cyclops—but Wiertz's version differs from all previous renditions. Apart from the crushed human bodies, what stuns you is the face of the Cyclops lugubriously munching one of the Greeks for lunch.

That Wiertz was as honest as he was irreverent comes out in a painting in which he portrays both Christ and the Devil as two very handsome young men. Since he had a peeve against the French, in one painting, *Napoleon in Hell*, he draws the Little Corporal as a detestable gnome, and in another canvas he shows a voluptuous nude perusing a prohibited novel while a horned demon stands behind ready to give her another one to read—the author's name is marked in plain letters, A. Dumas.

It's no wonder that up until 50 years ago, Wiertz's paintings could only be viewed through peepholes. The screens are gone now, and the effect of these macabre masterpieces is indeed tremendous. In all of Wiertz's works, the sensational aspects of his subject matter often hide his symbolism and his artistry. One prominent nineteenth-century writer said of these sinister works of art: "None should go to the temple of Rubens without also going to the temple of Wiertz. The two are not unworthy to be named in unison."

* * *

Nazi Tiger-Tank Souvenir

Celles

Once and for all the matter is now settled. The very biggest and best "souvenir" of World War II is to be found in this tiny Belgian village a few kilometers from Dinant. But behind the mammoth memento, which draws tourists from near and far (especially on Sundays), is the incredible story of how a Belgian woman, who owned a café here, singlehandedly stopped General von Rundstedt's offensive on Christmas Eve 1944—simply by telling a white lie.

When you get to Celles, you can hardly miss the "souvenir," for it occupies most of the area near the **Pavillon Ardennais Café**. It is a **GERMAN TIGER TANK** whose tracks and wheels have been removed, but whose long gun is still pointing toward the Meuse River. The gray steel of the stalled tank has now, after nearly 40 years of rest, turned to a rusty brown. Its armor is nevertheless still as impenetrable as ever, and you can bet it will be occupying this spot for a long time to come. Flanking the tank is a wooden sign on two legs that announces (in French) that "Here the von Rundstedt Offensive Was Stopped on 24 December 1944."

The name of Marthe Monrique has not made any of the history books dealing with the Second World War, but in Celles her name is golden. Then a plump 50, and never one to be intimidated by the Nazi officers or SS men who frequented her place for beer and snacks—she was known to refuse service to any German soldier who didn't mind his manners or spoke to her in an impolite way—it was this Belgian café owner who put a stop to Germany's offensive through the Ardennes. Most historians take her story with a grain of assault, but the local citizenry knows better and lets all tourists know what the hidden facts are.

The story really begins in September 1944 when the Nazi invaders occupying the area, both in Celles and nearby Dinant, were forced to retreat under the merciless pounding of the Allied armies. Despite the fact that Hitler's Wehrmacht was retreating to the Siegfried Line, an SS officer stopped his command car in front of the Pavillon Ardennais Café and yelled out that he and his men would be back soon, by Christmas. Unamused, the villagers just listened.

Nobody gave much credence to the boast, but on December 16, Nazi troops made a rather spectacular breakthrough in the Ardennes with armored divisions headed for the Meuse River. By Christmas Eve, the Germans had advanced back toward Dinant and Celles, but a German scout car had been blown up by a land mine at the entrance to Dinant, so the Nazis slowed down their forward move to a turtle's pace, fearful that the area had been mined by the Americans who were preparing to blow up the strategic bridge across the Meuse.

When the lead German Tiger Tank of the long column was blown up by a mine near the Café Ardennais, the commander gave the order to stop. Within the café were more than 100 persons who had sought shelter there, and Madame Monrique opened her door and walked straight up to the commandant who asked her for information. The Germans wanted to know if there were any Yanks in the area, and she said there were a large number of GIs all around (which was not true). She also told them that all the roads were heavily sown with mines because the Americans had worked all night (which was also not true).

Convinced that she was giving them the straight dope, particularly since there were two mined wrecks within vision, the Panzer troops decided to bivouac in the nearby Mayenne Woods until the next morning. Celles became, therefore, the furthest point reached by the Wehrmacht in Hitler's final gamble at victory because the next morning at dawn, wave after wave of Allied bomber planes pulverized the tanks since no Luftwaffe planes were in the area.

Meanwhile, Allied armored columns were rolling back, and the Germans now had to retreat once again. They had looked at the Meuse for the last time. Had they continued the few remaining miles to the Meuse the day before, they would have made it easily because there were no mines at all and neither were there any U.S. troops present.

The present owner of the Café Ardennais, who opens his establishment only sporadically, keeps a number of browned clippings from local newspapers in frames on the wall, and they tell how Madame Monrique became the savior of her town. There's one oldtimer here, however, who delights in relating Marthe's story in another way:

According to him, Marthe lied to the Germans for a personal reason. Because the road was blocked by the damaged Tiger Tank, she figured all the other tanks, in order to get by, would have to make a detour through her carefully cultivated garden.

HOLLAND

The Wooden Shoes of Holland

Marken

Color this Hans Brinker country any color you want, but no matter what, the inevitable things come through strong —the tulip gardens, the windmills and the wooden shoes. Like the tulip and the windmill, the wooden shoe is a Dutch treat. Unlike all other shoes, you can bet it will never go out of style.

Although most of the people of modern Holland opt for more conventional footwear, there are still places in this country—like the small fishing village of **MARKEN** some 15 miles northeast of Amsterdam—where the inhabitants wear wooden shoes almost every day, at work and around the house.

Known in Dutch as *klompen*—the name makes them sound clumsy or clompy—wooden shoes all sell very well all over Holland. Understandably, more than half of the sales each year are to tourists who like to buy a pair to take home as a souvenir or to use as flowerpot holders indoors or outdoors. The *klompen* come in a variety of styles that reflect both tradition and occupation: gardeners' shoes, for instance, have flat soles without heels; ice fishermen wear theirs with hobnails to grip the ice.

In Marken and some other small Dutch towns, tourists can watch *klompen* being carved. There are about 50 *klompen*-makers still left in the country who carve the shoes out by hand, an art that comes down from one generation to another. Machine-made wooden shoes, however, are turned out by some 700 Holland factories that produce a total of 3 million pairs a year. One factory in Eindovern puts out more than 6,000 pairs a week.

The shoemakers who still make the *klompen* by hand are

quite eager to show their fading art to anybody willing to watch. It's a fading art because it takes a long time to learn the craft, approximately eight years of training before you can transform a chunk of wood into a pair of good, usuable shoes. A skilled practitioner can fashion out a pair of shoes in about 90 minutes—truly a man who whittles while he works.

The shoemaking starts with a careful selection of wood, usually willow or poplar. The trunk of a tree is sawed into pieces almost the size of what the shoe will be, following which the maker begins to hack the wood into a general shoe shape with a long carving knife. Chopping, gouging and smoothing with at least a half dozen different steel, spoon-shaped scoops, he tackles the hollowing-out process like a dynamo. As you watch all this, you wonder about the cuts on his fingers and you wonder about splinters, but you don't bring up the subject. If the shoe fits, why ask?

Wooden shoes, of course, make marvelous gifts for friends and relatives back home. The cost is not as high as expected, especially in the small towns and if you buy directly from the shoemaker himself, many of whom will put onto the shoe any particular design of your choosing.

In the **Open Air Museum of Arnhem**, there is, among other things, the world's largest collection of wooden shoes. A lot of these have unusual patterns on them of a highly artistic nature. Each region has its own set of unique flourishes, but any shoemaker will put on a decoration you ask him to, like a windmill, painted-on shoelaces or tulip motifs. Even the toe shape will be made to your bidding, such as round and fat to thin and pointed.

Men's wooden footgear is invariably varnished black with the owner's initials emblazoned in white. Women's shoes are also often black, with colored patterns. When Dutch women marry, they frequently wear wooden shoes at the ceremony—and in the past the carvings on their wedding shoes were made by the would-be grooms who had given them to the brides-to-be as an engagement gift. This still goes on all over Holland outside the cities.

Contrary to all expectations, wooden shoes are not

clumsy to wear, nor are they heavy on the feet. Combined with thick woolen socks, they are warmer than ordinary shoes, more comfortable and more functional. One reason they are popular in the villages, especially those towns on or near the coast, is that where there are few paved roads, the flat klompen prevent the wearer from sinking into muddy ground. They are also leakproof—and if water should get into them from the top, they dry out much faster than leather. Good wooden shoes do not warp, either.

In some things Holland will never change. The wooden shoe bit is a prime example of how a people can show tourists a nice time by putting their best foot forward.

Norway

Huldra the Nordic Temptress

Lifjell

Okay, Loch Ness monster, get lost! . . . Norway has its own bewitching, phantom tourist attraction—**HULDRA THE NORDIC TEMPTRESS**. And she hides here and there and everywhere in Norway's vast forest region. Though nobody has seen Huldra lately, that doesn't stop guided tourist parties from going out into the woods for a fun-search of what Scandinavian folklore would have you believe is "the most beautiful woman ever," albeit she is over eight feet in height.

Who is Huldra the Nordic Temptress? According to Norwegians who grew up with stories about her, she's many things to many people. She:
- makes the woods of Norway her home;
- skips over rocks and streams;
- appears suddenly and evaporates into the fog;
- has long blond hair flowing like a mountain river;
- lures lonely men or hunters into the thickets, keeping them as prisoners;
- is often seen with a herd of cows, etc. and so forth.

According to unverified eye, witness reports, Huldra is a monster of a female being who can change herself into a fair maiden and have a life-shattering influence on any man who meets her—for all of them immediately fall in love with her and ever so willingly go off with her, only to disappear forever. This legendary figure who inhabits Norway's woodlands has a distaff beauty that is marred only by one factor—beneath her ankle-length skirt there is to be seen the long tail of a cow. This is Huldra—a witch, beautiful beyond all adjectives.

As explained by Dr. Birgit Hertzberg Johnsen, a researcher at the University of Oslo Institute for Folklore Science, sightings of Huldra can be compared to modern-day UFO sightings.

"People believe they exist and imagine them when facing a combination of strange phenomena," declares Dr. Johnsen. "They really do think they have seen Huldra, who is invariably spotted at those times during the day when light and shadow can play tricks with the senses. Often it's a strange or unexpected sound that triggers off the experience. If a twig snaps or one hears an unfamiliar cowbell, the lone wanderer lets his imagination spin, especially if his fears as a youngster had already been fired by the stories his grandfather told on dark winter nights about people who were spirited off into the woods."

Despite any lack of scientific data about Huldra, there are thousands of Norwegians, mostly men, who claim to have seen her in the woods. Others have reported hearing her sweet voice, calling to her flock of cows—"Lulo, lulo, lulo, luuulo!" The word "lulo" is the only word Huldra utters, according to the reports, and it's a Norwegian phrase used to make animals keep together.

Police archives contain an official Huldra-sighting report that came from one Nils Smith. On the night between the third and fourth of July in 1950, Nils reported, Huldra came toward him in the extensive forest near Lifjell shepherding a number of cows. Twilight was falling over the forest and a fog had begun to settle in. Nils said that the temptation to follow her was very great but that he struggled hard and managed to resist her. As luck would have it, a church bell sounded clear and strong, and since Huldra is known to dread this sound, she disappeared quickly.

Unlike the Loch Ness monster for whom a photograph, allegedly of the lake creature rising from the waters, has been published many times, Huldra has not yet been captured on film, though any number of artists and painters have drawn their conception of her. Most of Scandinavia's newspaper editors have a standing offer to buy an authentic picture of the Nordic Temptress, but so far nobody has come up with one. The difficulty in locating Huldra is that she is not confined to one area or region because her home is the extensive forest ranges that cover thousands of square miles.

Supposed to be as strong as Sasquatch (North America's Abominable Snowman), Huldra belongs to the so-called *huldre* people, whose origins go back to the time of Adam and Lilith (who, according to one myth, was Adam's real first wife before Eve came along). Lilith is the woman who gave birth to all demons, goblins and creatures of the underworld. The Huldra legion maintains that the ugly hag/gorgeous creature can do a lightning-swift, chameleon change after she has seduced a lone man in the woods.

Whether Huldra exists or not, official government policy is to spice up its tourism for economic reasons. The giant woman with the cow's tail hiding out in the woods makes a nice story for visitors who don't care if the evidence is telltale or tall-tail.

SWEDEN

Viking Olympics

Gotland

That this historic island in the Baltic needs to be reached by boat from the mainland (a five-hour trip) or by plane (a one-hour flight) must not deter you from coming here—especially if it's the second week of July. That's the time when the Viking Olympics take place! And that's the time you will be watching some truly offbeat sporting events that have their orgins in bygone times, like pillow-fighting on a suspended log, leg wrestling, *varpa*, *stangstortning* and *paerk*.

You needn't bother looking up these words in your *Unabridged* because they're Swedish words that have no English equivalents, besides which they're little-known sports that have not changed at all over the centuries. With or without a sponsor, you'll never see any of these folkloristic Viking games on your television screen, but a sidebar trip to the Baltic Sea's biggest island (75 miles long and half as wide) at the right time will give you a chance to attend the annual **STANGA GAMES** on the meadows of the small peaceful village of Stanga in Gotland's south parish.

If you come as a tourist, theoretically you are invited to participate in any of the ancient sports, all of which require superb primed muscles and years of brute-strength practice, Viking style. But the real fun is in the watching—and you don't even have to pay any kind of admission fee. That's the way it was done centuries ago, and now in the twentieth century there is still nothing to remind you that you're not back there when men were men and Vikings were super-men (except for the crackly, *low-fi* public address system that must date back to the time of Marconi).

Easily the most popular of the Viking games is *varpa*,

one of the oldest sports known to man, according the
Institute of Folklore Science in Stockholm. The sport of
varpa, which, as archaeological evidence proves, goes back
to the time of the Stone Age. From Viking graves many flat
varpa stones, the basic item used in the game, have been
unearthed, and scientists believe they were used both in
sporting activity and also as a way to improve efficiency in
combat. Played by six competitors on two rival teams, the
game of *varpa* requires inordinate strength because the
varpa stone weighs over ten pounds and must be tossed at
an upright target pole 65 feet away. The object of the game
is to throw the stone in an underhanded sweep (no sidearm
or overhand flips permitted) and get as close as possible to
the stick without knocking it over or tilting it.

But perhaps the most difficult of all the Viking games is
the sport of *stangstortning*, which is as hard to pronounce as
it is to play. This game involves a thick pole that is 13 feet
long and weighs over 50 pounds. A contestant has the job
of tossing it as far as possible with two hands, but it must
land within an imaginary zone between the ten o'clock and
two o'clock position, based on the imaginary six o'clock
point where the man made the throw. If a tosser can get
the pole to land at exactly the twelve o'clock position (like
the hands on a watch), he gets extra points.

What is impressive about this particular sport is that the
mere act of tossing the pole requires special muscle-power,
balancing skill and acrobatic versatility while the toss is
getting underway. If a man topples over during the tricky
preparatory motions, he is disqualified. So total dead silence from spectators is mandatory as the approach is
being readied. The record for a *stangstortning* throw is 9.49
meters, set by Leif Sundman in 1978, which many Viking
Olympics regulars believe may never be matched.

Less demanding in muscle is the sport of *paerk* because it
can be played in an aura of calm and relaxation. Pitting two
seven-man teams against each other in a battle for points
and territory, the game is a liberal mixture of tennis and
cricket with a ball of yarn sewed into a sheepskin that is
either kicked or hit by hand. Each member of the team
serves the uneven ball to a receiver who must return it on

the first bounce or on the fly, and where the dead ball finally finishes, points are won or bartered for territory. Whichever team garners 40 points first is the victor. This game is believed to have been brought to Gotland by Dutch sailors who play a similar sport in Holland called *kaatsen*.

Pillow-fighting on a log raised about five feet and suspended between two wooden horses brings on plenty of laughter from the spectators. Two contestants, each armed with a colored pillow (green and orange are the usual choices), sit astride the log and take turns walloping each other's heads, the object being to send the opponent to the turf below.

The Viking games are a big hit—and a gold-medal winner!

*   *   *

The Wasa

Stockholm

After lying for 333 years on the muddy bottom of Stockholm harbor, the **WASA** is today one of those rarities among museums—in that it is a one-item museum. But what an item!!! Ask any of the 5,000 people who each day visit the *Wasa* which ignominiously sank on its maiden voyage on August 10, 1628, several hundred yards out from the dock in 110 feet of water, in sight of what is now downtown Stockholm. Thousands of Swedes and His Majesty and the royal family watched the "show" in utter astonishment.

As the pride of the Swedish fleet, the mighty *Wasa*, a three-masted, 1400-ton galleon—then the largest naval vessel in existence—set sail on a balmy Sunday for the Thirty Years War. So everyone expected, but no sooner had she gone a few hundred yards than a swift gust of south wind caught her sails and tipped the gaudy crimson-and-gold warship precariously.

With water gushing into the open gun ports, the *Wasa*

went to the bottom, just like that. And it lay there until 1961 when the unlucky ship was raised. It took nearly 12 years for more than 360 tons of harbor water to be extracted from the *Wasa*'s boards and sails for its restoration. It is now the world's oldest salvaged and restored man-of-war.

Before it was brought up and mothballed, the *Wasa* was considered an exceptional boat, according to historical records—but not until it came up again did Swedish authorities realize how exceptional it was. Built only a few years after the *Mayflower* and half again as big, she turned out to be longer and taller than anybody had figured. It had over 700 ornamental pieces of intricate wood carvings, most of which were retrieved.

These pieces are now on display in a new drydock museum that also includes figures of warriors, sea creatures, mythological heroes, knights and a number of lions' heads, not to mention a grand aftercastle with the figures of two-foot-high cherubs playing musical instruments. Some 24,000 items salvaged from the ship—precious antiques and interesting memorabilia recovered from the wreck—form a truly fascinating permanent exhibit called Life on Board. It is today a treasury of information about seventeenth-century Swedes.

The unusual finds include, besides heavy cannons and ammunition, utensils for cooking and eating, barrels for salt fish and salt meat, flour and fresh water, some 4,000 copper coins, a pewter flask with a liter of liquor that resembled 300-year-old rum, and a butter box (its rancid contents still identifiable). Although the crew of the *Wasa* consisted of 133 sailors and 300 soldiers, the skeletons of only 18 persons were found in the ship.

One of the grisliest sights in the museum is the skeleton of a sailor who had been pinned beneath his lower-deck gun carriage at the moment of disaster. In his early thirties at the time, he wore a sheath knife and in his pants pocket was a leather money purse with square copper coins. His linen shirt and stockings, homespun jacket and buckle shoes are well preserved. About five-feet-eight-inches tall, he also wore leather mittens, a wide-brimmed felt hat and carried a clay pipe and sewing kit.

One wonders how all this could survive three centuries of immersion, and the museum gives the answer. Because the Baltic Sea has a low saline content and the temperature is cold, its waters are free of shipworms and other marine insects that would have attacked the carved decorations. Everything aboard the ship was preserved by the mud and water.

As luck would have it, the *Wasa* was still holding together when it came up, and that is explained by the fact that it had been built with wooden pegs and not nails. Had nails been used, they would have rusted away completely over the centuries, whereas the wooden pegs survived the ravages of the salt water. Even so, during the restoration work the Swedes had to put in about 5,000 new bolts to keep the shaky ship shipshape.

The three types of wood used on the *Wasa*—oak, pine and lime—would have rotted in the open air, and to stop this process, an automatic sprinkler system sprays the whole ship once a day with a polyethylene solution. Of course, this is done during the night after the museum has closed its doors. Visitors who come to look at the old girl are not permitted to walk on any of the five decks or the poop deck. There is a railed, but sometimes slippery, cat-walk that circles and hugs the *Wasa* completely that tourists follow. Once around takes about 15 minutes, but a visitor can tour it many times.

The *Wasa* museum is open in the summer from 10:00 A.M. to 8:00 P.M. and in winter from 10:00 A.M. to 5:00 P.M. English-language tours are conducted every hour in summer and every two hours in winter; there's a showing of a 28-minute film about the *Wasa* at two-hour intervals beginning at 11:00 A.M. The film won't win any Academy Awards, but the *Wasa* itself clocks in as a winner for being the world's most unusual time capsule.

LIECHTENSTEIN

The Other Liechtenstein

Triesenberg

In act 3 of many operattas, the inhabitants of a tiny principality dance in the village square, shored up with spontaneous choruses of gaily dressed, rosy—cheeked peasants. Liechtenstein is no alpine Ruritania, as you might find in an operetta, though many tourists who come here expect something along those lines.

As far as the tourist flow is concerned, all roads in Liechtenstein lead to **Vaduz**, the capital, which is certainly a logical place to head for if you've never been here before. Vaduz has the reigning prince's fourteenth-century castle (not open to the public, by the way), the spectacular art museum, the postal museum (a philatelist's delight), star hotels and double-starred restaurants and a national museum with artifacts from the Roman period.

But listen to the director of Liechtenstein's tourism, Berthold Konrad, who is firm in his belief that visitors do not spend enough time in his country.

"Tourists come here," he says, "in buses or automobiles (we have no railroad station or airport), stay a few hours in Vaduz, do a little buying in the souvenir shops, manage to sit at an outdoor café or restaurant for a drink or a meal and get their passports stamped so that they can tell their friends back home they've been to Liechtenstein."

Sad to relate, the rest of Liechtenstein is virtually unblemished by mass tourism. Although it takes about 20 minutes to drive from one end of the country (Switzerland) to the other (Austria), visitors can turn off the main highway at almost anytime and go into one of the 11 parish districts, each of which has its own character and most of which provide picturesque hamlets.

Liechtenstein's boundaries have not changed much since the early fifteenth century when two large estates (Schellenberg, known as the lowlands, and Vaduz, known as the uplands) were combined. In 1719 the two areas—comprising a total of 61 square miles—became the Imperial Principality of Liechtenstein, named after its prince, who today is Prince Franz Jošef II Maria Aloys Alfred Karl Johannes Heinrich Michael Georg Ignatius Benediktus Gerhardus Majella von und zu Liechtenstein. He is the twelfth sovereign ruler of this country, which is a constitutional monarchy with a democratic parliament.

By staying on in Liechtenstein a few days extra (after you've done the Vaduz bit, of course) you can visit every one of this principality's 11 communities, each a former earldom. The largest sector is **Triesenberg** (2,000 inhabitants), which has a strong alpine character and magnificent walks through forests and meadows. Of special attraction is the so-called **Prince's Climb**, which begins in the town of **Gaflei** and winds its way up through the mountain peaks. This climb is named after Prince John II who had the path cleared and made safe in 1898. Triesenberg, which rises to 5,250 feet at the town of **Malbun**, and which is a big snowsport center in winter, has one of the best bobsled runs in Europe.

Schaan, which is Liechtenstein's second largest parish, contains much of the country's industry—such as false teeth, feather pillows and quilts and pharmaceutical products. Its **Theater am Kirchplatz** brings in international artists and has become the cultural focus of the whole country. The smallest parish of all, **Planken**, is nestled in a woodland utopia and commands a marvelous panorama of the Rhine Valley.

Regarded as the oldest compact community in Liechtenstein, Triesen was first founded in Roman times and is the home of several noble families. The old quarter of the village is a must-explore visit, not to mention its nature reserve and a small scenically impressive lake. The southernmost parish of **Balzers** is worth a look because of its **Gutenberg Castle** (open to the public), which since 1919 has been a regular arena for operetta performances.

As the main locality of the Liechtenstein lowland, **Eschen**'s excavations of the new Stone Age culture and its prehistoric settlement should be viewed. Another parish, **Gamprin-Bendern**, which embraces two localities, has been continuously inhabited since 2500 B.C. The **Virgin's Grotto** is the only underground shrine in central Europe, and on the *Kirchhügel* (church hill), the men of Liechtenstein swore loyalty to their new Prince on March 16, 1699.

Schellenberg, distinguished by its two castles built during the Middle Ages, houses a community of people (population 581) who have lived there over 5,000 years. Calling itself "the village of seven hillocks," **Mauren-Schaanwald** has a bird sanctuary and a local nature trail that attracts many Europeans. Characterized by water meadows, **Ruggell** has 225 acres of land designated as a "protected area" to prevent the extinction of its special flora and fauna that can't be found in other parts of Europe.

If you have that snack in Vaduz, why not stick around and drink in the rest of this land.

* * *

Liechtenstein's Naafkopf Peak

Malbun

So explored and explained is the Continent that there seems to be no place in Europe anymore that remains unknown. True? Well, maybe. Of those few "undiscovered" nuggets, however, some are more undiscovered than others. Take **NAAFKOPF PEAK**, for example.

Naafkopf Peak is not a conversation piece, judging by the way hundreds of thousands of tourists flood into this matchless mini-state every year and pay not the least attention to the Naafkopf. The last statistics put out by the tourist office show that for every million travelers who come to Liechtenstein, maybe one makes an inquiry about Naafkopf peak.

What makes the Naafkopf more than just a peak-a-boo

site is that nowhere else in Europe can you find a piece of ground where you can sit down and be in three countries at the same time. Liechtenstein, Austria and Switzerland meet at exactly that point—and a huge wooden cross has been erected at the spot where the triumvirate of lands kiss and embrace.

Getting to the Naafkopf Peak—which is not really a peak but more of a high plateau—won't require any kind of special mountain-climbing gear in the summer or spring other than a pair of sturdy shoes. Except for two short stretches on the cliff-hugging path where you have to watch your footsteps, the walk to the Naafkopf is quite negotiable and not dangerous at all. Give yourself a full day to go and come back, if you're staying at a hotel in the capital.

Leave Vaduz during the morning and make your way through the town of **Steg**, which in this country of 61 square miles is less than ten minutes away by auto or bus. Quaint beyond all description, and mostly unvisited by tourist hordes, Steg is a starting point for various walking trails, where peaks of three mountains, known as the Three Sisters, seem to be extending welcoming hands to hikers exploring a kind of never-never land. During the ski periods, however, the cozy lodgings are always booked solid.

From Steg you drive uphill to the town of Malbun, which is the end of the 760f bus line, if you're taking public transportation from Vaduz. Here you can go on a ski-lift to a wonderful sun-terrance at an altitude of 6,500 feet where you can enjoy a cup of coffee and a Liechtenstein pastry before you depart on foot toward the Naafkopf.

It's an easy uphill hike of about 90 minutes to your first stop on this mountain-ridge path, the Bettlerjoch Pfälzer hut at 7,900 feet, where you can stop for a rest and a cuppa. Now, with another half tramp, you reach the Naafkopf Peak at 8,400 feet. In winter this makes a good starting point for a ski run downhill all the way to Malbun.

Once you arrive at the Naafkopf and the three countries that converge on top, there may be still another "bonus" in store for you, if the weather is clear. You can make out in the distance the silvery waters of Lake Constance and Germany, which therefore means that atop the Naafkopf a visitor can see four countries at one time—Germany, Switzerland, Austria and Liechtenstein. There is no piece of land elsewhere in the world where such a thing is possible.

On the Naafkopf you are privileged to put your John Hancock into a special book that is kept up there. The sturdy volume has been there since the wooden cross, which stands three meters high (almost ten feet), first went up. The reigning prince of Liechtenstein, Franz Josef II, his wife, Princess Georgina, and their five children have also put their signatures into the book. In fact, the prince's four sons and daughter are frequent visitors to the Naafkopf during ski periods.

If you want to walk all the way down to Malbun, instead of taking the ski lift from the terrace, allow yourself about five hours from the Naafkopf. It's advisable that you begin your descent well before dusk since in a few places you have to pay attention to the rough footpath.

Stay as long as you can on the summit of the Naafkopf and enjoy still another rarity—the most invigorating fresh air anywhere. Since Liechtenstein is four-fifths covered by forest, up there you have all to yourself one of Europe's most tree-mendous views.

GREECE

Mount Athos:
No Women Allowed

Mount Athos
The law says: *No Women Allowed*!

So if Ms. or Mrs. Tourist, or little Mary has a hankering to peek in on Greece's holy **Athonite Republic**, the only way for her to see it—sans fuss or botheration—is through binoculars from a rented motor launch or with an organized Aegean Sea junket from Piraeus. Yup, they barred milady from its sacred real estate with a law that goes back to the year 1060 A.D.

Travel-wise, **MOUNT ATHOS** is a novelty supreme, whether you see it from afar bobbing the waves or on land. But it is no place for a daring damsel to don a disguise and try to sneak in, because people in the past who were caught doing so received a standard punishment of six to sixteen lashes and immediate expulsion. If you, however, have all your dues paid as a certified member of the male fraternity, then the 900 monks of this monastic state offer you their gracious hospitality.

Its geography untouched by the presence of the opposite sex—and that even includes most female domestic animals—Mount Athos is probably the last male stronghold on planet Earth, a sanctuary where barricaded bachelors want to live out their days in undisturbed tranquility and contemplation.

As one of the curiosities of history, Athos considers itself independent of Greek jurisdiction and is governed by the Greek Orthodox Church. Rising 6,350 feet above sea level, the hunk of jutting land has 20 monasteries in 12 "towns." The inhabitants have no radio, no television, no newspapers, no phones, no telegraph and only one vehicle.

Besides the restrictions on Suzy-Q and her sisters, the monks also have severe laws against all musical instruments, smoking, singing and horseback riding.

What sort of people are the hermits of Athos? Most of these men were brought here immediately after birth and therefore have never seen a woman in their lives. But why have they remained cut off from civilization and content to spend their days perched atop a craggy peninsula of 150 square miles? One journalist (me), determined to try (briefly) the spartan life, forewent the usual 20th-century touristic conveniences to find out firsthand.

What I found in one monastery after another were immaculate sleeping quarters, substantial vegetarian food with plenty of fresh water or wine, and no-problem plumbing. The **Vatopedi Monastery**, which smells like the winery it is, runs the closest thing to a "hotel" (emphasis on the quotation marks). Meals, which are eaten in silence, consist of lentil soup, fish, salad and home-baked bread, plus wine or water. When you leave, if you feel like making a modest contribution in any currency, your generosity will not be declined. Nobody, however, will ever ask you for money or even suggest your having to make any kind of payment.

To get into Athos, male tourists have to obtain a special permit through the Greek Ministry of Foreign Affairs in Athens or the Ministry of Northern Greece in Salonika. This consists of a card (it costs a few dollars and is called a '*diamonitirion*') that you get from the Athos governmental agent, entitling you to free room and board. Your entry into Athos is through the port of **Dafni**, reached by a coastal boat leaving the town of **Ouranoupolis** at 7:30 A.M.

The gentlemen's utopia rises above the lazy brine of the Aegean like an overgrown pyramid to a steep summit of white marble. Along the flanks of the mountain are the monastic villages, the first of which was established in 274 A.D. Each of the monasteries was built with massive stone walls and watchtowers with slit windows and the buildings give the impression of being able to hold out against heavy aerial bombardments.

High on the list of monasteries to visit has to be **St. Pantaleimenos**, which has enough rooms and cells to house about 1,500 persons. Used by the monk Rasputin as a military stronghold, the monastery stored rifles, machine guns, and light artillery in its subterranean pits, which Rasputin's soldiers, disguised as holy men, had quietly infiltrated. After the revolution of 1917 broke out, members of Russia's ruling Romanov family were supposed to have fled to Rasputin's cozy cubbyhole.

But the big gossip about St. Pantaleimenos is that at one time it used to get $75,000 a year in subsidies from Moscow, apparently because some Kremlin bosses had been planning to use it as a hideaway for themselves, if and when they ever had to run for cover. Whether true or not, the monastery, with its dozens of narrow archers' windows, welcomes visitors today and is proud of its magnificent collection of icons. A monk with a huge key dangling from his waist will open the heavy door guarding these treasures on your request.

Another monastery you should visit is **St. Denis**. Here you come upon awe-inspiring icons, a priceless collection of rare Byzantine documents, the alleged preserved hand of John the Baptist and a splinter from the cross of Christ—the monastery's most prized relic. At St. Denis, the food and wine are the best.

Sooner or later, you walk into a skete, which is a monastic village dominated by an abbey. The one with the most dramatic landscape is the skete of **St. Anne**, whose buildings cling to the clefts of vertical rocks. Though its streets have no names everybody knows where to go, especially at suppertime when all the monks emerge from their individual dwellings to gather at the abbey for a meal that consists of fish, eggs, salad, cheese, fruit and wine. Because silence is not the order of things at St. Anne, the conversation is jolly and takes unexpected pathways. Without giving his name away, I suggest you ferret out the Irish monk who left behind a wife and nine-year-old son in London, where he ran a shop near Carnaby Street. His brand of English will keep you enthralled.

Since the monks all over Athos are scholarly types, quite a few of them speak book-English and are eager to practice it. "Why shouldn't I stay here?" one monk said through a ruddy-olive face, one of the healthiest mine eyes have seen. "The life here is good. It is quiet. And it is rewarding. There is no stress, there are no problems, we have no fears of any kind. We live together in Athos, and we live longer than people do anyplace else in the world."

Because the law against females states specifically that not even so much as a cow or a she-goat can cross the frontier, young women in recent years have attempted to edge in dressed as Tom, Dick, or Harry, via one ruse or another. So the monks have redoubled their preautions against women, and now anybody who wants to cross into Athos must undergo a personal physical examination as authorized by law.

Yet there have been some "border incidents," and even a few extremely embarrassing situations for the Athosians. One, some time ago, involved an American exchange professor, Cora Miller, a teacher of home economics in nearby Salonika. Miller put ashore in Athos one early morning with a rowboat and paraded around the beach in her bathing suit for at least an hour before being detected. Athos officialdom was so incensed by the outrage that they enacted a special law making it possible to sentence an undesirable alien to three months of incarceration. Despite her bravado and "insult," Cora got off rather easily and was let go after an overnight stay in a dungeon.

Even royalty has tried to get behind the Gender Curtain. The late queen of Romania, Marie, dressed up as a boy and almost wormed her way past the frontier. She was caught and sent home immediately. On that occasion the Athosians exhibited some fancy diplomatic talent and avoided what could have been a rather messy international episode.

The honor of being the first known human female actually to get into Mount Athos goes to the wife of munitions maker Paul Louis Weiler. She was one Alice Diplarakou, Miss Europe of 1930. Having strapped her breasts down with a tight sheet, Alice disguised herself as a sailor, landed at a deserted strip of beach and made her way on foot to Karyes, the capital. In Karyes she got a young monk to pose next to her for a snapshot. Later Miss Europe wrote an article for a Greek newspaper about her adventure. To prove she had actually been on Athos soil, she published the picture of herself and the cleric. Athos executives branded her a no-good schemer and dismissed the matter as a crass hoax. So far as the monks are concerned today, Mount Athos has kept its record intact.

The Athosians point out that even during the Second World War, when the German army marched in and occupied the land, the Nazis gave full respect to the monks' strange law against the female. None of the high-echelon officers—who governed Athos with an iron hand—ever brought in their wives or mistresses. However, the Nazis did make one change. They allowed a gaggle of hens to grace Adam's Seventh Heaven, and after the enemy soldiers retreated, there followed a hotly contested parliamentary debate about the hens. The final decision went in favor of the hens.

"After all," explained Abbot Basilidos, clutching a crucifix of diamonds that symbolizes his status as a government executive, "the chickens provide us with eggs for breakfast each morning."

CYPRUS

The Island of Love

Cyprus

For a start there is the legend of Aphrodite emerging from the sea in the buff. . . .

The there are two wisecracks about the much-heralded Greek islands—all 1,700 of them: the first is that visiting tourists have a choice of sweltering inside their hotels or sweltering outside; and the second wisecrack is that the first one is true.

But hold on a moment. Surprise! You can beat the island heat and oppressive humidity by trying the one Greek island that is no longer Greek and that is best described as the Mediterranean's coolest beauty spot—the place where the Greek goddess of love, Aphrodite, was given life and rose from the foaming waves fully formed and totally undraped.

Well, Aphrodite herself is now a revered statue in the **Museum of Cyprus**—but Cyprus has its share of other live goddesses who cover their elegant forms with G-strings, bikinis and other skimpy apparel that passes for legal swimwear, as defined by island law.

Appropriately identified as the "Island of Love," Cyprus is a place of beauties and beauty, but it's a place that has had its tourism battered because of strife between the resident Greeks and Turks who don't like each other. Both ethnic factions, however, make it plain that they like you, and genuinely welcome all foreign visitors with open arms.

Although Cyprus has yet to resolve the political differences between the Turks in the north and the Greeks in the south, tourists who come here don't feel any of the tension at all, because *Kypriaki* (its Greek name) has remained quiet for more than a decade. In fact, even though the northern

231

part of the island used to boast of having most of the hotels (located at Famagusta and Kyrenia), the energetic Greek Cypriots have spectacularly built up new resorts along the indented southern coastline.

Today such towns as **Limassol**, **Larnaca**, **Ayia Napa** and **Paphos** have drummed up a tourism business that attracts British, German and Scandinavian visitors each year. Last year the south coast resorts hosted some 900,000 Europeans but very few Americans.

At Limassol, Richard the Lion Hearted married Queen Berengaria of Navarre in **St. George's Chapel**, with a royal reception at **Kolossi Castle** where the rich, sweet commanderia wine, the island's specialty, became an instant favorite of the English monarchs and the British at home.

History reports that Berengaria followed the king in one of his ships when Richard was on his way to the Third Crusade in 1190. When the fleet was scattered by a storm, the king seized and conquered the island, rescuing his bride-to-be from the deposed ruler. Cyprus subsequently passed into the hands of the Venetians, the Turks and finally the British (in 1878), until independence in 1960.

To the west of Limassol lies Larnaca, a town that sports a marina equal to and very much exuding a French Riviera atmosphere. Larnaca houses one of Europe's strangest sites—the so-called Great Salt Lake, which not only gives Utah a run for its money but one-ups Utah: in the summer the lake is dry and snowy white like the American lake; in the wetter and colder months, the Cypriot lake turns to a remarkable pink because of the plumage of the thousands of flamingos wintering there. Another commanding temptation on the shores of this lake is the Moslem shrine of the **Tekke of Hala Sultan**, tomb of the Prophet Mohammed's foster mother.

Cyprus's other attractions include the not-to-be-missed **Stavrovouni Monastery**, more than 2,250 feet high on an eastern peak of the Troodos Mountains. The monks who live here give you a big welcome, but they do have a sign up warning women that they will not be admitted if they wear shorts, sleeveless shirts or have lipstick and rouge on their faces.

Although the Cypriot coastline has more than 400 snug, sheltered-water inlets that are used by swimmers, the most popular of these is the inlet resort of **Ayia Napa**, which is built on a rise and dips gradually to the sea. Even with the cluster of smart hotels in this area, the place never seems to be overcrowded, and draws the Scandinavian topless set.

Further west is Cyprus's best resort today, **Paphos**—the place where Aphrodite is purported to have risen from the waves in the frothy waters of the coral bay beach. It was at Paphos that Alexander the Great built Cyprus's first harbor and it was from here Cicero ruled the island for 15 years as the Roman pro-consul. Both St. Barnabas and St. Paul came to Paphos and converted the people to Christianity, and one of the noted sights here is the **Pillar of St. Paul**, to which he was tied and given 39 lashes for preaching Christianity on the island.

Also worth seeing are the rocky **Tombs of the Kings** (a third-century necropolis), the **Frankish baths** and the harborside **Byzantine castle**. The area also has a temple to Aphrodite, and people (especially lovers) flock to **Aphrodite's Rock**, which pokes out from the brine. A Paphos farmer made history when he uncovered something unusual while ploughing his field—it turned out to be the **House of Dionysus**, a Roman villa with 22 rooms, each with a mosaic scene from mythology. The villa had been hidden under a thin layer of earth for 16 centuries.

Two other villages require mention: **Kornos** specializes in pottery making (one of your best buys); and **Lefkara** is outstanding for its lace making. All over town women sit in the bright sunlight in front of their doorways, producing their famous lace mats, tablecloths and gloves. It is said that no tourist has ever left Lefkara without some lacey souvenir.

Gearing itself to tourists in every way, Cyprus has begun to push its winter tourism with reduced prices in hotels and shops. From January through March you can ski in the Troodos Mountains in the morning and go for a dip in the afternoon down at one of the beaches where the winter temperature often reaches 65 degrees Fahrenheit. The translucent sea makes for come-hither, year-round skin diving. Frequently, frogmen whoosh up with ancient coins or pieces of pottery from the Hellenistic or Roman period from sunken Greek or Roman ships.

Dotted with relics of a rich past that spans more than 8,000 years, Cyprus is an island of 3,572 square miles, boasting a dozen civilizations that have left their dent. So here the past is always present and very close to the future.

Most of the 696,000 people who live on the Island of Love believe that one day Cyprus's sweetheart, the Greek goddess of love, will reemerge from the bubbly sea to blow another kiss to the island's love affair with her.

TURKEY

Turkey's Art of Belly Dancing

Istanbul

Who are the world's greatest athletes? Triple-threat quarterbacks, homerun hitters, slalom ski whizzes? Guess again, guess again. . . . My own hearty vote goes to a small army of women. No, they're not Marines or Green Berets, and they don't pack six-guns. But they do obey a certain commando impulse—they dance almost nonstop, incessantly, in such a way that every muscle in their gyrating bodies moves in a different direction.

So who are they? They are Turkey's irrepressible, irresistible belly dancers. An art form that goes back to antiquity still provides tourists—especially those armed with videocameras—with a show that is a showstopper.

Recently I watched one such sturdy athlete do her thing to a musical piece that kept going on and on and on until the clock ran out of time. Without once huffing or puffing as she took her innumerable bows to a dinner audience of travelers from abroad who had been wowed beyond description, the zdftig danseuse moved graciously off stage, only to come back about an hour later for the second part of her act. That kept her going with nary a pause until well past dessert for another interminable workout of music and muscle in action.

Although belly dancing is as natural in Turkey as square dancing is in North America, the Turks look upon this ancient type of footwork as more aesthetic than erotic because of the considerable coordination required by the performer, who also click-clacks the brass cymbals on her fingers as she accompanies the music. Her hands must at the same time be expressive and suggestive, while her head must shift on a horizontal plane as her shoulders and arms move in the opposite direction from her head. Long hair is required for the dance—and this is held up with her hands while she twists her hips. It is de rigueur that she not be skinny.

For onlookers, especially the Turks in the audience, it is customary to get up and place a coin on the dancer's forehead when she does the most difficult movement of all—that of bending backwards while still undulating in rhythm.

Belly-dance experts in Istanbul—which is considered the best place in the world to view this traditional art form at its most accomplished best—say that female youngsters here learn to do the dance from their moms who learned it from their mothers, and so it goes. At social gatherings at home, young girls are often asked to belly dance for guests.

Of the many thousands of Turkish women who try to become professionals later on, only a few manage to make it to the top—but once up there, their names become household words, and they are celebs who command the highest respect. Women with mobile midriffs in other countries like Greece, Egypt and the Arab capitals are not considered authentic by the Turks, since the women in those countries learn the dance late in life from profession-al teachers and not at home as kids.

As we know it today, the major emphasis in belly danc-ing is on the undulations of the midsection. Quite likely these movements were part of prehistoric rituals to honor the female's ability to create life, especially a son. The better the undulations, the more likely that a new-born baby would be a boy—or so is the belief here. If nothing else, the belly dance is believed to prepare a woman's body for good health in childbirth.

Despite the fact that the dance seems to be the same no matter who does it, the belly dance is essentially impro-vised, for the individual does not follow a set choreography—she performs some basic steps and inter-prets the music of the strings as the tempo slows down or picks up. The movements are generally slow and liquid, coordinated to the so-called *ciftetelli* rhythm, arms snaking about the body, hips swaying, belly rippling. Like Jamilah in the *Arabian Nights*, the dancer has one purpose: to give good entertainment by doing the *gobek dans yapmak* and its ancient movements with total command of her every fiber.

Belly dancing reached a fine art of perfection in the days of the Turkish harems, when as many as a hundred women in the same harem did their best to catch the sultan's eye. As the blindfolded musicians stroked the strings of their instruments in a kind of perpetual motion, the sultan sat on his cushions deciding who would be his *ikbal* (the glorified one—or the sultan's favorite).

Before the great Kemal Ataturk formed the secular Turkish republic and passed modernizing reforms in the 1920s and 1930s, the strict Islamic moral code kept women veiled and segregated to a point that the belly dance was never seen in public until after the Second World War when the minister of the interior gave an official okay to recognized professionals to perform in nightclubs, hotels and restaurants. Slithering across the floor back and forth between courses of meze, shishkebab and baklava, the likes of Fatma, Semra and Emel have given Turkey's tourist business a thunder and lightning boost.

To catch some belly dancing there are actually dozens of places in Istanbul, but the best dancers are employed by those restaurants and night spots booked into the "Istanbul by Night" tours where some of the famous performers of today—like the sinewy Nesrin Topkadi and the beautiful Sibel Cam—hold forth with their utterly amazing talent. Talk about a Turkish delight. . . .

UKRAINE

The Kiev Cave Monastery

Kiev

So you think you've been everywhere in Europe? You've had lunch atop the Eiffel Tower, watched the sun rise behind the Matterhorn, posed next to Pisa's learning tower while holding it up with one finger, danced a dozen waltzes at Vienna's fabulous Opera Ball. Feeling a bit ho-hummmmm now? Don't!

There's still another destination for the sophisticated traveler who has one green pin left over to stick into his wall map. Come to Kiev on the banks of the Dnieper River and make a beeline for the city's most . . . er, ummm . . . unbelievable attraction—the cave monastery.

Created over a period of nine centuries and founded by a monk called Antony, the **PECHERSKY MONASTERY** is mostly beneath the earth, actually occupying nine underground levels of hollowed-out passageways. It draws adventurous tourists who must carry long lighted candles, following a guide who makes all the correct turns and leads the way down steps that are rather uneven, tricky enough to make for slow negotiating.

Down below, you inevitably find a priest giving mass in a corner chapel all by his lonesome. In fact, what is surprising is that a mass is going on at all times of the day in one of the tiny chapels at any of the levels. There are no electric lights in the subsurface monastery, so everything is lit up by flickering candles.

Ukrainian Catholics number more than 5 million. Defying the Soviet rules on formal religion almost since they were instituted, the Ukrainian Church went underground, literally. Before glasnost, in the case of the cave monastery, when a priest said mass somewhere below, no KGB man could ever know when or where it was taking place. Though all pilgrims who came to the church to hear mass knew about the secret services to honor Christ, were a policeman ever to enter the premises, he could never zero in on just where the mass was being performed. If he did, by the time he got there, the alert would have been relayed, the altar candle would have been blown out, and the presiding cleric and those in attendance would have swiftly vanished into one of the dark corridors.

More than 100,000 tourists a year descend into the cave monastery and most find it astonishing to see the many perfectly preserved bodies of mummified priests, some of whom have been dead for hundreds of years. The mummies in the Kiev catacombs, blessed with a natural ventilation, are said to be better preserved than any of those in Egypt. What's even more unbelievable, when the bodies were buried, none of the methods of preservation known to the Egyptians thousands of years ago was used. In the caves here every mummy stayed intact because of certain laws and phenomena of nature.

Of course, there is scientific reason, and your guide makes it all clear in lay terms when she tells you why. To explain the lack of decomposition in the caves, the determining factors are found in the soil. Since the makeup of the soil is both sand and clay, the top sand layer, therefore, sops up any all moisture, keeping the bodies at the various deep levels totally dry. Also, the temperature down below is constant, at around 59 degrees Fahrenheit. Because bacteria cannot live below a depth of 16 feet, no microbes have had a chance to destroy the bodies, of which there are 170 buried in the catacombs, each one very well preserved.

Today 75 monks live in the monastery, which has three underground churches—**St. Antony's**, **St. Barlaam's** and the **Church of the Presentation of the Holy Virgin**. Their walls are laced with graffiti in the Slavonic, Polish and Armenian languages, and the passageways of the caves are more than a half kilometer in length. Fragments of paintings are also visible on the walls.

Sitting on the ground or on benches both outside and inside the monastery vestibule are many peasants (most of them women) who have traveled long distances (often on foot) to make Mecca-like pilgrimages. Most of these people are very poor, so when they arrive at the monastery, there is a free bed for them to sleep overnight. In addition, on top of the main altar there are always fresh loaves of bread and cakes, most of which are baked daily by the monks, or brought in as offerings by Kiev housewives.

The caves in question have been there for centuries, and it is believed that they now fan out under most of Kiev. Scientists are getting ready to make explorations in the near future to determine how widespread they are.

Impressively vibrant, 1,500-year-old Kiev was nick-named Hero City during World War II because of its valiant fight against the Nazi hordes. Yet is has deservedly earned another name, Mother of Russian Cities, since it was here that the Russian nation had its beginnings. Rank-ing third in size (after Moscow and Leningrad), Kiev is quite unlike her two big sisters and inordinately proud that she is usually considered by foreigners on tour of the country as the most beautiful of the formerly Soviet cities.

The city's center for shopping, theaters and cinemas, businesses and promenading is **Kreschchatik Street**, the tree-lined main thoroughfare that is to Kiev what the Champ-Elysées is to Paris. Formerly the jewel of the Soviet Union, the capital of the Ukraine has more parks and public gardens than any city in Europe. Its **Park of Eternal Glory**—a gigantic hill complex of church buildings, muse-ums and statues—provides panoramic view of the Dnieper River, which divides the city in two. Dominated by an 85-foot-high obelisk (the tomb of the unknown soldier), this park is where brides traditionally place wedding bouquets around the eternal flame.

And in case you've been wondering, yes, Kiev is the original home of chicken Kiev—a delicacy with a surprise inside—but it's not surprising that the city's specialty dish tastes better here than anywhere else.

YUGOSLAVIA

The 16 Lakes That Connect

Plitvice

Before the country that called itself Yugoslavia disintegrated, its people were forever pointing out that their land had two alphabets, four languages, five nationalities and six republics. Now, you can take this type of nimble numerical nonsense one step further and add that one of Yugoslavia's republics—today the Independent Republic of Croatia—could calculate still another progressive statistic because it has 16 lakes. The Croatians hasten to assure you that although statistics, admittedly, can be big liars, those 16 lakes do indeed add up to a touristic plus.

Witness the **16 LAKES OF PLITVICE** that are chained to each other by crazy-quilt waterfalls in an immense forest landscape, playing leapfrog as they tumble from one to another. By creating this unreal cavalcade of intercommunicating lakes and cascades, Mother Nature has unleashed one of the great superwonders of Europe.

Opened by the government as a national park in 1949, the 47,300-acre Plitvice Lakes region is located midway between **Zagreb** and **Zadar** in the rural interior of the Yugoslavian republic of Croatia. Though about 85 miles southwest of Zagreb, and a bit off the routine tourist path, it is easily reachable by private car or by a tour-group bus—either from the center of Zagreb or Zadar.

Riding to Plitvice (pronounced PLEET-veet-zay) provides a never-to-be-forgotten adventure, taking you along excellent paved highways, climbing steeply over the coastal limestone mountains and crossing the crest of the range into a hilly farm area, where soon the rumbling of falling water seems to come at you like a Concorde jet from everywhere.

Once the up-to-now hidden water cacophany reaches you, a map is no longer necessary, for here you get your first glimpse of terraced, sparkling lakes through the dense grove of ancient beech trees. Clusters of waterfalls jump out at you amid luxuriant foliage in the upper area of the Plitvice Lakes, they then snake down and roar on in endless variety from one watery catch to the next. As you might suspect, at no time at any spot is it possible for you to ogle all the lakes or waterfalls at once, since they cover a course of about three miles. But there are vantage points from which you can actually view several simultaneously—great for the viewfinder of an eager camera.

In the upper stretch, the lakes have names like **Proscansko**, **Kozjak** and **Galovac**. Galovac gives you an electric jolt because of the adjoining waterfall that bursts left and right into a great circular veil of foaming water and precipitously plunges 65 feet into another pool. The other two lakes behave themselves and bubble from moss-draped cliffs into the forest's deep shade.

Scientists explain the formation of these upper lakes as a biodynamic phenomenon: the calcareous earth is formed when calcium and magnesium carbonates, suspended in the water, come in contact with growths of certain kinds of algae and moss, thereby slowly building up natural rock dams. This ecological process still goes on today.

A number of government-run hotels in this area provide rooms with an unbelievable panorama of Kozjak Lake. In addition, you can walk along its delightful shore-path, which you won't forget for a long time, especially if you choose late afternoon when the sun accents the foliage colors. You'll be impressed, Impressed, IMPRESSED!

If you can imagine such a thing, the best part is yet to come, for even more spectacular are the Plitvice Lakes in the lower half of the park. Offering a landscape of an entirely different kind, the waters of the second series of giant pools, bordered by bulrushes and thickets of fragrant willows, are emerald green in color and are framed by sheer canyon walls of whitish limestone that amplify the echo of the falling water.

Unlike the upper lakes, here you can cross the water stretch between **Lake Novakovica** and the multifingered **Sastavci Falls**. At certain points there are ferry boats that span a lake and also boatmen who will row you across for a small fee. You should, however, give high priority during your visit to the network of lacustrine trails that visitors can follow and walk on in an upward direction, many of them through shaded forests flanking the peaceful lakeshores, with some prehistoric bonus caves gaping at you.

The "stars" of the lower portion include another 65-foot waterfall that is actually an arc of falls that spill and parachute from many spots and different levels all the way down the face of a cliff. Close by and high above to one side, another stream creates the park's highest and most spectacular Nigara-double, dropping with a muffled bellow into a mist-shrouded basin 250 feet below. Most of the time there's a rainbow gracing the spray, a splendiferous stunner that turns all amateur photographers into pros.

The multifalls/multilakes combo is Yugoslavia's sweet-sixteen tourist attraction and rates a "10" on anybody's monitor. You can count on its making a swashbuckling splash.

HUNGARY

Budapest's Island in the Danube

Budapest

Tourism provides inlets and outlets for loyal devotees of one stripe or another—there are organic-music buffs Bach-ing around Central Europe, railway enthusiasts engineer-ing rides on the Continent, and dedicated garden fanciers blooming all over the map. One new 24-carat goal some travelers are "collecting" these days are river islands, and if you have not yet joined the growing ranks of collectors, why not start off by investing some time on Budapest's insular paradise in the fast-flowing waters of the river Danube?

The vivid green, boat-shaped oasis, that was built up by the Danube's pebbles washed in from faraway countries over the centuries and then enlarged by the city govern-ment, is called **Margaret Island**. It's an escapist's Eden for people who, weary of the guff of metropolitan living, want to get away from it all. Called in Hungarian, **Margitsziget**, it extends a mere 1.8 miles in length and bulges 550 yards at its widest part, as it graces the middle of the old Danube weaving through the very bosom of Budapest. If Hunga-ry's capital city is the "Queen of the Danube," then Marga-ret Island is the "Budapest Princess."

Coming nearest to the Tennysonian ideal, the isle is a romantic novelty. God must have been in a generous mood when He sketched the map of Budapest and created this river-girt fairyland where an idyllic serenity captures all visitors. Margaret Island, covered with age-old oaks, thou-sands of wonderful flowers, therapeutic springs, and plen-ty of kaleidoscopic history, has more enchantment per square foot than any other hunk of water-kissed real estate in landlocked Central Europe.

It is said that Budapestians know Margaret's refreshing

tranquility from childhood, frequent its marvelous play facilities during the teen years for games and sports, go there to hold hands in young adulthood and visit in their older years to rest and reflect. A tourist from abroad does not have that much timespan on his hands, but when he comes here for a brief look around, he just does not want to leave so soon. Margaret has that kind of engaging personality.

Once known as *Insula Leporum* (Island of Rabbits), the river patch got its present name from daughter of King Bela IV. Margaret retired from the vanities of the royal palace of Buda in the 13th century, put on the coarse habit of a nun and entered the Dominican convent located on the island. Centuries later the Church canonized her, and in time the Hungarians renamed their beloved island after her.

During its history, Margaret Island was occupied by the Knights of Malta, ravished by the Turks who used it as a military base, and acquired by the Habsburgs in the early 19th century. Perhaps the island's proudest moment came when the czar of Russia, the emperor of Austria and the king of Prussia disported on the enchanting islet all at the same time.

Margaret also became a hangout for personages like Alexandre Dumas, who called it "the pearl of Budapest," Franz Liszt, who came to "drink the music of the leaves" before composing a piece, and Imre Kalman, the king of Hungarian operetta, who frequently listened to the "tunes and warbles of the island's thrushes" and incorporated them into his scores. Hungary's immortal poet, Janos Arany, inspired by a circle of seven giant oak trees (which he called the Seven Sisters), spent many hours under their boughs finishing his great epic trilogy. Composer Richard Wagner adored the island, even though he once almost lost his life while trying to reach it in a rowboat that got caught in some rapids.

Today Margaret Island is connected to Buda on one side of the Danube and to Pest on the other side of the river by two modern bridges at each end. You can reach the island on foot from downtown in no time flat, but all automobiles and buses must use the one bridge that reaches the hotel-end of the island—only one bus is allowed to slice through the island, and it travels Toonerville-trolley style carrying passengers from the island to Buda and to Pest on the other bridge. Mostly, people get there by walking, and everyone revels in the clean air, free from traffic and noise.

Kicked around by civilization, the locals often go there, especially on Sundays, just to lie under a tree and unwind. But for the more active types, there are tennis courts, soccer fields, terraced café-restaurants, two luxury hotels, a game reserve, rose gardens, waterfalls, shady promenades, water-lily fish ponds, dance pavilions, a children's camp, a musical fountain, a tiny church, some easily explorable ruins of the convent, and an outdoor thermal-water swimming pool that can accommodate an awesome 20,000 bathers at one time, romping among artificially induced waves.

There is also open-air opera staged at the sky-high, landmark tower from June to September when there are performances almost every night at 8:00 P.M. Verdi and Wagner sung in Hungarian still sound like Verdi and Wagner—but what is usually interesting to opera buffs is that often some of the country's star singers will do important arias in Italian or German, even though the rest of the cast and chorus are singing in Hungarian.

Margaret Island has two natural-spring pools that provide warm medicinal waters the year round. These thermal waters, which were first brought to the surface in 1866, have made Margaret a therapeutic spa of renown. The **Thermal Hotel Margitszget** at the north end of the islet is staffed with a team of doctors and nurses. Whether you go to Margaret for the hydrotherapy or for its other pleasures, the river island is a good healthy place to be because it is 100% waterproof.

* * *

The Puszta, Hungary's Wild West

Debrecen

The Wild West, Hungarian style. . . . It's called the **Puszta** and it translates into English as the Great Plain. It's a giant lowland that covers more than half of the country or an area of some 20,000 square miles. The largest plain in Europe, it cannot be seen in its entirety, but the most thrilling parts are what your six-hour tour-bus tour gets to on a hither-thither, semiwild journey through the awesome, treeless, flatland most tourists don't visit. Sounds dangerous, doesn't it? Well, not really.

Your Puszta tour into East Hungary—organized by the official government tourist agency, Ibusz—takes you into an area of former outlaws, onetime runaway serfs, clans of once-hostile gypsies, the infamous "3 million beggars" (all of them now totally gone), and roving packs of teeth-baring wolves that at one time were known to be eager to eat you with or without paprika.

The Puszta is the nefarious geographic expanse where the powerful plum brandy was first created, where people still swash this firewater down like lemonade and where you will be served a jigger of the potent stuff (optional for the nondaring) when you sit down for lunch at a *czarda* (rustic restaurant).

Although time may have taken its toll on the Puszta, there's still enough derring-do left for tourists to get in on—great fun once they have seen delightful **Budapest** and its irresistable attractions.

One of the paramount stops of this land tour is where you see the most rousing horseracing demonstration by Hungary's bareback riders, the *czikos*, who do their super-spectacular show wearing soup-bowl turbans and flowing black pantaloons. Snap-cracking their long whips, these absolutely reckless gypsy horsemen—the cowboys of the Puszta—stand with one foot on each of the backsides of two stallions, while controlling a team of five speeding horses with an intertwined set of reins.

The rider raises his snaky whip and cracks it out to full length over the heads of the stampeding horses, tearing past you at no speed limit whatever. Open-mouthed spectators are always stunned by this equine phenomenon, but some people put it all on videotape for back-home instant replay proof of what sounds like a tall tale.

There's yet another "horse" attraction in store for you, as your bus wends its way across the Puszta to the town of

Nagycenk. This is Hungary's famous iron horse (the number 394 locomotive from the **Szechenyi Railroad Museum**), which you have an opportunity to drive yourself for a mile or so at no cost when you volunteer. In the cab with you is a veteran, standby engineer who advises you *how* to do *what* and *when* and *where*. The big thrill comes when you can give a loud toot of the whistle.

After the experience of driving your own train, you are awarded a diploma with your name inscribed on it, citing you as an honorary locomotive engineer. (My diploma today hangs proudly in the office and is in constant vision, even though I can't read Hungarian.)

Another place you visit is **Kalocsa**, a two-street town that is on the map only for its famous "painting women." These persons of yesteryear made their mark in Hungary's history by specializing in flowery murals and their Kalocsa embroidery. Upstairs in the **Viski Karoly Museum** is a stunning array of overstuffed bolsters and quilts, at one time mandatory for a bride's dowry. Not only is the passion for floral motifs evident here, but also at the **Folk Art Museum** where you are swamped with a plethora of boldly painted flowers bordering the rooms. Even the walls of the Kalocsa railroad station are covered with this vivid art form, and the sight of these decorations is enough to warrant your shooting a whole roll of film on them alone.

Straddling the mighty Tisza River, which cuts the Puszta into two equal parts, is the town of **Szeged** where the goddess-worshipping Koros culture had its heyday some 4,000 years ago, and where prosperity came after the year 1225 A.D. because of the royal salt monopoly. When the Great Flood of March 1879 washed away all but 300 homes, Szeged had to start all over again, with the result that the Puszta now can boast of a small city with 180,000 people with a downtown that has a pleasing but very eclectic architectural style.

Szeged's big tourist attraction, which dates back to 1913, is its open-air festival during July and August. Held on a huge 660-square-yard stage in **Dom Square**, which can seat an audience of 7,000, the annual events are big boxoffice draws.

Tours to this least frequented region of Hungary can be booked in Budapest or in **Debrecen**, the capital of the Puszta. Located some 150 miles east of Budapest, Debrecen has been inhabited since the Stone Age and is today a stronghold of Hungarian Protestantism. Directly to the west of the city is the **Hortobagy**, the most romantic part of the Great Plain, which teems with wildlife like herons, long-legged curlews, magpies, hares and brilliant dragon-flies, and where herds of wild horses can often be seen. The real character of the Puszta has been preserved here in tiny villages.

Puszta history shows that up until the invasion of the Turks in 1526, the hundreds of settlements here lived peacefully by agriculture. Unleashing a scourge upon the land, the Turks kept up nearly 150 years of unceasing warfare, as village after village fell into ruin and vast tracts of forest land were burned. Denuded of vegetation, the Puszta became swampy and pestilent with mosquitos. Nearly everybody fled, and the Puszta turned into an abandoned, deserted, bleak and uncontrolled enclave. In time all the misfits of society were drawn to the Puszta, to which even soldiers and police dared not venture. Is it surprising that most Hungarians shunned this massive parcel of land for a long period in history and only went there out of dire necessity?

In a calculated endeavor, prewar and postwar regimes crushed the "romance" out of the Puszta and forced the unruly peasants into collective-farm work units. Though the zone remains poor today, there is an uncompromising abundance of originality and vitality to the Puszta. Yesz, sztrangers szhould szee the szights of the Puszta, szince szecurity hasz szalvaged the szenery szuccesszzfully. . . .

CZECHOSLOVAKIA

Prague's Laterna Magika

Prague

However eagerly you may traipse the well-worn paths of tourism, nowhere will you find a magnetized lure like Prague's **LATERNA MAGIKA** theater, which plays to packed houses all the time. Though some critics have called it "illegitimate theater," others whip out rave-prose for the clever triple-threat amalgam of live theater, cinema and stereophonic sound—a marriage of trickery and deception that leaves audiences totally wowed. So, it's go-go-go!

Whether you understand Czech or not, language is *no* problem with a performance of Laterna Magika (Magic Lantern), for the storyline of the show biz sorcery comes across clearly, through the use of film and live actors on stage. The unique presentations, which are done in a 420-seat theater in the heart of Prague's so-called New Town at 40 Narodni Trida, employ ten screens, five projectors, a dozen or so live performers and another dozen technicians. Actors on the stage commune with actors on the screens, mixing reality and illusion. Indeed, with all the gimmickry involved, you never have a dull moment at a Laterna Magika show.

Tours in some foreign countries have proved so successful that they have spread the theater's fame, exciting the public by the confrontation on stage between the actors and the filmed events. Up to now the greatest undertaking of the Laterna Magika is the *Odysseus*, Homer's epic about the adventures of Odysseus (Ulysses)—presenting breathtaking stormy sea scenes with actor-sailors on stage who climb up real ropes to reach the sails depicted on a screen that is slanted from the stage-boat's deck upward and toward the audience. When the gigantic waves "spill" over the deck and the crew members hurtle themselves here and there from the force of the water, you as the spectator instinctively duck and then heave back into your seat ready for the deluge to hit you.

Further escapades have Odysseus burning out the eye of the menacing Cyclops with a red-hot stake, safely negotiating the temptations from the sirens, and the danger from Scylla and Charybdis (either meeting the monster or being swallowed by the maelstrom). Hero or villain, Odysseus nonetheless makes the Laterna Magica's audience-participants literally sit on the edge of their seats. The more calm moments of Odysseus's wanderings fill the viewers' eyes with spectacular land- and seascapes and tender relationships with some lovely ladies in equally fantastic ballet presentations.

One of the most popular shows of the recent past, and perhaps one of Laterna Magika's all-time number-one hits, is the *Tales of Hoffmann*, based on Jacques Offenbach's bizarre opera. Using all kinds of screens—round, square, narrow, triangular and CinemaScope, about a dozen in all, that are illuminated by projectors—the projection is 90-minutes long. The main character, Hoffmann, wanders from one screen to another while making appearances on the boards and singing with the help of a number of loudspeakers, set up literally everywhere.

The "live" Hoffmann sometimes slips behind one of the screens, which are transparent, and appears to be playing in the picture. And sometimes Hoffmann sings from three screens at the same time, in black-and-white, in color and in reversed negative—all done with a multiplicity of mirrors that gives Laterna its very Magika effect.

What else does Laterna Magika offer? The range of variations is infinite since the shows change from performance to performance. It's potluck what you draw, but it can be something like a pianist (on stage) playing an entire concerto by himself, handling all the different instruments of an orchestra (on screen). All of it is precisely and beautifully coordinated. Or you might see a male ballet dancer do a perfect pas de deux with a ballerina whose image is projected on the screen.

For those spectators who prefer action, Laterna Magika might offer a chase sequence. There is a version of a roller skater pursuing four girls who have boarded a bus that careens downhill on narrow streets, dodging oncoming traffic, fire engines, pedestrians, cyclists, baby carriages, lampposts and policemen. As the unsteady skater weaves out of the one medium into the other, it's even more exciting than that now-famous roller-coaster ride in the original Cinerama of some years back.

Basing some experiments on a 1918 show—that Russia's celebrated movie director, Sergei Eisenstein, once tried out but which failed miserably—two Czech brothers, Emil and Alfred Radok, gave birth to Laterna Magika in 1948. The Radok brothers, however, added their own ideas to the idea of combining live stage with film scenes and created their own brand-new works and storylines. Laterna Magika's first appearance outside Czechoslovakia was at the Brussels World's Fair in 1958, where it became a blockbuster hit. Although the Du Pont Company and the Texas Company very successfully used some of the Laterna Magika techniques at fairs in various parts of the United States, when the way-out Czech company made its debut at Carnegie Hall in 1964, the Broadway critics were harsh on it, saying that it was too much technique and not enough substance. After a later attempt in Germany with only mixed reviews, Laterna Magika went back to Prague to take up its permanent home. Since 1977 all performances have been uninterruptedly sold out, so visitors from abroad should either book seats before coming to Czechoslovakia or, once in Prague, see their concierge.

Admittedly heavy on hocus-focus and fraud-ian psychology (that's the fun part), the Magic Lantern shows have improved a lot during their home-stays in Prague, and instead of technical artifice being an end in itself, drama, humor and meaningful action have emerged strong in the evolutionary process. New authors exploring all the potentials have written many new works for Laterna Magika. One of the best of these is a vehicle called *The 11th Com-*

mandment, which couldn't work effectively as a film alone, nor could it go on with live performers only. In Magic Lantern, however, they click dramatically.

Yes, Laterna Magika is all a trick—and a treat!

* * *

The Oldest Store in Europe

Prague.

The tourist hot on the hunt for odd-infinitum will be rewarded the next time in this city's people-pulling-magnet **Old Town Square**, for just a few paces away is Number 3 Tyn Street, where he will stumble across the oldest store in Europe. As the only privately owned store in all of Czechoslovakia during the Communist regime, this sec-ondhand hardware emporium, that some folks would call a junk shop and others an antique shoppe, reminds you of a scene in a movie.

But be forewarned—only about half of the items on display and in disarray in "the shop on Main Street" are for sale, not because they are state-protected heirlooms, but because the present owners, Hans and Peter Capek, watch over the merchandise like mother hens and won't sell cer-tain things to which they and the family are "attached for sentimental reasons." Indeed, some of the items do have historical value—so, paradoxically, that makes the Capeks "custodians of an antique museum" as well as "dealers in old junk."

"People who come into the store," says Hans in the bookish English he learned in school, "are asked to sign my visitors' tome whether they buy anything or not. My father, Anton, who lived till ninety, and his father before him, Eduard, who died shortly before his ninetieth year, always made sure that customers and browsers alike put their signatures down."

An inspection of the ancient volumes (there are now seven) shows autographs from chiefs of state and other political VIPs who have signed their names in Arabic and Indian scripts, in Chinese and Japanese characters and in the Cyrillic alphabet. Most of the signatures, however, are of curious guys like you and me—some of whom even take to writing laudatory messages in the book.

One of the names pointed out to you belonged to the son of a man who owned a shop a few doors away, a shy boy who came around a lot to look in the windows but would not go into the store. Eduard Capek used to greet him through the open doorway, and one day he managed to get the young man to enter and sign his name: Franz Kafka!

The visitor books now contain signatures from people from every country in the world. But for a long time, Eduard Capek lamented the fact that no one from Turkey had ever come in. He wondered and waited. Shortly before his death in January 1974, a professor from the University of Istanbul wandered in, the drought was broken, the word spread in Turkey, and since then hundreds of Turkish people have paid calls.

And what does the Capek curio collection include? Well, around the dust-covered premises, you quickly spot thousands of keys to locks that will never be unlocked again, chains of all kinds and sizes, diverse tools from miniature pincers to blacksmith hammers, swords, daggers, clocks, candlesticks, torture instruments, iron lamps, copper engravings and a potpourri of unidentifiables whose purpose has been lost in a metalliferous assortment that has seen an eternity go by.

Nicknamed the Shop of Ten Thousand Things, the half store/half museum has never been shut for a single day (except Sundays). Located in a building that is about 700 years old, the place has had a lot of history attached to it and is today classified as a national monument. Over and over again, the owners have to turn down lucrative offers from people who want to buy the whole shop outright. The answer is always no. One movie producer tried very hard and kept raising the price far beyond any reality, but the answer was still no. In the end, he settled for renting the store to use as a setting for a film.

Filmmakers are constantly coming in to look for artifacts that are not to be found anywhere—like old chandeliers, ancient weapons or antique metal coffee grinders from one century or another. While a reporter was visiting Anton Capek a few years ago, a woman burst in and announced: "This is my last hope—do you have the hand wheel to a 1920 Singer sewing machine?" He did. And without batting an eyelash, he conjured up the required part quicker than you could thread a needle.

Once, when a representative of the Czech Academy of Sciences came in, he bought a number of copper plates of old engravings—one of which depicted a Russian czar on a bear hunt. It turned out that this particular engraving was not just a piece of junk: it had a value of over $10,000 and is now on display in a Prague museum.

To explain why he let such a valuable item leave his store, Capek shrugged his shoulders. He said that being around so many metal things has indeed given him an iron constitution—but that unfortunately he sometimes gets a little rusty.

ODDS AND ENDS

Willi's Place

Copenhagen, Denmark

Willi's Place gave some tourists the willies. Starting with that clock of his on the wall. . . .

Okay, the hands kept accurate time, but Willi's tick-tock had a face that would stop (ahem) a clock because its numbers read 1, 5, 8, 19, /, 2, 4, 2, 13, 6, 0 and 17. If you asked Willi himself what time it was, his answer would be that you could find out in the nick of what a stitch saves, 9. So much for Willi's clock. Now here comes Willi!

Willi was the owner of the International Soda-Fountain, which wasn't a soda fountain in the dictionary sense of the word but a sort of coffeehouse. Be that as it may, it was a coffeehouse that was certainly the craziest coffeehouse in Europe, not excluding Willi himself who was the craziest coffeehouse proprietor in or out of captivity.

At Willi's for instance, you couldn't order one hamburger—you had to take seven at a time, unless it was Wednesday. And when you paid for them, you—like every other customer—went to the cash register yourself, rang up the sale and made your own change.

Willi never had time to watch over the cash receipts because he was usually at one of the three constantly busy chessboards near the death mask of Dante. It frowned down on everybody in a room that had the skyline of New York painted on the walls, movie posters plastered all over the ceiling and pennants from Harvard, Purdue, Northwestern and Ohio State. From an old tangerine-colored bandanna Willi fashioned still another pennant that read: University of Hoboken, New Jersey.

Most of Willi's regulars always said that Willi looked crazy all right—but he was not so crazy as he looked.

Witness that cash register of his! By the end of the day it was jammed full—and when the bills and coins reached to overflowing, you merely tossed the money you owed him into the empty trash can underneath. No problem.

Victor Borge, himself a bit on the zany side, used to spend a lot of time at Willi's when he wasn't on the road doing his satirical one-man music shows. He felt that if someone was visiting Copenhagen and did not pay a call on Willi's Place, then that someone was something rotten in the state of Denmark. Located in the heart of downtown Copenhagen, Willi's Place was at 21 Vester Volgade. You went up two flights of stairs to the door that said No Admittance in Sanskrit.

No liquor was ever served at Willi's. The strongest stuff you could get was black coffee. In fact, there were over 300 white mugs hanging up on display, each with a name printed in gold. These represented the steady patrons. After you had been a customer for three years and 33 seconds, Willi would buy you a cup, ring a bell to get everybody's attention, play a scratchy LP of Wagner's over-ture to *Die Meistersinger* and forthwith make a presentation of the magnificent mug. You now belonged.

Anyone so honored, according to the rules of the house (rules?) had to buy a round of Danish pastries for every-body present, including Willi's mom and mother-in-law who ran the kitchen. Besides being a status symbol, the cup was not only used when you came in for coffee, but all messages and letters for you were stuffed in it like a mail-box. Having your own mug also meant you were the only person allowed to wash it.

Not the least of the Willi attractions were the photogra-phers' models who used his place as a hangout. The models went there to meet the photogs, and the customers (male) went there to meet the models. One of the fashion models caught the eye of an agent there, and he promoted her into winning the Miss Denmark of 1958 title before she went to Hollywood where she married a producer.

All told, Willi's Place accounted for 40 marriages, cou-ples whose friendships began right on the premises. Even one of Copenhagen's marriage-bureau officials met his wife at Willi's after he performed a ceremony and accepted an invitation to attend the reception at Willi's. Pleased by such events, Willi always made it a point to attend the weddings.

Willi ("No last names, please!"), who put his age as "somewhere between 7 and 77," worked for five years as a shipboard waiter for the East Asiatic Company, sailing the route between Copenhagen and Hoboken. On shore leaves in New Jersey and New York City he learned all about banana splits, cheeseburgers and other drugstore specialties. When he gave up the sea in 1950 to settle down, he opened up his own idea of an American-style soda joint.

Willi's oldest customers came to him practically from the very first day he opened. With their own permanent table, they were a group of eight Danish businessmen and seven lawyers who came in every day for lunch. These 15 stalwarts, convinced that the java at Willi's was the best in Scandinavia, were quick to advise you, however, not to order Willi's 007 Sundae: It was, no kidding, a lobster-and-crab banana split.

Paradoxically pessimistic about life, Willi had a sign near the cash register that said: NOTICE: IN CASE OF ATOMIC ATTACK BE CALM, PAY YOUR BILL. THEN RUN LIKE HELL. Asked about this sign, Willi had a standard answer that he delivered with his inevitable straight face: "When the bomb comes, it will prove that all men are cremated equal. Um . . . would you like a hard-boiled egg in your malted milk?"

Willi closed shop in 1970—suddenly—after having run his den of incongruity for 20 successful years. Nobody ever knew why. Nor did anyone ever find out where he went. When the building super and the police finally had to break down the door to get inside, the cash register was still open and still full of money. So was the trash can. That was Willi all over. . . .

All of us miss Willi's Place terribly. He was one of God's delightful mistakes. Be a good joe, Willi, and come back—the world needs you. And please, run like hell. . . .

* * *

When You Drive in England

When an American tourist rents a car in England, he's playing around with the United Kingdom version of "Rushin' Roulette" on two scores: (1) driving on the left-hand side of road, and (2) driving under the guidance of English road signs.

Enough prose may have already been dispensed about motoring on "the wrong side of the road," which—as one Yankee pun puts it—is not the right side. But an unanticipated danger for a U.S. traveler doing the U.K. on wheels is the English language—the Queen's English, that is. Matey, you jolly well should be on the alert with British road signs because some of them could just as easily be printed in Sanskrit or the Cyrillic alphabet, as far as an American is concerned.

Take this as a for-instance: You're driving along on the left side of the road, a bit j-j-jittery and plenty c-c-careful that you don't blunder because you're accustomed to driving on the right, when you suddenly meet up with a traffic sign that warns, "Keep to the Nearside Lane."Oy, now just *what* does *that* mean exactly?

With your car going at, say, 30 miles an hour, you may not have more than a split second to figure what that means in American English. It's so un-cricket. And here's another traffic sign that will drive you queasy; "Don't Go Into The Box Unless The Way Out Is Clear." By jove, that one on a recent motor trip through the Tight Little Island had me, literally and figuratively, coming and going. A smiling, patient bobby later explained it—and it means simply, don't block an intersection. Elementary, wot?

But then let's say you pull up to ask an Englishman for directions, and this is what he tells you (the italics and caps are mine):

"Take the *Dual Carriageway* to the first *Roundabout*, keeping a sharp eye for the *Left Coming* signs. Take the *Way Out* just beyond the first *Flyover* after you pass the *Car Park* next to the *Petrol Station*. Beware of the *Loose Chippings* and the *Crown Strollers*. Follow the *Road Diversion* and make sure you bypass the *Road Up*. If your motor car breaks down, you can use the *Lay-by* or any the *Verges* to look under your *Bonnet*." The translation of all this can be gotten from the Royal Automobile Club, which offers this British-American glossary for motorists: *Dual Carriageway* (divided highway); *Roundabout* (traffic circle); *Left Coming* (traffic merging from the left); *Way Out* (exit); *Flyover* (overpass); *Car Park* (parking lot); *Petrol Station* (service station); *Loose Chippings* (fallen rocks); *Crown Strollers* (road hogs); *Road Diversion* (detour); *Road Up* (road under repair); *Lay-by* (place to pull off the road); *Verges* (road shoulders), and *Bonnet* (hood).

Once you get onto a British motorway (their word for superhighway), you pick up the Englishman's automotive lingo pretty fast. You learn that what the English call a *klaxon* or *hooter* we call a horn, you learn that a *tyre* is your tire, a *windscreen* is your windshield, a *boot* is your trunk, a *silencer* is your muffler, a *wing* is your fender, a *gear lever* is your gear shift, a *number plate* is your license plate, a *puncture* is your flat tire and a *garridge* is your garage.

Also, let's not overlook that a *lorry* is a truck, an *articulated lorry* is a trailer truck, a *van* is a delivery truck, an *estate car* is a station wagon, a *caravan* is a trailer or a mobile home, a *moped* is a motorbike or motorscooter, and a *tram* is a trolley car. And lest we forget: a *centre reservation* is a median strip or divider, a *level crossing* is a grade crossing, and *public convenience* is a comfort station. By the way, your motor car is parked at the *kerb* (pronounced the same as our curb).

Yes, re Anglo-American linguistic differences, there are many pitfalls once you slide into an auto here. I'm reminded of a superhighway jam-up in the Midlands one afternoon. A triangular metal sign had been temporarily erected that read: Police Accident Ahead. To a neighboring motorist at his steering wheel I chanced a remark to the effect that I thought it indeed strange the police would give publicity to their own accidents.

"Nothing of the sort," chuckled the Englishman, who could have played Sir Alec Guinness without makeup. "What that sign means is that an accident has taken place, the police have arrived at the scene, and the situation is rather well in hand."

Now back to "Keep To Nearside Lane." Still a bit puzzled? Okay, it just means, stay to the very left. In England, if you stay to the left, you'll always be right, old chap.

*   *   *

So It's Goodbye to the Camel

Cairo, Egypt

So it's goodbye to the camel. . . .

Just as Old Dobbin was replaced by the horseless carriage, so too is the Arab world's faithful "ship-of-the-desert" being replaced by wheels and wings. Lo, the poor camel. The twentieth century is slowly automating him into the ranks of the unemployed, and it won't be long before the age of the single-humped *Camelus dromedarius* comes to an end.

He doesn't have a chance anymore. What was once his monopoly—the rolling desert sands that stretched for hundreds of miles between drinks of water—is now becoming motorized, civilized, organized and internationalized. At best, the camel today is something all travelers to the Middle East gape at, a living oddball out of the pages of Arabia.

Though he may survive as some kind of touristic testimonial from yesteryear, the desert mammal has lost his main job today, a job he held for better than 3,000 years for wages somewhat below the union scale. But because there is no Amalgamated Brotherhood of Caravan Dromedaries, his co-workers and the bottom-liners are deserting him for the bane of all beasts of burden, the internal combustion engine.

"The camel's golden age is past," explains a Moroccan businessman who knows the desert intimately. "We don't need him anymore. There is not an oasis left in the Sahara which cannot be reached by motor today. And the routes are getting better all the time. Thirty years ago it took several months to cross the desert by camel; now I can make the trip in a few days."

So efficient has the motor vehicle become, for instance, that truck caravans now penetrate forbidding empty desert regions that even the camel teams used to avoid. The wheel is showing every Arab that long trips on the hoof are strictly bush.

Another sign of the times is the airmail. Once upon a time the camel had much to do with transporting airmail letters. If you posted an air letter in an Arab town, it would travel the first leg of the trip by camel to the nearest airport—which might have been seven days away. With commercial airlines now flying in and out of most Arab cities, the camel no longer services the post office, a fact that has upped unemployment in the dromedary ranks.

Since fewer and fewer of the sand mammals are being used in caravans, today many camels are not working, but their owners are not letting the beast just sit on their haunches. For at least 10,000 years the camel has endured human domination, and now his masters are giving him a new role—this time in the field of tourism. In whatever Arab country you visit, there are enterprising turbanded cameleers waiting for tourist buses to pull up, because his nibs the Camel is now bedecked with a fancy saddle and a clean blanket to accommodate any visitor from abroad who opts for a once-in-a-lifetime ride.

Understandably, you can get a bit edgy watching someone else boarding a camel and holding on for dear life while the big brute is being prodded into standing up. But after you mount up, your nervous system is due for another jolt when the ride finally ends and the camel kneels to let you dismount from your wobbly perch. Now's the time—and you are warned beforehand—to grasp the supportive hand of the camel's owner, who is there to see that you are not catapulted forward to the ground and on your face.

Every rider exudes a sigh of relief once on terra firma again, but judging from the zillions of pictures taken of tourists getting on or off camels, the experience brings on plenty of laughs and spirited conversation. A camel ride is recommended for the strong of heart and for all those uneasy watchers on the sidelines.

Veteran camel-men like to tell tourists that their animals are the strangest domesticated animals on this earth. A camel has the feet of an elephant, the neck of a swan, the teeth and stomach of a mouse, the blood of a bird and the temperature of a reptile. He has two sets of long silky eyelashes to provide protection from the sun's glare. He can see with his eyes shut, and when necessary can plug up his nostrils against sand. Since pure water will make him dizzy, he prefers brackish water for its salt content.

Unknown to most visitors, who are attracted to but are nonetheless wary of him, the camel was responsible for the discovery of butter, which came about when an unknown desert tribesman of prehistoric times loaded a skinful of milk on his camel to take on a journey, but the peculiar ambling gait of the animal churned it into butter, thereby enriching mankind's table with a new food.

As a pack animal the desert breed made a monkey out of the donkey by proving he could travel for days without water, and, as is not generally known, even without food— even though he would be carrying 900 lbs. of weight or pulling as much as two tons of goods.

From time immemorial, therefore, the camel was in his glory. Indeed, he made possible the overland trade routes between the realm of the Queen of Sheba on the Indian Ocean and the lands on the North African shores of the Mediterranean Sea. Arabian kingdoms became richer because atop the ugly beast's humped back they could export bales of frankincense, sacks of myrrh and the whole range of valuable spices.

Working as man's servant for longer than any other animal, the awkward, popeyed, stiff-legged, goose-necked,

shaggy quadruped with his docile, sad expression on a face
far too small for the rest of his strangely shaped body has
always carried out his heavy duties without a complaint.
History has never recorded any hubbub among the humps.
And after he gets too old to lift his heavy packs, some tribes
use him for food. Camel meat, albeit a bit chewy, has a
pretty good taste.

Though he never showed any affection for his master,
either with a cheerful whinny or a nose-rubbing push, the
camel had a good track record with the sand men who, in
turn, treated the sullen critter as a colleague. Now the Arab
is turning his back on his four-legged friend, except for
when he is tourist bait and a videocamera star. Today, alas,
there aren't many Arabs here who would walk a mile for a
camel.

* * *

The Fabulous Swiss Army Knife

Ibach, Switzerland

With the aid of thousands of sharp-eyed, quality-
minded tourists, the greatest success story in this country
is—next to Heidi—the Swiss Army knife. Its Champion
model, with 24 blades and tools, is packed into a red case
and inlaid with the official silver cross of Helvetia, making
the knife an evergreen best seller in the souvenir shops of
Switzerland—a cut above all competitors.

When foreign travelers here want to take "something"
home as a gift, what they like about this prestigious piece of
cutlery is that it does not take up much space when packing
and yet is a mighty versatile tool (spell that f-r-i-e-n-d) for
any man or woman who is on the move. Though hardly a
secret weapon, the sturdy knife impresses at first, but its
performance over the years impresses you even more so.

Look what you get when you acquire the Swiss army
knife's Champion model, a compact gadget that fits snugly
in the palm of your hand and weighs about 160 grams (5.6

ounces): it has two blades, four screwdrivers, scissors, a can-opener, a reamer, a magnifying glass, a wood saw, a metal saw, a fish scaler, a hook disgorger, a fingernail file, a fingernail cleaner, a metal file, an inch and metric ruler, a bottle-opener, a wire-stripper, a toothpick, tweezers, a key-ring and a corkscrew. It has about everything in it but the kitchen sink. The Champion—which when opened up looks like a red centipede—had the distinction of being chosen by the Museum of Modern Art in New York to be part of its collection of unique, well-designed functional articles.

Home of the elegantly sumptuous pocketknife is the village of Ibach, 40 miles south of Zurich, where the Victorinox Company produces 4 million of the rust-free knives yearly. It must be said, however, that not all of these are the Champion, for the company makes 240 models in four sizes with a choice of four different handles. These also sell well. Once model in particular is a "ladies' knife," which has especially wide blades so that it can be opened without breaking a fingernail. It also fits neatly into a purse. Another popular model is the Spartan with nine tools—two blades, a screwdriver, a bottle-opener, scissors, a can-opener, a punch, a borer and a corkscrew—and is the one many tourists choose to take back home. If all the knives that left Switzerland for foreign shores were laid end to end, they would probably cut a swath from here to outer space.

Convinced of its functional pluses, Uncle Sam has chosen the Master Craftsman model with 17 tools for use by astronauts in both the Skylab and Space Shuttle programs, and the knives have now displaced a myriad of separate tools that would have been needed.

For its own use, the Swiss Army orders about 50,000 a year, and these are handed out to every citizen who takes the oath of allegiance when he first serves as a soldier. When Carl Elsener of Ibach started up a cutlery plant in 1884 that produced knives of high quality and durability, he persuaded Swiss Army authorities to abandon a German model they were isssuing to troops and adopt his. That has been going on since 1897. Elsener then got the government to authorize him to stamp the official Swiss cross on his product, and the rest is history.

Both the Victorinox and another company, Wenger S.A. (also officially permitted to use the Helvetian cross on the handles), are constantly on the lookout for innovations or additions to make the knife more efficient. Wenger has introduced a wrench into its models, but Victorinox has ruled against this one. Curiously enough, admirers of the Swiss Army knife even write in unsolicited fan mail suggesting sensible new additions like a tiny flashlight or crazy ones like a power saw.

One prominent fan of the multiblade wonder was an occupant of the White House. So taken with the Swiss Army knife was President Lyndon B. Johnson that he ordered 4,000 of them, encased in black, to be embossed with his signature and the gold presidential seal. He handed them out to his co-workers and friends all over the country.

Even President Ronald Reagan was fascinated with what many users call "the ultimate survival weapon." Soon after taking office in his first year, he asked the U.S. Embassy in Berne to place an order for 2,000 pocketknives with blue plastic covers embossed with a gold presidential seal and his own signature.

So popular have the knives become all over the world that several countries started to produce imitations—countries like Japan, Taiwan and Spain have manufactured cheap knives with red handles that look like the official Swiss Army ones. Victorinox keeps a table full of these on display in its lobby with knives that have twisted blades and others showing rust spots. Overhead is a contemptuous sign that reads: JUNK IMITATIONS.

It's a cutthroat business. . . .